Christadelphian
Biblical Interpretation
Annual 2010

Published by:

WILLOW PUBLICATIONS
13 St. Georges terrace
East Boldon
Tyne and Wear
NE36 0LU. U.K.

ISSN 1755-9227
ISBN 978-0-9563841-2-6

Printed by www.lulu.com and available from:

www.lulu.com/willowpublications

Other Publications by WILLOW include:

Fellowship Matters
Beginnings and Endings
Head-Coverings and Creation
Before He Was Born
Demons, Magic and Medicine
Demons and Politics
Job
Joel
Isaiah 40-48

Christadelphian EJournal of Biblical Interpretation (Quarterly)

www.christadelphian-ejbi.org

Christadelphian EJournal of Biblical Interpretation

Annual 2010

Jan 2010

Editorial, 6

John 1:3-4, 7

Misogynist Alterations of Scripture, 13

Being Jesus, 23

Wickedness in Shinar, 24

Numbered with the Transgressors, 30

Survey Results, 37

Babylonian Echoes in Isaiah 40-48, 39

The Nassouhi Prism, 47

SOTS Report, 50

Marginal Notes: Gen 2:23; John 10:35; 1 Cor 6:9, 51

A Tally of Two 'Theres', 55

Postscript: Writing and Printing in a Digital Age, 57

Apr 2010

Editorial, 63

The Babylonian Reading of Isaiah 40-48, 64

The Rich Young Man, 71

Evangelicals and the Doctrine of the Trinity, 77

El Shadday, 85

Should 'was' be 'became' in Genesis 1:2, 96

Reviews: Dever and Dunn, 104

Letters, 108

Marginal Notes: 1 Cor 11:3, 109

Christadelphian Writing, 110

Supporting Biblical and Historical Research, 113

New Websites and Blogs, 114

Jul 2010

Editorial, 116

Where the Vultures Gather Together, 116

A New Age, 123

Three Prophetic Utterances, 134

A Faithful and Wise Servant, 135

The Shema of Deut 6:4, 142

Marginal Notes: John 17:5, 155

Reviews: P. Pulman—The Good Man Jesus, 157

Report: The Great Trinity Debate, 159

Postscript, 162

Oct 2010

Editorial, 164

Galatians 3:28—An Equality Text?, 165

The Philippians Hymn and Pauline Theology, 174

Seals, Trumpets and Vials, 182

The Spirit of the Lord in the History Books, 183

Quirinius, 187

Pre-historic Genealogies, 190

Was the Ark a Practical Size?, 195

Marginal Notes: Isa 41:3, 198

Book Notice, 199

Letters, 200

Web Resources, 201

News: New Editor, 202

Postscript, 203

Supplement: Dating Revelation, 205

Editors: Andrew.Perry@christadelphian-ejbi.org
Paul.wyns@christadelphian-ejbi.org
T.Gaston@christadelphian-ejbi.org (Church history)
J.Adey@christadelphian-ejbi.org (Text and Language)

Christadelphian EJournal of Biblical Interpretation

Contents

- Editorial
- John 1:3-4
- Misogynist Alterations of Scripture
- Being Jesus
- Wickedness in Shinar
- Numbered with the Transgressors
- Survey Results
- Babylonian Echoes in Isaiah 40-48
- The Nassouhi Prism
- SOTS Report
- Marginal Notes: Gen 2:23; John 10:35; 1 Cor 6:9
- A Tally of Two 'Theres'
- Postscript: Writing and Printing in a Digital Age

Editorial Policies: The *Christadelphian EJournal of Biblical Interpretation* seeks to fulfil the following objectives: offer analytical and expositional articles on biblical texts; engage with academic biblical studies that originate in other Christian confessions; defend the biblical principles summarised in the common Christadelphian statement of faith; and subject the published articles to retrospective peer review and amendment.
Submission of Articles: Authors should submit articles to the editors. Presentation should follow *Society of Biblical Literature* guidelines (www.sbl.org).
Publication: E-mailed quarterly on the last Thursday of January, April, July, and October. Published as a collected annual paper-back obtainable from: www.lulu.com/willowpublications.
Subscriptions: This is a "free" EJournal to communities and individuals whose statement of faith is broadly consistent with the Christadelphian common statement.

Editorial

"Dumbing Down" is an expression you hear in the media. It refers to TV programmes or magazine and newspaper articles that present their content in a simple rather than a complex way, cutting out detail, the use of complex ideas, and instead using graphics, illustrations, pictures, photographs, video and sound-bites. Such media presentation looses the deeper analysis in favour of the surface treatment.

The apostle Peter observed that in Paul's letters there were things hard to understand (2 Pet 3:16) which implies that Paul did not "dumb down". If an inspired apostle wrote difficult things, it is certain that the OT scriptures also contain difficult material, pre-eminently the Prophets. What is more, the presence of such difficult material tells us something about what we should do in our reading and writing. We should not expect things to be simple, and neither should we always write what is simple. We should endeavour to write about the difficult and move forward our understanding of scripture and doctrine.

There is a reason why scripture contains difficult material. God appears to have included such material for his children down the ages, and we might ask and object by saying: *Why do this*, we don't *want* difficult holy writings? On the other hand, we might just ignore those parts of the Word that are difficult or just read over them in a superficial way. We may not "put the time in" to engage what is difficult preferring the quicker fix that is the surface. We are deceiving ourselves in such behaviour, saying, in effect, that we do not want what is difficult if it means too much effort. We might choose to fill our spiritual time with the easier things of speaking (and its correlate – listening) and singing, but this may well miss the lesson that the Word presents us, namely, that we need to spend our time in spiritual *thinking*. It is perhaps ironic that among the four *ings* of speaking, listening, singing and thinking that we neglect the thinking.

If we are to put the time into spiritual thinking, then one course of action in this endeavour is to seek out and collect Christadelphian writing from the older magazines which tended to go deeper in its treatment of topics.

John 1:3-4
P. Wyns

Introduction

This paper answers a question raised by John 1:3-4: What was made by the Word? The KJV renders the relevant text as follows:

> All things were made by him; and without him was not any thing made that was made. In him was life; and the life was the light of men. John 1:3-4 (KJV)

The New American Bible (NAB) renders this as follows:

> All things came to be through him, and without him nothing came to be. What came to be through him was life, and this life was the light of the human race. John 1:3-4 (NAB)

We can revise this to bring out the difference with the KJV as follows:

> All things came to be through him, and without him nothing came to be. That which was made in him was life, and this life was the light of the human race. John 1:3-4 (NAB revised)

The two versions differ in that whereas the KJV has the Word creating "everything", the NAB avers that "what came to be **through him** was life". The difference is clearly one of punctuation but the issue affects doctrine. The KJV will allow someone to believe the Word created all things, the universe, but the NAB will not allow this belief to get started.

Punctuation

There is a punctuation issue here: Should the relative clause (ὃ γέγονεν, "that which was made") go with v. 3 or v. 4? The earliest manuscripts have no punctuation (P⁶⁶,⁷⁵* ℵ* A B Δ *et al*).[1] Many of the later manuscripts which do have punctuation place the clause before the predicate "was life" thus putting it with v. 4 (Ì⁷⁵ᶜ C D L Wˢ 050* *pc*). Nestle-Aland²⁵ placed the relative clause in v. 3 but Nestle-Aland²⁶ moved the words to the beginning

---

[1] B. M. Metzger, *A Textual Commentary on the Greek New Testament* (2nd ed.; Stuttgart: Deutsche Bibelgesellschaft, 1994).

of v. 4. In a detailed article, K. Aland defended the change.[1] He sought to prove that the placement of ὃ γέγονεν ("that which was made") in v. 3 began in the 4th century C.E. in the eastern Greek church (see the Appendix). This development was engendered by the Arian Controversy and was intended as a safeguard for doctrine; the change was unknown in the West. Aland is probably correct in affirming that the clause was originally attached to v. 4; only when the Arians began to use the clause was it attached by the Eastern Church to v. 3. But this history does not rule out the possibility that, by moving the words from v. 4 to v. 3, one is restoring the original reading. Understanding the words as part of v. 3 is natural and adds to the emphasis which is built up there, while it also leaves a terse, forceful statement in v. 4. Accordingly, it can be argued that taking the phrase ὃ γέγονεν with v. 4 gives a complicated sentence. C. K. Barrett says that the two obvious ways of understanding v. 4 with ὃ γέγονεν included "are almost impossibly clumsy":[2]

> That which came into being – in it the Word was life.
> That which came into being – in the Word was its life.
>
> ὃ γέγονεν ἐν αὐτῷ ζωὴ ἦν...

Barrett's rendering of this "clumsy" punctuation is not unequivocal or impartial. We might render his form of v. 4 more neutrally (but still following him) as,

> That which came into being – in it/him (the Word) was life.

Barrett makes several points in support of taking ὃ γέγονεν with v. 3:

> (1) John frequently starts sentences with ἐν (*en*) and so such an opening word in v. 4 is normal for him.
> (2) John repeats himself frequently and so "nothing was created that has been created" is in keeping with his style.
> (3) The statements of John 5:26 and 6:53 both give a sense similar to v. 4 if it is understood without ὃ γέγονεν.
> (4) It makes far better Johannine sense to say that in the Word was life than to say that the created universe (that which was made, ὃ γέγονεν) was life in him.

---

[1] K. Aland, "Eine Untersuchung zu Johannes 1, 3-4. Über die Bedeutung eines Punktes" *ZNW* 59 (1968): 174-209.
[2] C. K. Barrett, *The Gospel according to St. John* (London: SPCK, 1958), 157.

So it is that Barrett takes the phrase with v. 3.

> All things were made by him; and without him was not any thing made that was made. In him was life; and the life was the light of men. John 1:3-4 (KJV)

And we might support this choice by referring to John 5:16,

> For as the Father hath life in himself; so hath he given to the Son to have life in himself... John 5:16 (KJV)

New Life in Christ

Barrett's view is wrong and he is misled by his reading of the clumsy alternatives as ones involving the notion of a created universe. It is rather the case, as the NAB has correctly discerned, that "new life" in Christ is the topic of v. 4 and this proposal is supported by John 6:3,

> Then Jesus said unto them, Verily, verily, I say unto you, Except ye eat the flesh of the Son of man, and drink his blood, ye have no life in you. John 6:3 (KJV)

The NAB renders the Greek as "what came to be **through him** was life". The assumption is made that the "coming into being" is referring to the physical universe, but John 6:3 demonstrates that it is the believer who "comes into being" through Christ and therefore can be said to have life in him.

Although fourth century Arianism understood Jesus as divine, their doctrine taught that Jesus was a created being – therefore at some point in time he did not exist. As Aland shows, orthodox writers preferred to take ὃ γέγονεν with the preceding sentence, thus removing the possibility of heretical use of the passage to the effect that life was made in Christ at some point in time. The different emphasis on punctuation by orthodox writers was therefore influenced by their anti-Arianism. The KJV punctuation expresses the Nicene view that "In him was life", as Jesus is thought to be co-eternal with God; Jesus himself could not therefore be a created being (but rather an incarnation of God); he had the life-principle "in himself" (eternally).

Staircase Parallelism

The balance in assessing the grammatical issue between both versions (KJV/NAB) is very fine, but the staircase parallelism in the text favours the NAB translation. Translations that are aligned with the NAB can employ "staircase parallelism" to justify their rendering of this passage. Staircase parallelism takes the rhythmic balance of John's Prologue into account, where the end of one line matches the beginning of the next, resulting in a "staircase of parallelisms"—see diagrams below:

In John 1:1 we have transliterated the Greek in a straightforward way so that we can see how the major term (coloured yellow) of the former clause is picked up in the next clause. Commentators have dubbed this a "staircase" which we have shown in Diagram 1. The same point can be made with regard to John 1:3-5, and we show this in Diagram 2. In Diagram 2 we can see that the "staircase" can only be preserved if ὃ γέγονεν (O GEGONEN) is placed on the third line above and therefore as part of v.4. On this basis, we can argue that the correct punctuation of John 1:3-4 is that which is given in the NAB.

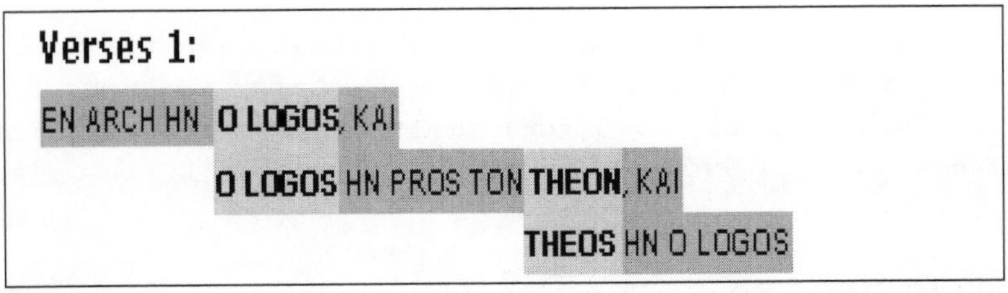

Verses 1:

EN ARCH HN O LOGOS, KAI

O LOGOS HN PROS TON THEON, KAI

THEOS HN O LOGOS

Diagram 1

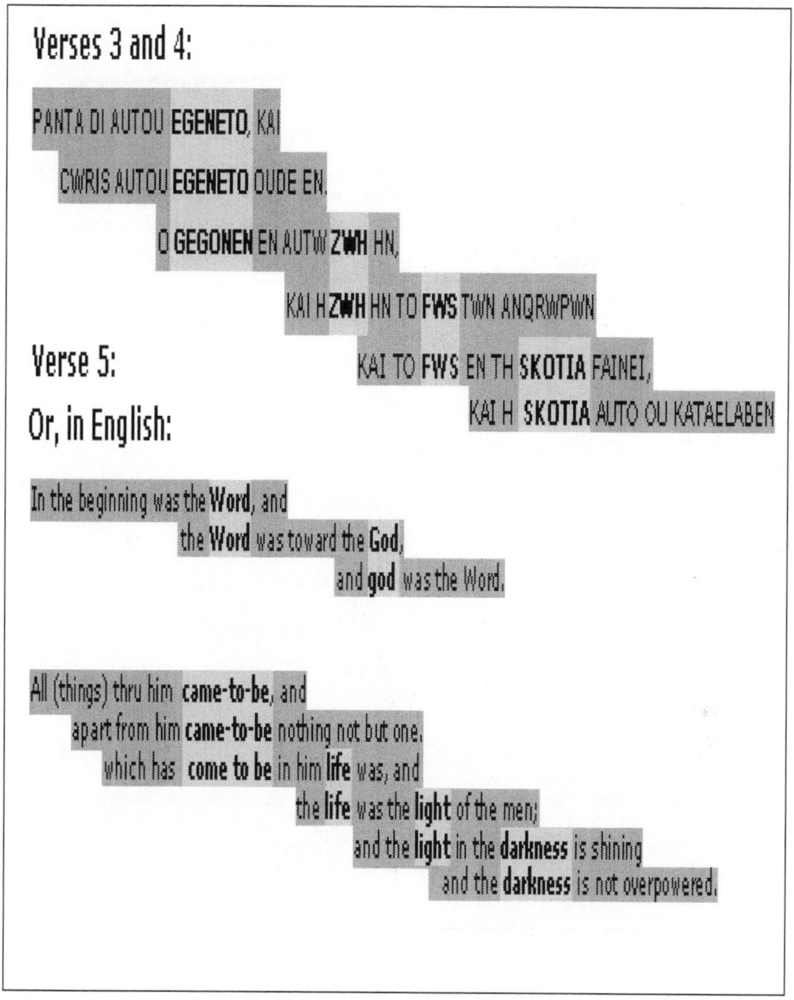

Verses 3 and 4:

PANTA DI AUTOU EGENETO, KAI

CWRIS AUTOU EGENETO OUDE EN.

O GEGONEN EN AUTW ZWH HN,

KAI H ZWH HN TO FWS TWN ANQRWPWN

Verse 5:

KAI TO FWS EN TH SKOTIA FAINEI,

Or, in English:

KAI H SKOTIA AUTO OU KATAELABEN

In the beginning was the Word, and
the Word was toward the God,
and god was the Word.

All (things) thru him came-to-be, and
apart from him came-to-be nothing not but one.
which has come to be in him life was, and
the life was the light of the men;
and the light in the darkness is shining
and the darkness is not overpowered.

Diagram 2

Conclusion

Translations are often biased; sometimes it is only a matter of emphasis or punctuation. The aim of this article is not to introduce an alternative translation, but to show why translations that follow the NAB are correct.

Appendix

Patristic usage (gathered from the Nestle Aland 27th edition) demonstrates a shift in translational emphasis for John 1:3-4 after Nicaea; see table below.

What came to be through him was life, and this life was the light of men. NAB	...and without Him nothing was made that was made. NKJV
Naassenes II/III	
Theodotus (ac. to Cl) II	
Valentinians(ac.to Ir) 160	
Diatessaron II	
Ptolemy II	
HeracleonII	
Theophilus 180	
Perateni III	
Irenaeus 200	
Clement 215	
Tertullian 220	
Hippolutus 235	
Origen 254	Adamantius 300
Eusebius 339	Alexander 373
Ambrosiaster IV	Ephraem 373
Hilary 367	Didymus 398
Athanasius 373	Epiphanus 403
Cyril (Jerusalem) 386	Chrysostom 420
Epiphanus 403	Jerome 420
	Nonnus 431

Misogynist Alterations of Scripture
J. Burke

Introduction

Egalitarian scholars identify anti-feminist bias in the later Greek manuscripts of the NT, and on this basis they speculate about such bias in earlier manuscripts; this paper examines one such presentation.

Misogyny in the 'Western' Greek New Testament

An argument found among egalitarian scholars is that the New Testament text was altered by later generations of Christians in order to validate developing misogynist attitudes. This argument is articulated in particular detail by egalitarian B. Witherington III:

> In view of the above evidence, it appears that there was a concerted effort by some part of the Church, perhaps as early as the late first century or beginning of the second, to tone down texts in Luke's second volume that indicated that women played an important and prominent part in the early days of the Christian community.[1]

Witherington says, "**it appears that** there was a concerted effort by **some** part of the Church, **perhaps** as early as the late first century or beginning of the second",[2] but when it comes to presenting the actual evidence which can be observed, Witherington does not cite any textual evidence earlier than the 4th century,[3] some 200 years after the 2nd century.

Witherington refers to "D and others" as his range of manuscripts.[4] D is a Greek/Latin diglot, also known as Codex Bezae Cantabrigensis, or D^ea (where the superscript 'ea' refers to the content of the text: the gospels (known as 'Evangelium') and Acts (known as 'Apostolos'). D is a 5th century text but the Greek text type it instantiates, (called 'Western'), cannot be dated any earlier than **250 AD**, even if quotations from early Christian writers are used (there are no Western type Greek manuscripts or

---

[1] B. Witherington II, "The Anti-Feminist Tendencies of the 'Western' Text in Acts", *JBL* 103/1 (March 1984): 82-84 (83).

[2] Witherington, "The Anti-Feminist Tendencies of the 'Western' Text in Acts", 83.

[3] He only cites one text as early as the 4th century.

[4] Witherington, "The Anti-Feminist Tendencies of the 'Western' Text in Acts", 82; he does not specify which other texts he means.

papyri earlier than the 4th century). The texts that Witherington discusses are given in the table below:

Text cited by Witherington				
Passage	Text Name	Text Type	Date	What happens?
Matt 5:32	D, it[a, b, d, k]	Western	4th century, 5th century	Protection of male privilege
Acts 1:14	D	Western	5th century	Additional mention of children
Acts 17:4	D	Western	5th century	Reference to wives rather than women
Acts 17:12	D	Western	5th century	Men included as prominent
Acts 17:34	D	Western	5th century	Omission of Damaris
Acts 18:2, 3, 7, 18, 21, 26	it[h gig]	Western	5th century	Priscilla's prominence reduced
Col 4:15	D, G[pm]	Western	5th century, 9th century	House church allocated to Nymphas not Nympha

In addition to D, the table above identifies an African Old Latin copy of an earlier Greek text ('it'—the 'it' stands for 'Itala', meaning Latin, and the other superscript letters stand for various specific copies of this Latin manuscript). The reading in D of Matt 5:32 is supported by 'it' and it is also found in other Greek and Latin manuscripts according to the 4th-5th century Christian writer, Augustine. The table also refers to another Latin manuscript (it[gig]), which is a 13th century Old Latin manuscript, and to a text referred to as 'G[pm]' (the 'pm' stands for the Latin *permulti*, meaning 'very many', and indicates that many manuscripts of this tradition have this reading), which is a 9th century Greek/Latin interlinear diglot also known as Codex Boernerianus.[1]

---

[1] Witherington goes on and says 'D, G pm, **et al.** [and others]', but does not say to which other manuscripts he is referring— Witherington, "The Anti-Feminist Tendencies of the 'Western' Text in Acts", 84.

From this survey of Witherington's evidence it may be seen that he does not present any actual textual evidence earlier than the 4th century, and most of his textual witnesses date to the 5th century. It is significant that these variants are all found in the Western text type, since this text type is most well known, not for its anti-feminist bias, but for its general tendency to paraphrase and edit the text in a particularly arbitrary manner.[1] It is also significant that almost all of these variants are found in only **one** manuscript tradition of the Western text (D), with only three variants appearing in any other Western manuscript tradition (G[pm], it[a, b, d, k, h]), and this demonstrates that these are not even systematic changes to one particular manuscript tradition, let alone the entire Western text type. This is one of the reasons why modern textual scholars generally view few (if any), of these alterations as genuinely motivated by a desire to minimize the role of women in the early church. They are so few and far between, so inconsistently found, and some of them are so much more readily attributable to accidental scribal error or the desire to render the text more grammatical, that they contradict the idea that the New Testament was revised studiously by groups of anti-feminist scribes as a result of changing attitudes to women in early Christian history.

It should also be pointed out that Witherington is an egalitarian scholar, whose interpretation of these textual alterations is demonstrably influenced by his own sensitivity to the subject. A comparison of Witherington's statements on the texts with the statements of the United Bible Societies' Committee shows that in a number of cases there is a more likely explanation for the text's alteration than any anti-feminist attitude by a particular scribe. The comments from the UBS Committee in the following tables (our emphasis is added) were written by B. M. Metzger, and are considerably more moderate on the subject than his own previous comments in his book, *The Text of the New Testament: Its Transmission, Corruption, and Restoration*,[2] written two years earlier; comments are given after the text from Witherington and the UBS Committee. Each table

---

[1] B. M. Metzger states, "The chief characteristic of Western readings is fondness for paraphrase. Words, clauses, and even whole sentences are freely changed, omitted, or inserted. Sometimes the motive appears to have been harmonization, while at other times it was the enrichment of the narrative by the inclusion of traditional or apocryphal material. Some readings involve quite trivial alterations for which no special reason can be assigned"—*A Textual Commentary On the Greek New Testament* (2nd ed.; New York: UBS, 1994), xx.

[2] B. M. Metzger, *The Text of the New Testament: Its Transmission, Corruption, and Restoration* (New York: Oxford University Press, 1992).

presents the relevant data relating to Witherington's examples of anti-feminist bias.

Tables

Table 1

Acts 17:4	
Witherington	**UBS Committee**
While there is some ambiguity in the text of 17:4 as we have it in p74, K, A, B, E, P (so that γυναικῶν τε τῶν πρώτων might be translated "the wives of leading men" instead of rendering "women of the first magnitude"), D and others give us the unambiguous καὶ γυναῖκές τῶν πρώτων.[1]	**It is possible to translate** γυναικῶν τε τῶν πρώτων "and wives of the leading men," an interpretation that the Western text **enforced by reading** καὶ γυναῖκές τῶν πρώτων. A majority of the Committee preferred the reading supported by P74 ℵ A B E P Ψ 33 81 614 1739 *al*, not only because of superior external attestation, but also because it was thought much more likely that copyists would replace the less usual connective by the more common καὶ (or δέ, as in l1021).[2]

Comment: Both Witherington and Metzger agree that the text here is actually ambiguous in the first place, and could be read either way. This is therefore not clearly a matter of a deliberately anti-feminist reading being introduced, but a scribal decision as to which particular interpretation of the text made more sense to them.

---

[1] Witherington, "The Anti-Feminist Tendencies of the 'Western' Text in Acts", 82.
[2] Metzger, *Textual Commentary*, 401.

Table 2

Acts 17:12	
Witherington	**UBS Committee**
We find the same phenomenon at 17:12. **D* alters the text so that both the men and women are prominent** (καὶ τῶν εὐσχημόνων ἄνδρες καὶ γυναῖκες) and thus the women's prominence is lessened somewhat.[1]	After beginning the verse with a rather banal observation, τίνες μὲν οὖν αὐτῶν ἐπίστευσαν, τίνες δὲ ἠπίστησάν ("Some of them, therefore, believed, but some did not believe," cf. 28.24), **codex Bezae smooths the grammar of the generally received text** and reads καὶ τῶν Ἑλληνιων καὶ τῶν εὐσχημόνων ἄνδρες καὶ γυναῖκες ἱκανοί ἐπίστευσαν ("and many of the Greeks and men and women of high standing believed")...**Besides being better Greek** the readjusted order has the effect of lessening any importance given to women (cf. comments on ver. 34 and on 18.26).[2]
Acts 1:14	
Of a similar nature is the addition of καὶ τέκνοις at 1:14 by Codex Bezae **so that women are no longer an independent group** but are simply the wives of the apostles.[3]	**Instead of the colorless** σὺν γυναιξὶν codex Bezae reads σὺν ταῖς γυναιξίν καὶ τέκνοις ("with their wives and children"); **compare 21.5**, where the Tyrian Christians accompany Paul to his ship σὺν γυναιξίν καὶ τέκνοις...[4]

Comment: Metzger notes that the original text was 'colorless'. It is characteristic of the Western text type to alter the text to make it more stylistically 'interesting', and in this case Metzger also points out that the scribe altered the text to conform to the grammatical pattern already existing in Acts 21:5, an alteration which the scribe considered to be more likely to be in conformity with the original. Such 'harmonization' is also characteristic of the Western text type, so there is no necessity to attribute

---

[1] Witherington, "The Anti-Feminist Tendencies of the 'Western' Text in Acts", 82.

[2] Metzger, *Textual Commentary*, 402.

[3] Witherington, "The Anti-Feminist Tendencies of the 'Western' Text in Acts", 82.

[4] Metzger, *Textual Commentary*, 246.

this alteration to an anti-feminist motivation. In any case, does associating the women with the apostles as their wives really diminish them in any meaningful way? This sounds like the imposition of a 21st century cultural view onto the 1st century text. Metzger points out that the reason for Codex Bezae (D), altering the text was to smooth the grammar and render it into better Greek. Such alterations are a common feature of the Western text type, especially Codex Bezae, so this textual alteration is simply what the scribes of the Western text type typically did in any case. There is therefore no need to attribute to this alteration an anti-feminist motivation.

Table 3

Acts 17:34
Witherington
...the omission in Codex Bezae of καὶ γυνὴ ὀνόματι Δάμαρις at 17:34 **is in all likelihood more evidence of an anti-feminist tendency in this textual tradition.**[1]
UBS Committee
The omission in codex Bezae of the words καὶ γυνὴ ὀνόματι Δάμαρις **has been taken by some...to be another indication of the anti-feminist attitude of the scribe...It is, however, more likely...**that a line in an ancestor of codex Bezae **had been accidentally omitted**, so that what remains in D is ἐν οἷς καὶ Διονύσιος ὁ Ἀρεοπαγίτης εὐσχημόνων καὶ ἕτεροι σὺν αὐτοῖς ("among whom also was a certain Dionysius, an Areopagite of high standing, and others with them"). In either case, however, the concluding phrase σὺν αὐτοῖς suggests that Luke originally specified more than one person (Dionysius) as among Paul's converts.[2]

Comment: There is a case to be made here that the alteration is a deliberate attempt to diminish the importance of the women in the text. However, as Metzger says, it is more likely to have been due to an accidental omission, so there is no necessity to attribute to this alteration an anti-feminist motivation.

---

[1] Witherington, "The Anti-Feminist Tendencies of the 'Western' Text in Acts", 84.
[2] Metzger, *Textual Commentary*, 407.

Table 4

Acts 18
Witherington
In the Western text of chap. 18, there is a definite effort to reduce the prominence of Priscilla, **probably because she appears to the editors to be assuming her husband's first place** and also because she was **a well-known teacher of a male Christian leader, Apollos.**[1]
UBS Committee
Apparently the Western reviser (D it^{gig} syr cop^{sa} arm *al*) desired to reduce the prominence of Priscilla, for he either mentions Aquila first (as here) or inserts the name of Aquila without including Priscilla (as in verses 3, 18, and 21). The unusual order, the wife before the husband, must be accepted as original, **for there was always a tendency among scribes to change the unusual to the usual.** In the case of Priscilla and Aquila, however, it was customary in the early church to refer to her before her husband (cf. Ro 16.3; 2 Tm 4.19).10 On an anti-feminist tendency, see the comment on 17.12 above.[2]

Comment: Although it is possible to read the tendency in some of the Western witnesses to place Aquila first or insert Aquila's name without including Priscilla as a desire to reduce the prominence of Priscilla, there is also the fact (as Metzger observes), that the general tendency of the Western text type scribes was to 'change the unusual to the usual'. Since in their day (centuries later), it seemed to them unusual that Priscilla would be mentioned first, they altered the text to conform to what they considered to be more likely to be original. The fact that they did this with many other passages indicates that there is no necessity to attribute to this alteration an anti-feminist motivation, even though in this case it is entirely likely.

---

[1] Witherington, "The Anti-Feminist Tendencies of the 'Western' Text in Acts", 82.

[2] Metzger, *Textual Commentary*, 413.

Table 5

Matt 5:32	
Witherington	**UBS Committee**
Consider the Western text of Matt 5:32b. D, itᵃ, ᵇ, ᵈ, ᵏ, and other manuscripts omit καὶ through μοιχᾶται in 5:32b. Bruce Metzger suggests that some scribes felt that if the divorced woman is made an adulteress by illegal divorce, then anyone marrying such a woman also commits adultery. **Alternatively, this omission may reflect the tendency of the Western text to highlight and protect male privilege**, while also relegating women to a place in the background. In this case, the omission here is of material that reflects badly on men.[1]	The reading of B (ὁ ... γαμήσας) seems to have been substituted for the reading of the other uncials (ὃς ἐὰν ... γαμήσῃ) **in order to make the construction parallel to the preceding participial clause** (ὁ ἀπολύων). The omission of the words και ... μοιχᾶται (D itᵃ, ᵇ, ᵈ, ᵏ Greek and Latin mss. acc. to Augustine) **may be due to pedantic scribes who regarded them as superfluous**, reasoning that if "everyone who divorces his wife, except on the ground of unchastity, makes her an adulteress [when she remarries]," then it would go without saying that "whoever marries a divorced woman [also] commits adultery".[2]

Comment: Once again, Metzger makes the point that the scribal tendency to smooth the text (in this case to create a neat parallel), and to remove material perceived as redundant, is an adequate cause for the alteration, so there is no necessity to attribute to this alteration an anti-feminist motivation.

---

[1] Witherington, "The Anti-Feminist Tendencies of the 'Western' Text in Acts", 84.

[2] Metzger, *Textual Commentary*, 11.

Table 6

Col 4:15	
Witherington	**UBS Committee**
This anti-feminist tendency appears also to be in evidence at Col 4:15. While B, 6, 424ᶜ, 1739, 1881, *et al.* have αὐτῆς indicating a church in the house of Nympha, D, G pm, *et al.* have αὐτοῦ indicating a church in the house of Nymphas.'[1]	Νυμφαν can be accented Νύμφαν, from the feminine nominative Νύμφα ("Nympha"), or Νυμφᾶν, from the masculine nominative Νυμφᾶς ("Nymphas"). **The uncertainty of the gender of the name led to variation** in the following possessive pronoun between αὐτῆς and αὐτου. On the basis chiefly of the weight of B 6 424ᶜ 1739 1877 1881 syrʰ, ᵖᵃˡ ᵐˢ copsᵃ Origen, the Committee preferred Νυμφᾶν ... αὐτῆς. The reading with αὐτῶν arose when copyists included ἀδελφοὺς in the reference.[2]

Comment: Metzger notes that the gender of the name was uncertain to start with, giving rise to variations in the text. The difference between the female name Nympha and the male name Nymphas was a matter of accenting the Greek letters one way or another, but the earliest manuscripts did not use any accents at all, meaning that later scribes had to make interpretative decisions at times. There is therefore no need to attribute to this alteration an anti-feminist motivation, even given the fact that the ambiguity was settled in favour of the male name Nymphas.

---

[1] Witherington, "The Anti-Feminist Tendencies of the 'Western' Text in Acts", 84.

[2] Metzger, *Textual Commentary*, 407.

Conclusion

When all the facts are presented, the argument for significant alterations of the Greek text by anti-feminist scribes becomes significantly diminished. Instead of alterations being observed from the second century onwards, we find instead alterations only from the 4th century onwards, some 200 years later. Instead of evidence of systematic scribal bias in collaboration with emerging anti-feminist attitudes, we find a tiny handful of alterations in a mere handful of manuscripts, none of which contains all of the alterations, and most of which contain only one or two. Instead of clear evidence of anti-feminist motivation in the case of each alteration, we find clear evidence that normal Western scribal influences (a tendency to paraphrase, eliminating perceived irregularities in the text, smoothing the grammar, creating parallels, and harmonizing with other passages), were in most cases a more likely cause.

Witherington's own words are pertinent here:

> That the so-called Western text **has certain definite theological tendencies** not found in various other manuscript traditions is so **well-known that it hardly needs rehearsing**.[1]

The evidence for deliberate theological revision of the text within the Western text type is indeed well recognized by the scholarly consensus. The evidence is so apparent and so abundant, that the case is undisputed. This is completely different to the suggestion that the Western text type also contains evidence of deliberate anti-feminist revision of the text, as the evidence for the latter is not in any way equivalent to the evidence for the former.[2]

---

[1] Witherington, "The Anti-Feminist Tendencies of the 'Western' Text in Acts", 84.

[2] Together with brother Mark Olsen, the author has co-written a 40 page paper addressing commonly asked questions concerning New Testament textual criticism (especially with regard to the issue of identifying the most reliable manuscripts), which the interested reader may request from the address: dixit-dominus@thechristadelphians.org.

Being Jesus
P. Wyns

Moses *saw* the goodness of God "pass before him", but that goodness was expressed in the proclamation of the divine name. What Moses *heard* were the divine attributes, grace and mercy, articulated with the imperfect-future **I will be gracious** and **I will show mercy** (Exod 33:18-20), thereby establishing the hope of future God manifestation (cited by Paul in Rom 9:15 also using the future tense). The echo and allusion is with Exod 3:14 and **I will be who I will be**.

The phrase **I will be who I will be** begs the question: **Who will God be?** The covenant promise vouched safe to David answers the question:

> **He shall be** to me a Son 2 Sam.7:14 (KJV)

This is an obvious allusion to the texts of Exod 3:14 and Exod 33:18-20 – the son would manifest the qualities and character of the Father ("to him"). This passage is quoted in the future tense in Hebrews, "I will be to him a Father, and he shall be to me a Son" (Heb 1:5), within the context of a discussion of **inheriting a more excellent name** (Heb 1:4).

Perhaps this theology of God manifestation is best expressed in a formulation used by the apostle Paul in 1 Cor.15:8-10 which has multiple echoes with Exodus 3:

> And last of all he was seen (cf. 'appeared'—the same word is used in Acts 7:30 in the description of the burning bush incident) of me...For I am the least of the apostles....but by the grace of God **I am what I am**...yet not I but the grace of God which was with me. 1 Cor 15:8-10 (KJV)

The context of the passage (1 Cor 15:4) is redemption, salvation (cf. Exod 3:7-10, 17) and resurrection. Paul was an **apostle** (="sent one" cf. "send" in Exod 3:10, 12, 13, 14, 15), and God promised to be **with** him as with Moses (Exod 3:12).

Paul affirms **I am what I am**, echoing **I will be who I will be** in Exod 3:14. He uses the present tense **I am**, because he fulfils the terms of I will be **who** I will be—God was manifested through the Spirit in him. Jesus had said that he was a "chosen vessel **to bear my name**" (Acts 9:15).

In a similar fashion the blind man, whose sight was restored (like Saul's), could say: **I am** (John 9:9). The blind man uses exactly the same syntactic expression for which Christ was almost stoned in John 8:58—yet he was not claiming to be God. Jesus explained that the blind man had his condition so that "the works of God might be made **manifest** in him" (John 9:3). Hence, the blind man was inspired to say **I am** in order to show how he fulfilled the terms of the promise in I will be **who** I will be.

The name of Jesus is an abbreviated form of *Yahweh* prefixed to the Hebrew verb for "to save"—*Yahshua*. This name becomes *Iesous* in the Greek and is coupled with the third person future form "he shall save" in Matt 1:21-23,

> ...and thou shalt call his name Jesus: for **he shall save** his people from their sins...and they shall call his name Immanuel....God with us. Matt 1:21-23 (KJV)

Matthew's narrative at this point is a paronomasia that explains 'Jesus' in terms of redemption ("save") and fellowship ("with"). Isaiah called the Messiah "Immanuel" or "God with us" which picked up on the Exodus motif, "Certainly, **I will be with thee**" (Exod 3:12). Hence, Jesus was to claim that "I am come in my **Father's name**" (John 5:43) and that "I have **manifested thy name**" (John 17:6). He did this insofar as he too was a fulfillment of I will be **who** I will be.

Wickedness in Shinar
P. Wyns

Introduction

In the previous issue of the *EJournal*, T. Gaston[1] examined the tensions that led to the separation of Christianity as a distinct religion from Judaism based on the standard work, "The Partings of the Ways" by J. D. G. Dunn.[2] The catalyst in this development was the destruction of the Second Temple which necessitated the reformation and rebirth of Judaism as Rabbinical Judaism (the heir of Pharisaic Judaism). The article focused attention on the Jamnia community, which after AD 70 was authorized by the Romans to operate with a degree of autonomy unavailable to any other Jewish community and which therefore became the architect of a new

---

[1] T. Gaston, "The Parting of the Ways", *CeJBI* 3/4 (Oct 2009): 1-7.
[2] J. D. G. Dunn, *The Partings of the Ways* (London: SCM Press, 1991).

Jewish orthodoxy: Rabbinic Judaism. However, the importance (sometimes even the existence) of the Jamnia Council is challenged:

> The concept of the Council of Jamnia is an hypothesis to explain the canonization of the Writings (the third division of the Hebrew Bible) resulting in the closing of the Hebrew canon. ... These ongoing debates suggest the paucity of evidence on which the hypothesis of the Council of Jamnia rests and raise the question whether it has not served its usefulness and should be relegated to the limbo of unestablished hypotheses. It should not be allowed to be considered a consensus established by mere repetition of assertion.[1]

Whatever the contribution of the Council of Jamnia in the land of Israel may have been, it is certain that Roman support was squandered with the Bar Kokhba revolt led by Simon Bar Kokhba (AD 132–136). The revolt was supported by Rabbi Akiba.[2] The revolt was viciously crushed by the Romans, and the consequences for Judaism were even more devastating for the population than those of AD 70 as the majority of the Jewish population of Judea was killed, exiled, or sold into slavery after the Bar-Kokhba revolt, and Jewish religious and political authority was suppressed far more brutally, with the Jews even banned from entering Jerusalem.. After the revolt the Jewish religious center shifted away from the land of Israel to the Jewish scholars of **Babylon** under Parthian control, away from the influence of Rome.

Rabbinic Judaism gained dominance within the Jewish Diaspora between the second to the sixth centuries AD, with the codification of the oral law and the development of the **Babylonian Talmud** to control the interpretation of Jewish scripture and to encourage the practice of Judaism in the absence of Temple sacrifice and other practices no longer possible. Babylon became the main centre of Jewish religious, cultural, and political life; Judea would not become prominent again until the modern era. The destruction of the Second Temple and the emergence of Rabbinic Judaism in Babylon are predicted by the prophet Zechariah and confirmed by Christ.[3]

---

[1] J. Lewis "Jamnia" *ABD*, 3:634-7 (634).

[2] "Bar Kokhba" means "son of a star" (Num 24:17: "There shall come a star out of Jacob").

[3] [ED. AP.] Palestinian centres of learning (such as Usha) were also influential, especially during the second century. Babylonian prominence

Vision of the Flying Scroll

The vision in Zechariah 5 is about the destruction of a "house" in the land[1] and the establishment of a new "house" in the land of Shinar[2]. Zechariah is said to have prophesied in the second year of Darius the Persian (520 BC) but his ministry extended to the forth year (518 BC). Like Haggai, therefore, he is addressing and seeking to encourage the postexilic community.

At first glance Zechariah 5 is incongruous with the previous visions concerning restoration, but closer examination demonstrates that this is not so, for the restored community was being reassured that God had removed the iniquity, allowing the remnant a fresh beginning; thus Zechariah 5 complements earlier visions. However, the vision also carries an implicit warning; for what God had performed in the past – removing iniquity and exiling the nation, would happen again if the nation remained unrepentant. From Zechariah's standpoint (building the new temple) the vision is retrospective and reassuring, but it is at the same time prophetic of future events, for the iniquity that had been removed to Shinar in order to allow the community to flourish, could also at some future point return from Shinar and contaminate the nation again.

The flying scroll with the curse was of huge proportions – it flew so that it could be viewed throughout the land – it was written on both sides so that it could be read from above (by the angels, who act as witnesses?) and from beneath (by the people) – in other words ignorance of the divine will was not an excuse. The Hebrew word translated "curse" (Zech 5:3) alludes to the covenant sanctions that attend the violation of God's covenant with Israel (cf. Deut 29:12, 14, 20-21). Stealing and swearing falsely (mentioned later in this verse) are sins against mankind and God respectively and are thus violations of the two major parts of the Ten Commandments. These two stipulations (commandments 8 and 3) represent the whole law. The second part of the vision describes three women – two of them with wings bearing a basket containing a third woman called iniquity or "lawlessness." These "women" come out of the house that has just been destroyed:

---

develops towards the end of the second century especially with the Amoriam.

[1] The curse encompasses the whole "land" or "earth" (*eretz*, Zech.5:3); here in particular it concerns the land of Judah.

[2] "Shinar" is the "country of two rivers", the ancient name for the territory later known as Babylonia or Chaldea (Gen 11:2).

> Then lifted I up mine eyes, and looked, and, behold, there came out (i.e. of the house) two women, and the wind *was* in their wings. Zech 5:9 (KJV)

We are clearly dealing with a parody of the Ark of the Covenant – instead of two "ox-faced" cherubim with the spirit in their eagle wings we have two women (representing Israel and Judah) with the "wind"[1] in their unclean stork wings. Instead of the gold covered mercy seat—a lead weight, instead of the glory of God dwelling between the cherubim—a wicked woman called "lawlessness" in the "midst". Moreover, the description vouchsafed to Zechariah is similar to Ezekiel, "He said moreover, this is their resemblance (Heb., 'eye') through all the earth." (Zech 5:6; cf. Ezek 10:12; "and their wings, and the wheels, were full of eyes round about"). The two women are based on the matriarchs Rachel and Leah, "which two did build the house of Israel" (Ruth 4:11), except now a different kind of house was being prepared.[2]

Establishing a House in Shinar

> Then said I to the angel that talked with me, Wither do these bear the ephah? And he said unto me, to build it an house in the land of Shinar: and it shall be established (*kuwn*), and set there upon her own base (*mekunah*). Zech 5:10-11 (KJV)

The scroll that bore the curse had the same dimensions (20x10 cubits) as Solomon's porch (1 Kgs 6:3). This is not accidental, for the porch was supported by two pillars that symbolised the covenant made with David (1 Kgs 7:21):

> But I will settle him in mine house and in my kingdom for ever: and his throne shall be established (*kuwn*) for evermore. 1 Chron 17:14 (KJV); cf. 2 Sam 7:12

---

[1] The meaning of the Hebrew word *ruach* is to be deduced from the context. The main idea running through all the passages is that of invisible force. It is variously translated as either wind or spirit.

[2] The "two sisters" (based on Rachel and Leah) form the archetype for Ezekiel (Ezek 23:1-3). Contrast the removal of iniquity in Zechariah with the removal of the glory in Ezekiel: "Then the glory of the Lord departed from off the threshold of the house, and stood over the cherubims" (Ezek 10:18). Rachel and Leah "built the house of Israel" (Ruth 4:11).

God had promised (Exod 23:20), "to bring the people into the place which I have prepared" (*kuwn*). The first pillar was Jachin "He (*Jah*) will establish (*kuwn*)"; the other pillar, Bo'az, probably means, "He will strengthen".[1] Zechariah draws our attention to this by using poetic parallelism between the words "established" and "base".

The Hebrew *mekunah* ("base", related to the verb *kuwn* "to establish") is used eight times in 1 Kings 7 for the description of the brass base of the lavers and the base of the pillars that Solomon made for the temple. King Ahaz removed the brazen "sea" from its base (*mekunah*) of twelve oxen (2 Kgs 16:17); one can only presume that he used the base as support for a (portable?) throne or maybe an altar. He certainly copied and installed an Assyrian altar in the temple. Ahaz' action seems to be a response to Isaiah's message,[2]

> If ye will not believe, surely ye shall not be <u>established</u>. Isa 7:9 (KJV)

We might well add the words of the Deuteronomy,

> Do ye thus requite the Lord, O foolish people and unwise? *Is* not he thy father *that* hath bought thee? Hath he not made thee, and established (*kuwn*) thee? Deut.32:6 (KJV)

The divine response to the nation's corruption was to exile the people and the bases to Babylon:

> And the pillars of brass that *were* in the house of the Lord, and the **bases** (*mekunah*), and the brazen sea that *was* in the house of the Lord, did the Chaldees break in pieces, and carried the brass of them to **Babylon**. 2 Kgs 25:13 (KJV)

> And when it is established (*kuwn*), she shall be set there upon her own base (*mekunah*) Zech.5:11 (KJV revised)

---

[1] The meaning of "Boaz" is uncertain but most probably means "strength"—the word "strength" is twice used in Prov 31:17 (where the virtuous woman is modelled on Ruth) playing on the name of Boaz. The pillars formed an outward symbol of the promise made to David: "Yahweh would establish the seed of Boaz".

[2] Ahaz set the Assyrian altar in the temple area after the crisis of Isaiah 7.

> 'I will send out *the curse*', says the Lord of hosts; 'It shall enter the house of the thief and the house of the one who swears falsely by My name. It shall remain in the midst of his house and consume it, with its timber and stones'.
> Zech 5:4 (NKJV revised)

Leviticus 14 proscribes the procedure that the priest must follow in order to cleanse a leprous house. If the house could not be cleansed, the following took place:

> And he shall break down the house, the stones of it, and the timber thereof, and all the mortar of the house: and he shall carry *them* forth out of the city into an unclean place. Lev 14:45 (KJV)

Before condemning an unclean house, the priest would inspect the house three times before pronouncing his final verdict—similarly, Jesus inspected the Temple three times during his ministry, culminating in the last inspection during his final week (Matt 21:12, 13; Luke 19:43-48). The verdict pronounced by Christ is based on Zechariah's vision:

Matthew 23 & 24	Zechariah 5
A den of thieves (21:13). Stealing (23:23-25). Corban (Mark 7:11).	The house of the thief (v. 4).
Swearing (23:16-22).	Swearing (v. 3).
Your house left desolate (23:28).	Timber and stones of the house consumed (v. 4).
Not one stone upon another (24:1-3).	

Consequently "their house" ("your house") was destroyed by the Romans, for it was an unclean house, no longer fit to be his Father's dwelling place. The subsequent history of Israel demonstrates that the remainder of Zechariah's vision was fulfilled in Babylon, for the Jews, deprived of cultic ritual, established their interpretation of the Law as a substitute.

Conclusion

The vision in Zechariah 5 is about apostate Judaism not apostate Christianity. The temple was destroyed (again) as predicted by Zechariah (and Christ) and false religion was established in Babylon in the development of Rabbinic Judaism. Spiritually the Jews had regressed to the place of their exile.

Numbered with the Transgressors
P. Wyns and A. Perry

Introduction

The themes of "numbering" (census-taking) and plague as a consequence of failure to pay the **atonement price** are found in the parallel accounts of David's numbering of the people in 2 Samuel 24 and 1 Chronicles 21. Whenever a census was taken atonement money was paid as an offering to the Lord "for an atonement of your souls" otherwise a plague would afflict the people (Exod 30:12-16). Such a plague afflicted the people after David's census, and we can infer that it was *because the atonement price was not paid*. In this paper, we will examine this incident and conclude with suggestive parallels that are to be observed with the "suffering servant" of Isaiah 53 who was "numbered with the transgressors".

David Numbers the People

> Again the anger of the Lord was aroused against Israel, and He moved David against them to say, "Go, number (מנה[1]) Israel and Judah". 2 Sam 24:1

The action of "numbering the people" is usually regarded as an act of folly or pride by David and/or a capricious/arbitrary act by God.[2] Despite David's willingness to accept all the blame for what had been done, we are

---

[1] The same word is used in 1 Chron 21:1, 17 and Isa 53:12.

[2] R. Alter affirms that "The reason for God's wrath is entirely unspecified, and attempts to link the events in the preceding narrative are quite unconvincing…perhaps, indeed, there is no discernible reason for God's fury against Israel…He is decidedly an interventionist God, pulling the human actors by strings, and He may well be a capricious God, here 'inciting' David to carry out a census that will only bring grief to the people". *The David Story: A Translation with Commentary of 1 and 2 Samuel* (New York: Norton & Company, 1999), 353, fn.1.

left in no doubt that Yahweh (a 'satan' in 1 Chron 21:1) was the prime mover behind David's action to take a census. Hence, in the summary of his reign David, is only held accountable for his sin in the matter of Uriah the Hittite and the census-taking receives no mention (1 Kgs 15:5). These details invite a closer look at the whole episode:

1) The anger of the Lord was kindled against Israel rather than David. The preposition "against" (ב) is repeated in the description of the action of David, so that we know that the action "against them" was the numbering.

2) Yahweh "moves" (סות) David (1 Sam 24:1), which is rendered "provoked" in 1 Chron 21:1 (KJV). The verb is broad in meaning and the sense here is conveyed in any neutral verb of persuasion, with "provocation" a translator's interpretation.

3) The numbering takes more than nine months (2 Sam 24:8) and this detail illustrates peaceful conditions in the land allowing the commander of the army and a detachment to travel the length and breadth of the land collecting the census data.

4) A military catalyst for the census is therefore unlikely. Were David under attack in ongoing campaigns, it is implausible to infer that the commander of the army would collect census data with a view to a general conscription. This might be done ahead of a pre-emptive campaign the next year on the part of David, but not as a defensive response to an attack.

5) Thus, while the anger of the Lord is often kindled against his people, and this takes the form of attacks by the surrounding nations, this is not the case here because what is "against" the people is the numbering.

On the basis of (1)-(5), we should conclude that domestic politics are behind this incident rather than military threat. The persuasion of David by the Lord would naturally have taken the form of a word of prophecy.

What happens during the census-taking is indicative of the domestic situation. Levi and Benjamin were excluded from the census by Joab (1 Chron 21:6). This suggests that the census was taken *against* Israel and Judah as a means of asserting the authority of the Davidic king and that dissension was present at the highest of levels (Joab). It will be remembered that David was not accepted by the northern tribes for the first seven years of his reign at Hebron and we may surmise that Joab had support among the tribes.

If Yahweh saw that some of the people were hostile to David, his anointed, then this would explain his anger "against them" and how the action of numbering them would be "against them". By such an action they would be brought under the authority of the king. We can go further in specifying what the domestic situation might have been because Levi was one of the tribes not counted. Levi was not a northern tribe, but the priestly tribe spread among the people. They were the priestly ruling class among the people and were presumably on the side of Joab throughout the census-taking. Similarly, the mention of Benjamin hints at the politics of the situation. Saul was of Benjamin, and supporters of Saul's house (Benjaminites) were hostile to Davidic claims upon the throne. Benjamin had a history of trouble with David. They had violated the covenant made with the Gibeonites who served at the tabernacle in the days of Saul (2 Sam 21:1-6; cf. Josh 9:19-23). David had granted the Gibeonite request to have seven of Saul's sons executed because of the covenant violation.

In this connection it is important to recall that **census-taking was allowed by the Law** upon payment of an atonement price. Thus, a census is not in itself an act that is "against" the people unless there is the sort of background that we have sketched. God had imposed three years of famine for Benjamin's refusal to repent over their slaughter of the Gibeonites. This was action "against" the people and the census-taking was likewise "against" the people and in support of David.

Finally, we might note that the plague that was visited upon the people after the census particularly fell upon Benjamin. Interestingly, the parallel account in Chronicles[1] adds the following detail (not present in Samuel),

> For the tabernacle of the Lord and the altar of the burnt offering, which Moses had made in the wilderness, were at that time at the high place in Gibeon. But David could not go before it to inquire of God, <u>for he was afraid of the sword of the angel of the Lord</u>. 1 Chron 21:29-30

Gibeon was in the territory of Benjamin, and David was afraid to go there because the plague was presumably vigorous in that area.

David numbered the people and after receiving the census data he confessed that he had done foolishly.

---

[1] Chronicles is of later provenance than Samuel.

> And David's heart smote him after that he had numbered the people. And David said unto the Lord, I have sinned greatly in that I have done: and now, I beseech thee, O Lord, take away the iniquity of thy servant; for I have done very foolishly. 2 Sam 24:10

This is not a confession that the *census itself* was foolish, but rather that **the census had been carried out without regard to the atonement price being paid**. This is shown by David's choice of punishment: he chose the pestilence or plague that would be visited upon the people if they did not pay an atonement price. He had carried out the census without proper regard to the Law:

> When thou takest the sum of the children of Israel after their number, then shall they give every man a ransom for his soul unto the Lord, when thou numberest them; that there be no plague among them, when *thou* numberest them. Exod 30:12

There is a further dimension to this foolishness and the underlying politics. The atonement price was meant for the tabernacle and sanctuary (Exod 30:16) but the tabernacle was at the time of the census in Gibeon and in Benjamin. The Levites and Benjamin were the two tribes that would have been the beneficiaries of the monies taken through the census. Their non-participation in the census is all the more telling when we see that David had not collected the atonement price.

> And David said unto God, *Is it* not I *that* commanded the people to be numbered? even I it is that have sinned and done evil indeed; but *as for* these sheep, what have they done? let thine hand, I pray thee, O Lord my God, be on me, and on my father's house; but not on thy people, that they should be plagued. 1 Chron 21:17

It is possible to mis-read David's confession: he did command the people to be numbered, but this is not the sin. It is true that his confession of sin does not identify his failing to collect the atonement price, but this is implied for those with knowledge of the Law.

H. A. Whittaker proposes that the motivation for the census-taking (disguised as a military census) was the desire by David to raise funds for the building of the Temple and he suggests that the census-taking occurred early in his reign.[1] This proposal has not received the attention that it deserves, but the narrative has no mention of atonement monies being raised or not raised. We could surmise that David *was* raising such monies for a sanctuary, but not the sanctuary-tabernacle that was at Gibeon in Benjamin. We could hypothesize that he was collecting monies for a future temple in Jerusalem. Such a proposal would explain the opposition by Benjamin and the Levites if they were vested in the existing arrangements.

The problem with Whittaker's proposal is that it does not account for the confession of sin on the part of David since the taking of a census was lawful. If David *was* exacting the atonement price, his sin would become his keeping the monies for a new temple. We don't know if the Levites would oppose such an aspiration given that it does not diminish their role in Israel. Further, while Benjamin may have opposed such an action when the tabernacle-sanctuary was in their territory, we should remember that the tabernacle moved its location around Israel. Accordingly, we would say that Whittaker's historical reconstruction is a step too far. The justice in God afflicting a pestilence upon Israel requires a legal basis and the failure to collect an atonement price seems the simpler explanation.

We might query whether David was at fault in this episode. Did *he* determine not to collect the atonement price, or was this a failure on the part of Joab and his poll-tax collectors? Or was it disobedience on the part of the people as each city, town and village was visited by Joab? We need to look at David's confession of sin. This happens in two stages:

(1)

> And David's heart condemned (נכה *nakah*) him after he had numbered the people. So David said to the Lord, "I have sinned greatly in what I have done; but now, I pray, O Lord, take away the iniquity (עון *'avon*) of your servant (עבד *'ebed*), for I have done very foolishly. 2 Sam 24:10 (NKJV)

This is the initial confession and it is followed by the affliction of the people with a plague and 70,000 die throughout all the land. With Levi and Benjamin singled out, it is possible that these two tribes were more fully in

---

[1] H. A. Whittaker notes that; "there is general agreement that 2 Samuel 21-24 consists of an appendix to the history, made up of items divorced from their chronological setting". *Samuel, Saul & David* (Cannock: Biblia, 1993), 220-226 (220).

transgression. This settles the question of culpability – the whole people were involved.

David's heart condemned him, and this is an acknowledgement of guilt rather than any self-sacrificial taking of blame.

(2)

> And David lifted up his eyes, and saw the angel of the Lord stand between the earth and the heaven, having a drawn sword in his hand stretched out over Jerusalem. Then David and the elders *of Israel, who were* clothed in sackcloth, fell upon their faces. And David said unto God, *Is it* not I *that* commanded the people to be numbered? even I it is that have sinned and done evil indeed; but *as for* these sheep, what have they done? let thine hand, I pray thee, O Lord my God, be on me, and on my father's house; but not on thy people, that they should be plagued. 1 Chron 21:16-17 (KJV)

The second confession is different; it is an **intervention** on behalf of the people. In this intervention, David **takes** responsibility upon himself and his house and **excludes the sheep** from blame.

David shoulders all the responsibility and requests that divine retribution be visited against his "father's house" instead of the people. In other words, David was asking to be "numbered with the transgressors" – to be treated as the one who had not paid the atonement money at the census-taking. In this request, David was offering to pay the price. This is why he insists that he **purchase** the temple site from his own resources. An atonement tax has not been collected but the site for the temple had still to be bought; David pays with his own resources and this is the atonement price for the census.

The Suffering Servant

There are echoes of David's "transgression" in the Servant Song of Isaiah 52:13-53:12:

number the people (מנה *manah*)	**numbered** with the transgressors (מנה *manah*)
David's heart was **smitten** (נכה *nakah*)	we esteemed him stricken, **smitten** (נכה *nakah*)

take away the **iniquity** (עון ʿavon)	he shall bear their **iniquities** (עון ʿavon)
your **servant** (עבד ʿebed)	my **servant** (עבד ʿebed)
these **sheep**, what have they done (צאן tso'n)	we like **sheep** have gone astray (צאן tso'n)

These echoes might be judged as purely coincidence; this is a reading judgment. On the other hand, they may be part of a designed contrast between the Suffering Servant who is innocent and David who was culpable. David calls himself a "foolish" servant; in contrast the servant of Isaiah is a "prudent/knowledgeable" servant. David confesses personal "iniquity" and sin and empathises with the "smitten" people by being "smitten" in the heart. The Suffering Servant is esteemed by the elders of the people to be "smitten".

These parallels with the Suffering Servant are striking. Scholars, such as M. Barker, have clearly recognised that the **atonement ritual** forms the background to Isaiah 53.[1] It is beyond the scope of this paper to explore this theme, but we can note the two most obvious connections:

He shall **sprinkle** many nations (Isa 52:15)	He shall **sprinkle** the blood (Lev 16:19)
He **bare** the sin of many (Isa 53:12)	The goat shall **bear** upon him all their iniquities (Lev 16:22)

This suggests that the Servant was modelled on the one who performed the atonement rites in the first temple. We should not be surprised to find echoes of the **atonement price** paid by David as well as the **Day of Atonement** in the description of the Suffering Servant.

Conclusion

There are problems of interpretation in the episode of David's numbering of Israel. The main problem is the puzzle as to what is wrong. Census-taking was lawful and there is nothing intrinsically "against" anyone in the taking of a census. In order to solve this puzzle we are driven to reconstruct the history behind the episode. We have inferred that the sin of David was a failure to collect the atonement price. Someone might ask: why do we have to infer anything in the first place; the text does not actually specify any sin. Such an attitude is an understandable complaint on

---

[1] M. Barker, "Atonement: The Rite of Healing" *SJT* 49/1 (1996): 1-20. [Cited May 2009] www.marquette.edu/maqom/Atonement.pdf.

the part of the historian but it fails to appreciate the conditions under which the historical records of the Israelites were recorded.

> An Aside: Dating undated prophetic books is a judgment that can only be made through a careful comparison of the language of the book with what is known about the history of Israel and Judah in Kings and Chronicles (and any non-biblical sources). **Joel** is a case in point: it requires a comprehensive knowledge of the times of Ahaz and Hezekiah to know that this is the correct placement of the book.

Survey Results

In the table below we have laid out the results of the questionnaire that we circulated to the Subscriber List in October 2009; thanks to those who replied. The feedback leads us to the following conclusions and proposals.

(1) The EJournal project should continue to run and pretty much everyone files each issue away on disk. People have different requirements and would naturally have different preferences for types of article. The only two clear messages are: first, there is no need to engage *more* scholarship, and this is consistent with our intention to reduce the scholarly element during 2010; secondly, contemporary ecclesial issues should be given more space.

(2) Articles will sometimes be too complicated and too narrow; this is inevitable but we try and balance a dry and narrow piece, or a technical piece, with something with broader appeal and without technicalities. The lack of space given to technical and complicated material in the mainstream magazines of the community is one reason why the EJournal will continue to include such material.

(3) The EJournal is a vehicle for use by writers who want to write types of material and in a style that would not be acceptable to the mainstream magazines. Consequently, while we would like to cover all the areas that people would want, the editors are themselves working on a narrower range of topics at any one time, and coverage of a broader range of issues depends on others who may write and send in a piece.

(4) The size of the EJournal and its articles are about right. The Annual should continue to include the quarterly issues but in 2010 (GW) it should include new material (not circulated in the quarterly issues). In order to facilitate this, we propose to exclude the editorials, the contents pages and

newsy items from the Annual and re-organize it logically rather than chronologically by quarter.

(5) With online publication and print-on-demand facilities it is possible to retrospectively change published material and this flexibility has been used and will continue to be used.

	Yes	No	
Is the EJournal providing a resource?	93%	7%	
Are the articles bad in any way...	**Yes**	**No**	**Some**
a) Too complicated?	7%	29%	64%
b) Too easy?		100%	
c) Too narrow?		64%	36%
Do you file the issue away on disk or discard after review?	**File**	**Discard**	
	97%	3%	
Are there areas that need covering?	**Yes**	**No**	
a) More on defending the faith?	75%	25%	
b) More on ecclesial issues like the role of men and women in the church?	82%	18%	
c) More on Bible background?	71%	29%	
d) More on exegesis?	64%	36%	
e) More on engaging scholars?	34%	66%	
f) More on church history?	41%	59%	
g) More on theology?	62%	38%	
Should the EJournal continue to run or be folded?	**Run**	**Fold**	
	100%		
Should articles be shorter - longer? Issues bigger - smaller?	**Bigger**	**Smaller**	**Same**
	90%	10%	64%
Should articles be shorter - longer? Issues bigger - smaller?	**Bigger**	**Smaller**	**Same**
	60%	40%	64%
Should the Annual include just wholly new material?	**Yes**	**No**	
	32%	68%	
Do you look at the website now and again?	**Yes**	**No**	
	68%	32%	

Babylonian Echoes in Isaiah 40-48
A. Perry

Scholars have identified traces of Babylonian cultural expression in Isaiah 40-48 and concluded that this locates the author in a Babylonian milieu. S. L. Peterson has reviewed the older scholarship on this question (up to 1975), and discussed the texts that have been adduced and their characteristics of self-predication and self-praise.[1] His conclusion is that "Deutero-Isaiah[2] [Isaiah 40-55] intentionally adopted some details of Mesopotamian style and terminology".[3] Nevertheless, he notes that while there may be specifically Babylonian elements in Isaiah 40-55, it is more often the case that those characteristics that scholars highlight are not just Babylonian, but broadly Near Eastern in provenance, and just as comparable with the Assyrian period and the older periods of Mesopotamian history.[4]

This judgment has been supported by H. M. Barstad[5] and the lines of questioning that he puts forward include: i) Are the similarities nothing more than common forms of expression around the Near East and an older cultural milieu; and ii) does the influence show that Second Isaiah was domiciled in Babylon? To these doubts we can add our proposal that if there are Babylonian echoes and allusions, it is due to Isaiah of Jerusalem's engagement with the world-view of the Babylonian envoys (Isaiah 39) and his countering of the influence of the Babylonians that had settled in Northern Israel under Sargon II.

---

[1] S. L. Peterson, *Babylonian Literary Influence in Deutero-Isaiah: A Bibliographic and Critical Study* (Unpublished PhD Diss., Vanderbilt University, 1975), 2. This is the standard review up to 1975 and is often cited.

[2] Scholars typically regard Isaiah 40-55 as the work of a Babylonian prophet called Deutero-Isaiah or Second-Isaiah. We do not, but that is a different matter; our interest here is in Babylonian echoes in the text of Isaiah 40-48.

[3] Peterson, *Babylonian Literary Influence*, 4; see also p. 45—"Deutero-Isaiah cast his message in unmistakeable contrast to the dominant Babylonian world view".

[4] Peterson, *Babylonian Literary Influence*, 75.

[5] See H. M. Barstad, "On the So-Called Babylonian Literary Influence in Second Isaiah" *SJOT* 2 (1987): 90-110.

Scholars[1] have documented certain phrases and words common to Isaiah 40-55 and Babylonian texts, and while some of these are common to a broad range of Mesopotamian cuneiform texts, it is worth noting a sample of texts in order to judge the extent to which Isaiah of Jerusalem (or Second Isaiah if you are a critical scholar) uses Babylonian forms of expression. There are two types of text: i) those that describe Yahweh's claims about himself; and ii) those that describe the relationship between Yahweh, the Servant and Cyrus.

Yahweh and the King

Examples of texts in this category include:

1) Calling an individual by name and, moreover, doing so with favour and in grace, is a feature of royal texts.[2] The Servant states that Yahweh "made mention of my name" (Isa 49:1), and Yahweh states, "I have called thee in righteousness" (Isa 42:6). This compares with Marduk pronouncing the name of Cyrus as recorded in the *Cyrus Cylinder*,[3] and other comparable phrases such as "they favourably designated his name" used of Nabonidus and "they favourably called my name" used of Esarhaddon.[4] The rhetoric here is that Yahweh has called the Servant and he also calls Cyrus (Isa 45:4) **rather than Merodach-Baladan**; any so-called calling by other gods is an empty claim.

2) The "holding of the hand" is a common ritual motif in dealings between the king and Marduk:

> I shall lead him by his hand... *Verse Account of Nabonidus*[5]

---

[1] J. W. Behr, *The Writings of Deutero-Isaiah and the Neo-Babylonian Royal Inscriptions: A Comparison of Language and Style* (Pretoria: Pretoria University Press, 1937); W. Hallo, *Early Mesopotamian Royal Titles: A Philological and Historical Analysis* (AOS 43; New Haven: American Oriental Society, 1957).

[2] Behr, *The Writings of Deutero-Isaiah and the Neo-Babylonian Royal Inscriptions*, 20-21.

[3] The Cyrus Cylinder is an inscription on a clay barrel commemorating the capture of Babylon in 539—translation in ANET, 315-316. For an overview see A. Kuhrt, "The Cyrus Cylinder and the Achaemenid Policy" *JSOT* 25 (1983): 83-97.

[4] S. M. Paul, "Deutero-Isaiah and Cuneiform Royal Inscriptions" *JAOS* 88 (1968): 180-186 (182).

[5] *The Verse Account of Nabonidus* in ANET, 313-315.

...lead him [Marduk]... *Cyrus Cylinder*[1]

May thy heart turn towards him who takes thy hand...
New Year Festival Prayer[2]

This bears comparison with,

> Thus saith the Lord to his anointed, to Cyrus, <u>whose right
> hand I have holden</u>, to subdue nations before him; and I
> will loose the loins of kings, to open before him the two
> leaved gates; and the gates shall not be shut... Isa 45:1
> (KJV); cf. 41:13; 42:6

F. Stummer has identified a number of texts (hymns) addressed to Marduk
that use the phrase "to take by the right hand".[3] The point of the rhetoric
in Isa 45:1 is directed against Marduk and Merodach-Baladan: Yahweh was
the one who would hold the hand of Cyrus, **not of Merodach-Baladan.**[4]

3) In the royal texts, common phrases such as "the beloved of the god",
"the favourite of the god" and the "chosen/selected of the god"
correspond to phrases in Isaiah like "loved one/friend" (Isa 41:8; 43:4)
"my chosen one whom I desire" (Isa 42:1).[5] Following the call by a god,
the king would be given tasks to fulfil, and this is the structure of the first
Servant Song (Isa 42:1-9); the title of "Servant" is common for
Mesopotamian kings.[6] In nominating Cyrus, the rhetoric is directed against
against both Hezekiah and Merodach-Baladan.

---

[1] ANET, 315.

[2] S. H. Hooke, *Babylonian and Assyrian Religion* (Norman: University of
Oklahoma Press, 1963), 109.

[3] F. Stummer, „Einige keilschriftliche Parallelen zu Jes. 40-66" *JBL* 45
(1926): 171-189 (177-178).

[4] This rhetoric requires "Cyrus" to be "on the scene" and we have shown
in an earlier article how "Cyrus" was a throne-name for the Persian royal
house and noted the inscriptional evidence that Teispes (675-640) bore the
name—A. Perry, "Naming Cyrus" *The Christadelphian EJournal of Biblical
Interpretation Annual 2008* (Sunderland: Willow publications, 2007), 68-73.

[5] Paul, "Deutero-Isaiah and Cuneiform Royal Inscriptions", 181; see also
Behr, *The Writings of Deutero-Isaiah and the Neo-Babylonian Royal Inscriptions*,
21-22.

[6] Behr, *The Writings of Deutero-Isaiah and the Neo-Babylonian Royal Inscriptions*,
25-26.

4) The motif of being called while yet in the womb is a common feature of the divine right of kings.[1] S. M. Paul cites texts from seven Assyrian and Babylonian kings. For example, Ashurbanipal (669-632) affirms,

> I, Ashurbanipal, am the creation of Ashur and Belit…whom Ashur and Sin, the lord of the crown, already in the distant past had called by name for ruling, and who created him in his mother's <u>womb</u> for the shepherding of Assyria.[2]

This bears comparison with Isa 49:1,

> Listen, O isles, unto me; and hearken, ye people, from far; The Lord hath called me from the <u>womb</u>; from the bowels of my mother hath he made mention of my name. Isa 49:1 (KJV)

This common form of expression contributes to the identification of the Servant as a king. This point in turn casts doubt on the Babylonian exilic reading, since the Jews had no king in exile. It lends support to our reading that the Servant is Hezekiah.

Yahweh and the gods

Examples of texts in this category include:

1) The Babylonian New Year Festival was a weeklong ritual and various activities were assigned to each day. In respect of the making of images, it is stated,

> When it is three hours after sunrise he shall summon a craftsman; then shall he give him precious stones and gold from the treasury of Marduk for the making of two images for the sixth day. He shall summon a carpenter, and shall give him cedarwood and tamarisk wood. He shall summon a jeweller, and shall give him gold.[3]

---

[1] Behr, *The Writings of Deutero-Isaiah and the Neo-Babylonian Royal Inscriptions*, 21.

[2] Paul, "Deutero-Isaiah and Cuneiform Royal Inscriptions", 185; see also Behr, *The Writings of Deutero-Isaiah and the Neo-Babylonian Royal Inscriptions*, 21.

[3] Hooke, *Babylonian and Assyrian Religion*, 104.

This kind of language is echoed in Isaiah in texts such as,

> The workman melteth a graven image, and the goldsmith spreadeth it over with gold, and casteth silver chains. Isa 40:19 (KJV)

> They lavish gold out of the bag, and weigh silver in the balance, *and* hire a goldsmith; and he maketh it a god: they fall down, yea, they worship. Isa 46:6 (KJV)

While the rhetoric addresses the manufacture of idols, it also ridicules the Babylonian New Year Festival and is one of several allusions to the festival in Isaiah.

2) The prayers to Marduk offered during the Babylonian New Year Festival have points of contact with the defence of Yahweh in Isaiah:

> Who does pass through the heavens, dost heap up the earth; Who dost <u>measure the waters of the sea</u>, who dost cause (the fields) to be tilled; Dwelling in E-ud-ul, Marduk the exalted...[1]

This bears comparison with,

> Who hath <u>measured the waters in the hollow of his hand</u>, and meted out heaven with the span, and comprehended the dust of the earth in a measure, and weighed the mountains in scales, and the hills in a balance? Isa 40:12 (KJV)

Peterson suggests that there is a contrast going on in Isaiah: while Marduk passed through the heavens, Yahweh set their limits; while Marduk measured the waters of the sea, Yahweh did so with just the span of his hand; while Marduk heaped up the earth, Yahweh weighed the dust, mountains and hills.[2]

3) *Enuma Elish* is the Babylonian creation myth that was read during the New Year Festival. Part of the myth describes the formation of the gods,

---

[1] Hooke, *Babylonian and Assyrian Religion*, 105; Peterson, *Babylonian Literary Influence*, 83.
[2] Peterson, *Babylonian Literary Influence*, 83-84.

> Then it was that <u>the gods were formed</u> within them (i.e.
> the waters of Apsu and Tiamat)...Anshar and Kishar were
> <u>formed</u>, surpassing the others.

This mythology is addressed in Isa 43:10,

> Ye *are* my witnesses, saith the Lord, and my servant
> whom I have chosen: that ye may know and believe me,
> and understand that I *am* he: before me there was <u>no God
> formed</u>, neither shall there be after me. Isa 43:10 (KJV)

Peterson comments, "...we have here a type of intellectual dependence
upon a Babylonian tradition, which dependence is demonstrated by the
prophet's conscious rejection of, and polemic against, the tradition".[1]

4) Self-predication is a form of speech in which a god asserts something of
himself/herself. The form of speech is widely used in Mesopotamian texts.
For example, in the following Sumerian hymn to Enlil (c. 1000-1300), we
read,

> I am the Lord, the lion of the holy An, the hero of Sumer,
> I make the fishes of the sea glad, and see that the birds do
> not fall down, the wise countryman, who ploughs the
> field, Enlil, <u>I am he</u>.[2]

The sequence of "I am the Lord" with intervening claims ending with a
juxtaposition of the god's name with the expression "I am he" bears
comparison with many Isaiah texts:

> Who hath wrought and done *it*, calling the generations
> from the beginning? I the Lord, the first, and with the
> last; <u>I *am* he</u>. Isa 41:4 (KJV); cf. 43:10, 13; 46:4; 48:12; 52:6

The use of this form of speech is set against the competing claims of the
gods. It is a form uniquely common[3] in Isaiah 40-48 and used in Yahweh's

---

[1] Peterson, *Babylonian Literary Influence*, 97.

[2] W. Beyerlin, ed., *Near Eastern Religious Texts relating to the Old Testament*
(London: SCM Press, 1978), 101.

[3] That is, Isaiah 40-48 characteristically expands upon the self-predication
with relative clauses and participial phrases— Peterson, *Babylonian Literary
Influence*, 116.

polemical speeches.[1] There is an additional contrast to note: Peterson observes that the form is used to affirm the solitary power of Yahweh serving and saving his people; in Mesopotamian texts the self-predication is about self-honour.[2]

5) Shamash the sun-god is given praise in an old hymn found in the library of Ashurbanipal but thought to be older (c. 1000). Its theology has an obvious point of contact with Isaiah:

> O illuminator of the darkness...you suspend (?) from heaven the circle of the earth...[3]

> *It is* he that sitteth upon the circle of the earth, and the inhabitants thereof *are* as grasshoppers; that stretcheth out the heavens as a curtain, and spreadeth them out as a tent to dwell in... Isa 40:22 (KJV)

Again, the rhetoric is brought into sharp relief: the Isaiah text affirms that it is Yahweh who controls the circle of the earth.[4]

6) The incomparability of the god is an important claim, and this was attributed to several Babylonian deities as well as other Near Eastern gods. In one text from Ashurbanipal's library, celebrating the moon-god we read,

> O lord, who decides destinies in heaven and on earth, whose saying no one can alter, who holds water and fire in his hands, who guides living creatures – who among the gods is as you are?[5]

The emphasis on "Who is like Nanna?" bears comparison with,

> And who, as I, shall call, and shall declare it, and set it in order for me, since I appointed the ancient people? and

---

[1] Peterson, *Babylonian Literary Influence*, 109.

[2] Peterson, *Babylonian Literary Influence*, 113

[3] Beyerlin, *Near Eastern Religious Texts relating to the Old Testament*, 102.

[4] Or again, given the prominence of the light of the sun and the moon in Babylonian divination, Isaiah counters with the promotion of Yahweh as the light of the people or of the Servant as the light to the Gentiles (Isa 42:6; 60:19-20).

[5] Beyerlin, *Near Eastern Religious Texts relating to the Old Testament*, 105.

the things that are coming, and shall come, let them shew unto them. Isa 44:7 (KJV)

The moon was critical in deciding the destinies of nations and the science of divination explained how the moon in its various positions and configurations conveyed to the king what was going to happen on earth.

Or again, a Hymn to Sin (the Moon god) begins,

> O Lord, hero of the gods, who in heaven and earth is exalted in his uniqueness...In heaven who is exalted? Thou! Thou <u>alone</u> art exalted.[1]

Or again in a Hymn to Inanna,

> My father gave me the heavens, and gave me the earth. I am the lady of heaven. Does anyone, any god, measure himself with me?[2]

which compares with Isa 44:24,

> I *am* the Lord that maketh all *things*; that stretcheth forth the heavens <u>alone</u>; that spreadeth abroad the earth by myself... Isa 44:24 (KJV)

The greater frequency of this type of language in Isaiah 40-48 and its popularity in Babylonian hymns of self-praise, suggests that the language is directed towards these ideas.

Conclusion

The above examples establish that Isaiah's rhetoric is engaged with Babylonian and/or Mesopotamian ideas and particularly those of the relationship between god and king.[3] It is possible to extend the connections between Isaiah 40-48 and the thought-world of Mesopotamia with more examples. For instance, the idea of divine control over history and the interest of the god in his people are obvious shared ideas reflected in Isaiah and Mesopotamian texts. In such a context, the argument in

---

[1] ANET, 385.

[2] Westermann, 156; Peterson, *Babylonian Literary Influence*, 110-111.

[3] This is the thrust of Paul's paper and observed by Peterson, *Babylonian Literary Influence*, 60.

Isaiah is that Yahweh has such control and the Mesopotamian deities are without power and foreknowledge.[1]

The texts are used to support the idea of a Babylonian Second Isaiah. Our counter claim is that the echoes illustrate how Isaiah's rhetoric is directed against **the Babylonian envoys and Merodach-Baladan**. Isaiah's argument is that Yahweh is the one true God and the one who has chosen his Servant (Hezekiah). Since "the Servant" of "the deity" is a common motif for the Near Eastern king, Isaiah's argument requires a pre-exilic context of interpretation.

The Nassouhi Prism
A. Perry

Introduction

The Nassouhi Prism is not a new discovery but it presents a problem of interpretation and historical reconstruction to Persian scholars. In an earlier article the prism was cited as evidence of the use of the name "Cyrus" in connection with the royal house of Anshan as early as 646.[2] The point of this article is to add an historical reconstruction for the prism.

The Nassouhi Prism

The name "Cyrus" is typically Elamite/Persian (*Kūrush*) and it *may* be a **given name** or a **throne name** for rulers in Anshan/Parsumash at least as early as 646. A text, from the thirtieth year (646) of Ashurbanipal, king of Assyria, has Kūrush paying tribute through his first-born son, Arukku.

The Nassouhi Prism is an Akkadian clay prism, originating from Babylon and reads:

> (When) Kurash, king of Parsumash, heard of the mighty victory, which I had inflicted on Elam with the help of Ashur, Bel, Nabu and the great gods, my lords, (and that) I had overwhelmed the whole of Elam like a flood, he sent Arukku, his eldest son, together with his tribute, as

---

[1] For example, compare the *Esarhaddon Oracles* in ANET 449-450 for points of contact with Isaiah 40-48.
[2] A. Perry, "Naming Cyrus" *The Christadelphian EJournal of Biblical Interpretation Annual 2008* (Sunderland: Willow publications, 2007), 68-73.

hostage to Nineveh, my lordly city, and implored my
lordship.[1]

The identification of this Kūrush is disputed, with some scholars willing to
equate him with Cyrus I, while others regard 646 as too early for Cyrus I to
be the ruler of Anshan/Parsumash, who is given dates like 620-590 or 640-
600.[2]

If 646 is indeed too early for Cyrus I, our suggestion would be that
"Kūrush" is a given name for Teispes[3] (675-640), the father of Cyrus I, and
Arukku a given name for Cyrus I or an older son that did not succeed in
the dynasty. Persian scholars have not made this proposal, partly because
they have adopted consensus views about Second Isaiah and his prophetic
mention of Cyrus II.[4] If we instead take Isa 44:28/45:1 to be from Isaiah
of Jerusalem, this changes the possibilities for the history in question.

In order to avoid an equation between the Kūrush of the Nassouhi Prism
and Cyrus I, scholars hypothesize about the existence of another otherwise
unknown region with a similar name of "Parsumash" (further north).[5]
Their reconstruction is that the Nassouhi Prism is about the ruler of this
region rather than the well documented Anshan/Parsumash in the south.
However, if we factor in the evidence of Isaiah (see below), then we have
two texts that give witness to a "Cyrus" of Anshan/Parsumash, one from
700 and one from 646.

The chronology of the early Achaemenids is uncertain and texts are scarce
before Cyrus II,[6] and so an equation between Teispes and the Kūrush of
the Nassouhi Prism cannot be proven or disproven, especially if the texts
from Isaiah are discounted. If we factor in Isaiah's evidence—that he had a
historical reason to nominate a Cyrus—then an equation between Teispes
and Kūrush becomes a distinct possibility. If Teispes began his reign in
675 at age 40, then he might be a young prince in 700, age 15. We know

---

[1] A. Kuhrt, *The Persian Empire: A Corpus of Sources from the Achaemenid Period*
(London: Routledge, 2007), 53.
[2] On this see M. Brosius, *The Persians* (London: Routledge, 2006), 7; E. M.
Yamauchi, *Persia and the Bible* (Grand Rapids: Baker, 1990), 71; Kuhrt, *The
Persian Empire*, 54.
[3] It is significant that Cyrus II lists the dynasty from Teispes in the *Cyrus
Cylinder* which has a number of echoes with Isa 45:1—ANET, 316.
[4] See Kuhrt's treatment in *The Persian Empire*, 84.
[5] Kuhrt, *The Persian Empire*, 54.
[6] Kuhrt, *The Persian Empire*, 47-48.

that the party of Babylonian envoys included princes and it is possible Teispes was a member of the party learning the diplomatic trade. If we change the dates of Teispes' reign, the age we hypothesize for him in 700 can also change.

The practise of taking throne names upon accession was widespread in the Ancient Near East. Although it might be thought that "Cyrus I" and "Cyrus II" indicates that "Cyrus" is a throne name, this cannot be proved. If we equate Teispes and the Kūrush of the Nassouhi Prism, Kūrush would be one of his **given** names. A. Kuhrt notes that "Kūrush" is now thought to be an Elamite name,[1] meaning "He who bestows care" or "He gives fortune". The Nassouhi Prism is anti-Elamite insofar as it celebrates victory over the Elamites; the selection of "Kūrush" as Teispes' given name in the prism could be part of this **anti-Elamite propaganda**. This is our proposal for the historical reconstruction of the prism.

We have noted that scholars are unwilling to equate Cyrus I with the Kūrush of the Nassouhi Prism. If instead, we make the equation with Teispes, the name of his eldest son, "Arukku", would be the given name of Cyrus I, and this would then be evidence for "Cyrus" being a throne name, so adopted in deference to his father Teispes (and Isaiah's prophecy given in Teispes' presence?). The throne name was then continued in the grandson, Cyrus II.

Conclusion
Our conclusion remains the same as in our earlier article: In 700, the Achaemenid dynasty was just beginning with Achaemenes, and the region of Anshan would have been perceived as an active part of the Elamite Empire, traditional enemies of Assyria and traditional allies to Babylon. The house would have been perceived in terms of the minor nobility of Elam, the junior governing partner in the Elamite alliance.[2] It is not implausible to suppose that Isaiah would have nominated a future liberator from Assyrian dominance nominating a prince of this region especially if the royal prince was a member of the party of envoys. In this case, Isa 44:28/45:1 is primary evidence for "Cyrus" being a given name of Teispes (or even Achaemenes if we want to canvass all possibilities).

An Elamite-focused prophecy nominating a Persian prince is an inspired, historically plausible, prognostication by Isaiah in 700. It works because

---

[1] Kuhrt, *The Persian Empire*, 48. Compare the older view in Yamauchi, *Persia and the Bible*, 72.
[2] Brosius, *The Persians*, 6.

the prince is **representative** of the Achaemenid dynasty and the eventual succession of kings named "Cyrus".

News: SOTS Report 2010

About 150 people gathered at Fitzwilliam College in Cambridge for the annual Society of Old Testament Winter meeting 2010. The society is a few years away from its hundredth anniversary and its membership is comprised of current, retired, aspiring or wannabe academics that have been through or are in the academic system.[1] Membership is open to anyone with Hebrew, but with meetings held only in the UK, it is largely British. Talks vary in quality and relevance to the Bible Student, but there are discounted bookstalls, and opportunities to pick up useful information from the current scribal class.

Evening talks at the conference are meant to be lighter affairs and the first evening was regaled by J. Cheryl Exum talking about "Art and the Exegete"—how renaissance painters represented biblical scenes . She chose scenes such as "David and Bathsheba" and "Abraham sending away Isaac". Nothing revelatory was said, except to note the obvious point that painters choose to represent and misrepresent the biblical narrative. For example, she discussed how the biblical text represents the morality of the sending away of Isaac through its use of distancing and how painters have represented the emotions of the episode in the faces and postures of the characters involved. Yahweh talks of "the bond woman" and the "son of the bond woman" (Gen 21:12-13) rather than "Hagar" and "Ishmael". Renaissance painters had the opportunity to pass comment on the incident in how they portrayed the emotions of Abraham, Sarah, Hagar, Ishmael and Isaac—did they paint Hagar and Ishmael as "bond woman" and "son of bond woman", badly treated, or did they paint Abraham and Sarah in a good or better light?

The most interesting talk of the 2 day conference was by Ellen van de Wolde on "to create" (ברא, *bara*) in Genesis. Her thesis was that it carries the meaning of "to separate, distinguish, divide" in the narrative. She drew a contrast with the Hebrew for "to make" (עשׂה) and observed that while this verb is common in Genesis 1 and 2 (vv. 7, 11, 12, 16, 25, 26, 31; 2:2, 3, 4), the verb (as she sees it) "to separate, distinguish, divide" is rare (vv. 1, 21, 27; 2:3, 4). The puzzle then is to explain its incidence: why does God

---

[1] The only Christadelphian to have been a president of the society is Bro. W. G. Lambert (1984).

only *bara* the whales (1:21)? What does it mean to *bara* man (1:27)? Her argument for "to separate, distinguish, divide" is based on Gen 1:1 and what God actually did with the heavens and the earth: they came about through separation of the waters. It would be fair to say that the audience was not sympathetic to the thesis. The verb occurs in 45 texts in the Hebrew bible and it would take a monograph to demonstrate the thesis for the semantic domain.

Other talks at the conference included a presentation by S. Gillingham on "Psalms 1 and 2 as an Introduction to the Psalter". This examined the history of interpretation of the two psalms to see whether commentators had taken them to be one or two in number for the purposes of introducing the book of Psalms. While the KJV of Acts 13:33 has "second psalm" for Psalm 2, there is manuscript evidence for "first psalm" (mainly Codex Bezae) as well as "the psalms". The most interesting part of the talk however was the common vocabulary between the two psalms.

Another talk that had some useful data was that by M. Nissinen on the distribution of male, female and transgender prophets in Mesopotamia and West Semitic texts. His conclusion for Assyrian prophets was that intuitive prophesying was carried out by both male and female with corresponding bias towards male and female deities. However, technical divination and its prophets were male. His explanation was that divine agency meant that human gender was not critical in being a prophet as such; however, if technical skills were required, the profession was followed by males.

Talks are a mixed bag; some may be of no value, especially if they are from a historico-critical perspective, which generally dominates at SOTS. The value in attending lies mainly in the networking opportunities—to talk to academics who have written commentaries and monographs in the field in which you have an interest. Lunch, dinner and coffee, and their respective queues were the opportunities for talking.

Marginal Notes

Genesis 2:23—Naming Eve and Feminism—PW/AP

Naming can be and is an act of dominion on occasion. For example, if the name-giver is God, a patriarch, or a king, the name given is part of the intention to shape the destiny of the one named. We see this in the naming of Abraham or Jacob/Israel. Or again, in the naming that goes on in families upon the birth of a child, we see the authority of the parent expressed and the expectation for the child encapsulated in the name. For example, we might think of the naming of Jesus in this regard.

In attempting to subvert the order of creation, feminist interpretation of Genesis 2 asserts that Adam had no dominion or rule over his wife until after the Fall. The proposal is made therefore that in the New Creation, we should return to the ideal of Eden in which the man and the woman are equal as to role. Such an argument neglects to see or deliberately puts aside the teaching implicit in Adam's naming of Eve and the cultural significance that such naming carried in patriarchal times. The naming shows that Adam had authority over Eve. The harmonization of Genesis 1 and 2 in this regard would see Eve's authority in creation as derived from her husband.

John 10:35—Scripture Cannot Be Broken—AP

What does it mean to say "Scripture cannot be broken". The verb is a common one (λύω) and the semantic field is broad: to loose, to untie, to break, to free, to abolish, to break up, to tear down, to repeal, to annul, *and so on*. Some would say that it is a statement about **textual integrity** because Jesus' argument is about particular words in a psalm. This would be a significant inference for the history of the Second Temple period. Today, we will commonly say that the original autographs were inspired and fully accurate while accepting that our copies may have errors. In short, we do not insist on textual integrity for our copies of the text.

However, we know that in Jesus' day there were different text types with regard to the scriptures; this is clear from the DSS. Was Jesus of the opinion that, say, there were copies of Isaiah in his day that were textually without error—perhaps scrolls held in the Temple? Or is there here another concept of scripture at work in this conversation? Is Jesus adverting to a **canonical status** by saying "scripture cannot be broken"? Had the canon of the Jewish scriptures recently been fixed? Is his point one of authority?

1 Cor 6:9—Sodomites—TG

It is frequently repeated in certain quarters that ἀρσενοκοῖται ("sodomites" [NKJV]; "homosexual offenders" [NIV]) refers only to certain pagan practices, and therefore does not include all forms of homosexual activity. This assertion is based upon the claim that ἀρσενοκοῖται has a narrower semantic field than is generally accepted.

The difficulty in resolving on a translation of this word is not because its etymology is unclear. It is derived from the compound of two words ἄρρην ("male") and κοίτη ("bed", euphemistically "sexual intercourse"), and thus could be literally render "males who lie with males". The difficulty concerns the fact that ἀρσενοκοῖται is not widely attested, and is not known at all before the first century AD. Since some later writers appear to use the word, or its cognates, in the context of male prostitution or pedastry, it has been proposed that one or other of these might be its meaning in 1 Cor 6:9. Without considering these usages in detail, it is apparent that unless all these references can be shown to refer solely to male prostitution or pedastry then the argument for restricting the semantic field fails.[1] The fact that ἀρσενοκοῖται is used to refer male prostitution, and pedastry, and other homosexual activity (as indeed it is) demonstrates that these term as wide semantic field and can be (and is) used generically to refer to all forms of homosexual activity.

Perhaps more significant for the understanding of 1 Cor 6:9 are the linguistic parallels in Leviticus [LXX], where the command against homosexual activity is given:

καὶ μετὰ ἄρσενος οὐ κοιμηθήσῃ κοίτην γυναικός βδέλυγμα γάρ ἐστιν (Lev 18:22)

καὶ ὃς ἂν κοιμηθῇ μετὰ ἄρσενος κοίτην γυναικός (Lev 20:13)

The parallels between these verses and ἀρσενοκοῖται are unmistakably as in both cases the root words ἄρρην and κοίτη occur. The suggestion that has met with scholarly support is that ἀρσενοκοῖται came into usage by Jewish writers, influenced by the Septuagint, looking for a word to condemn the homosexual activity of the Greek world.[2] There are a variety of Greek words available for various forms of homosexual activity. The only reason to coin a new term like ἀρσενοκοῖται would be to refer more generally about homosexual activity, reflecting the prohibitions made in Leviticus.

Returning then to 1 Cor 6:9, the meaning of ἀρσενοκοῖται seems determined by several considerations: 1) Paul, steeped in the Old Testament, is likely to have categorized sins based upon the framework of the Mosaic Law, even if he did not accept that all its prohibits were applicable to the Christian believer; 2) there are better alternatives that Paul could have used had intended to refer to either male prostitution or

---

[1] These uses are considered in detail in D. F. Wright, "Homosexuals or Prostitutes? The meaning of ἀρσενοκοῖται (1 Cor 6:9, 1 Tim 1:10)" *Vigiliae Christianae* 38:2 (1984): 133-141.

[2] Wright, "Homosexuals or Prostitutes?", 145.

pedastry; 3) Latin, Syriac and Coptic translations of the Pauline writings all attest to a general translation of this term.[1]

In sum, we can have confidence that 1 Cor 6:9 refers generically to all homosexual activity. The remaining issue is whether the English word "homosexual" (NASB; HCSB) is a suitable translation. Since in common usage "homosexual" often refers to sexual orientation rather than sexual activity, a more literal translation such as "men who practice homosexuality" (ESV) or "men who lie with men" (NWT) is preferable.

---

[1] Wright, "Homosexual or Prostitute?", 144-5.

A Tally of Two 'Theres' *
J W. Adey

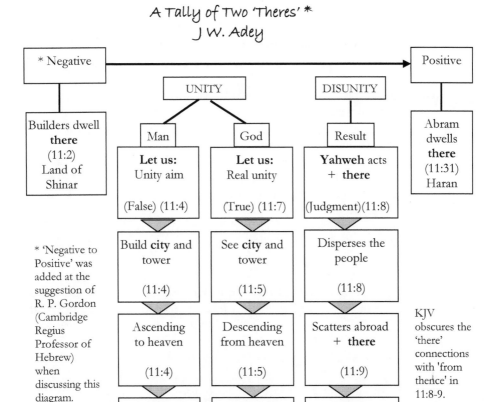

* Negative					Positive

UNITY   DISUNITY

Builders dwell **there** (11:2) Land of Shinar	Man	God	Result		Abram dwells **there** (11:31) Haran
	Let us: Unity aim (False) (11:4)	**Let us:** Real unity (True) (11:7)	**Yahweh acts + there** (Judgment)(11:8)		

* 'Negative to Positive' was added at the suggestion of R. P. Gordon (Cambridge Regius Professor of Hebrew) when discussing this diagram.

Build **city** and tower (11:4)	See **city** and tower (11:5)	Disperses the people (11:8)
Ascending to heaven (11:4)	Descending from heaven (11:5)	Scatters abroad **+ there** (11:9)
Make us **a name** (11:4)	Yahweh **+ there** (11:7)	**Yahweh** confuses **+ there** **Names** 'Babel'

KJV obscures the 'there' connections with 'from thence' in 11:8-9.

Text and context: As Gen 2:7 and 2:18, 20-23 complementarily unveil the making of man and woman briefly overviewed in 1:26-27, so the Babel incident of 11:1-9 peers into the past, providing an etiology of how the dispersal of the nations of chapter 10 came about, when (11:1): "the whole earth was of one language ('lip')".[1] Language was the Babel builders' social mortar. In 10:10, Babel heads a list of cities and is said to be the 'beginning' of Nimrod's kingdom. The new concept of 'kingdom' emerges and by implication Nimrod becomes the first king. His attitude is not godly; enthronement in Babel, this divinely judged 'there', is proof.

My diagram identifies an overall scene-setting in Gen 11 of a negative 'there' to a positive 'there'[2]; between what happens in Shinar at Babel versus Abram's arrival in Haran. Reading the Bible holistically shows the (designed) creation of counterpoint in this context.

Terms within this 'there' framework set up a significant contrast, or opposition, between Babel (Babylon) and the 'City of God'.

With Hebraic punning they occur in language about "the place God has chosen to put His **name there**" (Deut 12:5ff; 1 Kgs 14:21). The man-built heavenward Babel-'there' is a counterfeit, or inversion, of the heavenly, set-on-a-mountain-top, city, to be called 'Yahweh is **there**' (Ezek 48:35). This is Zion and Jerusalem. In this **there**, Divine **unity** will be manifested (Cf. "Song of **Ascents**" Pss 132:5, 13-17, and 133). In that day, in "a pure language", God's "**name** will be call[ed] upon, to serve Him with **one** consent" (Zeph 3:9).

Abram in the Haran-*there* introduces one who was 'looking for a city whose builder and maker is God' (Heb 11:10); a city to come (Heb 13:14); made without hands; not 'here and now'. With clean hands and a pure heart Abraham and his seed, which is Christ, will be able to enter Zion, the city of God, and ascend into the hill of Yahweh (Ps 24:3-4).

So, Babylon and Jerusalem are set in contrast and contestation. See the cultic 'high hills' in Israel (Babylonish 'theres') versus God's chosen place in Ezek 20:28, 40. But, 'Babylon the Great' is judged with ultimate finality (Rev 17). The holy city New Jerusalem, the Lamb's wife, those with the Father's **name** in their foreheads, descends and **unites** with him on Mount Zion (Rev 14:1; 21:2).

Notes
1. D. I. Block in "The Role of Language in Ancient Israelite Perceptions of National Identity", *JBL* (1984): 335 cites an ancient Babel-like parallel in a Sumerian text, mentioning one ("harmony-tongued") universal language before Enki, leader of the gods: "changed the speech . . . of man that had been one" (lines 154-156).
2. R. P. Gordon *Holy Land, Holy City: Sacred Geography and the Interpretation of the Bible.* (Carlisle and Waynesboro, GA: Paternoster Press, (2004): 40, re Ps 48: (v. 7[6]) notices that "The use of the adverb 'there' may imply something more definite than mere cultic re-enactment." He notes Ps 76:3-4 (2-3)'s juxtaposition of *Zion* and *there*.

Postscript
Editing and Writing in a Digital Age
A. Perry

The Internet with its websites, instant messaging, forums and e-mail, along with print-on-demand online publishing, has changed the possibilities in how written material is produced and circulated within the community. There is now no need (and this has been the case since the 90s) to incur costs for the following types of written material: ecclesial news, announcements, editorials, and articles. The annual subscription costs for magazines (which are not small, especially for those on a low wage or the unemployed and retired) can be avoided through the simple expedient of publishing online.

Ecclesial news could be posted online in a central place and copied to the news pages of forums (with suitable registration and password access). Archives can be kept online for reference. The same point goes for announcements and adverts of all kinds. In the same way that the ecclesial magazine was a structure of ecclesial life, changing times require a new structure in which the "ecclesial magazine" for whatever fellowship or part of the world is transferred to the Internet and made available on a free basis. For those who are without access to the Internet, local printing on desktop laser printers and circulation of material amongst ecclesial members can meet this need. And, for those who like to retain a traditional format for the magazine, this is also still possible.

The above proposal is a Western perspective and the traditional print magazine is needed in countries where the Internet is not widely available. It is a question of meeting need in the most appropriate way. For those who can and wish to access printed magazines through the Internet, there is no reason why the material should not be freely available online to individuals.

The distribution of traditional magazine content through wireless devices and mobile broadband devices such as e-book readers like the Kindle is the way forward in the next few years (should such years come along). In the same way that a person might have gone to a library or a newsstand, s/he will download the required content to an e-reader. This development is a further reason why the mode of circulation for ecclesial magazines needs to migrate from the printing press to include the Internet.

It is a fact that some, maybe many, like to hold a traditional magazine in their hands (e.g. me; I am blessed to be able to borrow and save the cost). The problem for our point of view is that only an economy of scale makes magazine printing viable; if ecclesial magazines migrate all their content to the Internet, the economic basis for a print equivalent produced and circulated on a monthly basis will be undermined. The way to meet this problem is to reduce the quality of the paper used, the print process, and the type of cover. Another way to meet the problem is to support magazines through the ecclesial donation bag. Another way is to consider the Internet as a revenue stream.

The Internet Portal could be subscription-based. There might be free areas and subscriptions areas. Ecclesias could hold a subscription pass to all areas; individuals could have access to free areas or use their ecclesial subscription pass. Some material could carry a charge, for example, PDFs, presentations, Sunday School material. Classified adverts could carry a fee, *and so on.*

The decline of one media in favour of another is unavoidable. The management of the decline does not lie in a refusal to embrace the new media. All ecclesial news, announcements and adverts should have a central location on the Internet. This Portal should also contain the content of the other print magazines produced around the world. The decline of print as a medium for magazines should be managed and several management strategies are possible.

First, there may be sufficient demand for a print magazine to justify the exercise of printing. In widening the availability of all magazine content by placing it online, there is no necessary rule which states that print magazines become unviable; it depends on the laws of demand. Secondly, magazine issues can be aggregated and printed to reduce costs. It is a simple fact that aggregating monthly issues into quarterly, half-yearly or annual print copies is cheap using print-on-demand publishing.

This strategy requires a new model in our thinking about the circulation of writing. Ephemeral content like editorials, news, announcements, and adverts do not warrant preservation in print if they are archived online. Collating the more valuable spiritual material into a quarterly, half-yearly or annual book, with proper indexing and a logical structure, satisfies the need for printed reading matter in the community in this area.

The change envisioned is not small; instead of the "ecclesial magazine" people would think of the "ecclesial internet presence". As a matter of course, most would reference the site for news, announcements, adverts, editorials and articles. From the site it would be possible to link to all ecclesial magazines that are published worldwide and participate in forums; reference individual ecclesial websites, preaching sites, *and so on*. The site would have archived magazines and e-commerce facilities to facilitate the purchase of print copies of collated collections of issues of magazines.

The mindset and role of an editor change in this scenario. S/he is no longer a writer and editor with an eye on the next book for printing or the next issue for printing. Rather, s/he is an editor of a web presence where only a small part of the job description involves handling the work of supplying copy for printing. The management of a web presence involves work with e-mail, forum management, web design, document preparation and upload, news updates, instant messaging and video conferencing—and, of course, there is the research and writing to be done.

Moving to a free model for the distribution of all magazine content has the obvious benefit of reaching greater numbers and arrests the decline in the circulation of print magazines because it circumvents this problem; it also reaches a new demographic which does not purchase a print magazine but which is active online.

Moving to an online model of distribution also requires a different attitude towards what is written. It is no longer the case that a book is written and it remains unchanged until the print run has been exhausted. Rather, with print-on-demand, a book is a work in progress. It has to be written to a certain standard for initial publication, but once in print, there is no need to regard the text as sacrosanct. It can be changed easily and uploaded as a "new impression" or, if the changes are substantial, a new edition. The quick and easy exchange of peer review of written material that the internet affords allows such change to be made in a timely manner. The same principle applies to articles published online.

There is nothing sacred about the word "monthly". News, the need for announcements, the urgent requests for prayer, the requirement to advertise—these things happen in real time and not in monthly intervals. The opportunity and the urge to share writing happen in real time and not on the first of the month before the month of publication. Moving to an online basis of publication allows sharing to happen in real time or perhaps weekly. As it is, there is news, adverts and announcements made monthly to some; to others such things happen more immediately through forums such as Facebook, e-mail, blogs and Twitter. Certainly, there is enough foreign news in the Middle East to justify a regular news comment in the appropriate area of the Portal.

Traditional Christadelphian magazine publishing needs to develop in the direction of the internet so that there is holistic approach to the circulation of written material, one where forums, blogs, websites and print-on-demand media are handled together as part of the same editorial enterprise.

The Internet is a medium of equality. Anyone can set up a web presence in the name "Christadelphian". Anything can be said when there is an arbiter of one. Discussion forums allow the exchange of any opinion around the world. The consequences of speaking out online are usually hidden. As matters stand today, there is no authority in any of the Christadelphian websites. As a result there is (as ever) the presence of false teaching. The way in which the presence of Christadelphians on the web has grown—unstructured, uncontrolled—exacerbates problems of doctrine.

The piecemeal upload of some magazine content to a website that has a domain name matching the name of a magazine does not address the needs of the situation. The ethos that has driven the magazines of the community needs to shift wholesale from the concept of "the next issue of the magazine" to the "day-to-day management of the website content". The magazine needs to be seen as an adjunct to the Internet presence from the website to the downloaded e-magazine on an e-reader.

Such a shift can only come from the editors and the committees that control the ecclesial magazines. It requires editors to assume an active online presence; it requires agreement by the main magazines to move all their content to the web and make this accessible through a central Portal; it requires good and changing web design; it requires co-operative editing and administration of the various web presences – editors/administrators both young and old.

There are some points to make by way of conclusion. In this new world the concept of what a magazine is and what an editor is changes. One way in which a magazine changes is that limits on content can be lifted. Thus the policy of including only generalist and introductory material with pictures and illustrations can be lifted so that the internet Portal includes material of a more advanced type. The concept of the "single editor" changes since web site management allows and requires cooperative editors for the various types of content. These are major changes, albeit evolutionary if they are strategically managed.

What might be the vision in such a development? The goal is a unity expressed in Eph 4:13-16,

> Till we all come in the unity of the faith, and of the knowledge of the Son of God, unto a perfect man, unto the measure of the stature of the fulness of Christ: That we *henceforth* be no more children, tossed to and fro, and carried about with every wind of doctrine, by the sleight of men, *and* cunning craftiness, whereby they lie in wait to deceive; But speaking the truth in love, may grow up into him in all things, which is the head, *even* Christ: From whom the whole body fitly joined together and compacted by that which every joint supplieth, according to the effectual working in the measure of every part, maketh increase of the body unto the edifying of itself in love.

As things currently exist the Internet is not being used in a way that fulfils the goals of this passage. Discussion forums toss people around by every wind of doctrine instantly and worldwide; websites can be set up under the name "Christadelphian" and promote contrary views, often derived from church writings, with the aim to promote a "movement" or a cause. Of course, the interplay between the Man, the Woman and the Serpent is not going to go away. But the Man has a responsibility here for teaching, and one way to facilitate and foster the unity required by Eph 4:13-16 in the context of the Internet is to bring the mainstream Christadelphian magazines and discussion forums under one Portal and to migrate all content to that Portal, supported with a shift in the mindset of the editors towards web site management and co-operative editing. This kind of strategy has a unifying effect and it acts as a counterweight to the disunity engendered by the current state of affairs.[1]

> Apologies to readers who may have noticed that that the website has been down for more than a month. This has been due to domain name registration renewal delays.

---

[1] [Ironical Footnote: It may appear as if this opinion piece is trying to do the EJournal "out of business".]

Editors: Andrew.Perry@christadelphian-ejbi.org
Paul.wyns@christadelphian-ejbi.org
T.Gaston@christadelphian-ejbi.org (Church history)
J.Adey@christadelphian-ejbi.org (Text and Language)

Christadelphian EJournal of Biblical Interpretation

Contents

- Editorial
- The Babylonian Reading of Isaiah 40-48
- The Rich Young Man
- Evangelicals and the Doctrine of the Trinity
- El Shadday
- Should 'was' be 'became' in Genesis 1:2ᵃ
- Reviews: Dever and Dunn
- Correspondence
- Marginal Notes: 1 Cor 11:3
- Christadelphian Writing
- Supporting Biblical and Historical Research
- New Websites and Blogs

Editorial Policies: The Christadelphian EJournal of Biblical Interpretation seeks to fulfil the following objectives: offer analytical and expositional articles on biblical texts; engage with academic biblical studies that originate in other Christian confessions; defend the biblical principles summarised in the common Christadelphian statement of faith; and subject the published articles to retrospective peer review and amendment.

Submission of Articles: Authors should submit articles to the editors. Presentation should follow *Society of Biblical Literature* guidelines (www.sbl.org).

Publication: E-mailed quarterly on the last Thursday of January, April, July, and October. Published as a collected annual paper-back obtainable from: www.lulu.com/willowpublications.

Subscriptions: This is a "free" EJournal to communities and individuals whose statement of faith is broadly consistent with the Christadelphian common statement.

Editorial

"It is just a phase" is a common expression, and life does go through phases. In terms of writing, if you review the last fifty years of your local ecclesial magazines, you should notice that writers have phases. They appear for a number of years and then there is nothing. It is not because they have died, but rather they have passed through a phase. If they were good writers for you, then you miss their ongoing contributions. Of course, several people write for a long time, perhaps for a lifetime, and contribute regularly. This may be a good or a bad thing; they may not be good writers for you. I say "for you" to keep things subjective, but I believe there is an objectively "good" and "bad" for writing about Scripture.

Editors have to write; writing is their hobby, and so this is just as well. If an editor is not a good writer for you, then this is a problem. If a magazine has several editors, there is a greater possibility that they will write something of value for readers, but this is not guaranteed. It is said that speakers can love the sound of their own voice and speak well beyond the time they have been allocated. The same is true of writers; they can love their own writing and give preference to that writing when filling the pages of a magazine. For an editor, this is a danger—s/he can exclude other writers' submissions because they love to see their own words in print.

Fortunately (we do not believe in the god of Fortune), the editors of the EJournal do not experience the temptation to prefer their own writing to that of those sending in material; the editors do not get very much material (obviously). It might be thought that the kind of material that we print and circulate is not being written in the community. This is partly true; however, there are Christadelphian websites where the EJournal's kind of material does appear—and this is a valuable alternative medium.

Is this editorial a lament? I don't think so; it does not matter where deeper study materials appear in the community (print and/or online); all that matters is that it does appear. It would be bad for the community if the only writing it produced was comprised of "devotion", "introduction" and "sentiment", even if these are valuable forms of writing.

The Babylonian Reading of Isaiah 40-48

A. Perry

Introduction

The Babylonian reading of Isaiah 40-48 dominates scholarship. To a considerably lesser extent you find a Babylonian reading of Isaiah 49-55, and there are still some who read Isaiah 56-66 through a Babylonian lens. Go back a hundred years and there was little doubt about the Babylonian provenance of Isaiah 49-55 and a few more willing to read Isaiah 56-66 in a Babylonian context. Christadelphian commentary has tended to follow the scholars and the Babylonian line with one or two exceptions.

One exception, H. A. Whittaker, has commented, "I am satisfied, to the point of dogmatism such as I normally decry, that Hezekiah and Isaiah (all 66 chapters) lean on each other considerably".[1] However, G. and R. Walker state, "But when we continue to read into chapter 40, we find no obvious historical markers to Hezekiah's day, such as those which made the background of chapters 1-39 so clear. Instead, all the references are to a time of redemption after a scattering and captivity – a captivity which did not take place in the days of Hezekiah, for Jerusalem was saved through the faith in the remnant therein. And the name of Cyrus appears in the text as the one who does God's will in causing the captives to return".[2] Walker and Walker follow the scholar's Babylonian reading,[3] whereas Whittaker offers an eighth century reading.

Eighth century readings of Isaiah 40-66 are rare; exilic and post-exilic readings dominate. Whittaker is able to reference a monograph by J. W. Thirtle[4] and a commentary by W. A. Wordsworth.[1] In the journal

---

[1] H. A. Whittaker, *Isaiah* (Cannock: Biblia, 1988).

[2] G. and R. Walker *The Second Exodus* (Norwich: Bible Student Press, 2001), 20.

[3] See also R. Roberts and C. C. Walker, *The Ministry of the Prophets, Isaiah* (2nd ed.; Birmingham: CMPA, 1923); or more recently in M. Vincent, "What Happens in Isaiah?" *Christadelphian Magazine* 137 (2000): 18-22; 59-62; 99-102; 138-142; 179-182; 218-222; 258-262; 299-302; 338-342; 378-382; 418-422; 459-462.

[4] J. W. Thirtle, *Old Testament Problems* (repr. Hyderabad: Printland Publishers, 2004; London: Henry Frowde, 1907). Thirtle's work is noted by W. H. Cobb, "Where Was Isaiah 40-66 Written?" *JBL* 27 (1908): 48-64 (49).

literature, there is a three-part article by J. B. Payne.[2] Apart from these writings, you have to go back to the 18th century to dig out commentaries that read the entire book of Isaiah against the background of the life of Isaiah of Jerusalem, which, you would think, was the obvious thing to do. What happened to change this situation in English scholarship was the rise of higher-critical scholarship in Germany in the 19c.

Are church commentaries right? Is the consensus right? Should Christadelphian commentary follow the church position? Over the years the Isaianic material assigned to a Babylonian provenance has narrowed so that today most would only agree upon Isaiah 40-48. Should we further restrict the Babylonian material?

These may appear arcane questions, and it is the biblical text that counts. The main argument for a Babylonian provenance of Isaiah 40-48 is the mention of Cyrus, but if we place to one side Isa 44:24-28 and 45:1-7, do we need a Babylonian reading for the rest of Isaiah 40-48. In this article, placing the Cyrus oracles to one side, we will argue two points: i) the implied geography of Isaiah 40-48 is Palestinian; and ii) the implied history of Isaiah 40-48 cannot be the times of the Exile.

Palestinian Provenance

A Babylonian exilic reading of Isaiah 40-48 can be given in a general way, but the devil is in the detail and the following details[3] do not fit a Babylonian reading:

---

[1] W. A. Wordsworth, *En-Roeh: The Prophecies of Isaiah the Seer* (Edinburgh: T & T Clark, 1939). Wordsworth's work is noted by R. K. Harrison, *Introduction to the Old Testament*, (London: Tyndale Press, 1970), 794-795.

[2] J. B. Payne, "Eighth Century Israelitish Background of Isaiah 40-66" *WTJ* 29 (1966-1967): 179-190; *WTJ* 30 (1968): 50-58; 185-203.

[3] The "evidence" we list has been compiled and adjusted from J. D. Smart, *History and Theology in Second Isaiah* (Philadelphia: Westminster Press, 1965), 20-23; C. C. Torrey, *The Second Isaiah* (Edinburgh: T & T Clark, 1928), 20-37; C. R. Seitz, *Zion's Final Destiny the Development of the Book of Isaiah: a Reassessment of Isaiah 36-39* (Minneapolis: Fortress Press, 1991), 205-207; R. J. Coggins, "Do we still need Deutero-Isaiah?" *JSOT* 80 (1998): 77-92, (85); H. M. Barstad, The Babylonian Captivity of the Book of Isaiah: 'Exilic' Judah and the Provenance of Isaiah 40-55 (Oslo: Novus Forlag, 1997), 23-33; P. R. Davies, "God of Cyrus, God of Israel: Some Religio-Historical Reflections on Isaiah 40-55" in *Words Remembered, Texts Renewed* (eds., Jon Davies, Graham Harvey and W. G. E. Watson; Sheffield: Sheffield University Press, 1995): 207-225, (213-215); J. A. Maynard, "The

1) Who is at war with Jacob/Israel (Isa 41:12)? Why is there so much fear (Isa 40:9; 41:5, 10, 13, 14; 43:1, 5; 44:2)? How would the people become a new sharp threshing instrument (Isa 41:15)? How were they to fan and scatter their enemies (Isa 41:16)? Obviously, there are no nations in and around Babylonia to satisfy these conditions. Rather, there is a state of war in the land, for which we have no corroborating evidence if this is the end of the Exile. This fits better the circumstances of Isaiah's times. Thus, there is corresponding fear on the part of the people and the reassurance that they will thresh their enemies—details that fit with the aftermath of 701.

2) Who are the Mesopotamian nations that are being called to a meeting (Isa 41:1, 21)? How had they been hostile to God's people in the Exile? There is nothing in the records of Kings and Chronicles to contextualize such a meeting. Yahweh summons the nations and islands/coastlands (see also Isa 41:5; 43:9) to a meeting place; it is more probable that this is *in* Judah rather than Babylon, because the word for islands/coastlands refers to cities towards the coast.[1] This indicates a location for the prophet proximate to the Mediterranean.

Diplomacy fits the chaotic conditions in the land after 701, with local nations and city states vying for power in the situation left by the decimation of the Assyrian army. Hence, there is a call to a meeting between Judah and the nations.

3) The anti-idol polemics are directed towards the nations (Isa 41:5-7, 21-29) in addition to the Babylonians (Isa 44:25; 46:1; 47:9-13). Cyrus was the ostensibly emergent power at the end of the Exile, so why is the prophet concerned with other nations and their idols? Where are they in the politics of the Exile? Babylonian idolatry was prevalent in the land in Hezekiah's day as a result of Sargon II's deportations to Northern Israel, and the

---

Home of Deutero-Isaiah" *JBL* 36 (1917): 213-224; M. Buttenwieser, "Where did Deutero-Isaiah live?" *JBL* 38 (1919): 94-112; W. H. Cobb, "Where Was Isaiah 40-66 Written?" *JBL* 27 (1908): 48-64.

[1] The RSV and NASB have "coastlands" and the KJV has "islands" for the Hebrew אִי. The LXX often renders אִי with νῆσος which means "island" (e.g. Isa 41:1; 42:10, 42:12, 15; 49:1; 51:5; 60:9; 66:19; cf. Acts 13:6; 27:26; 28:1, 7, 9, 11). A clear example of אִי meaning a literal island is Ezek 26:18 (RSV), and Job 22:30 is a clear figurative example of אִי meaning "city". We propose that the term refers to the city states along the coast.

idolatry of other local nations was prominent in their diplomatic interaction with Judah.

4) The state of the people is one that is "robbed", "spoiled" and "in prison" (Isa 42:7, 22); this does not fit the Exile. At the end of the Exile, the people were a settled community in Babylon and Judah. This is the sort of remark that would fit the aftermath of an invasion (701) rather than the state of a people after seventy years living off the land under Babylonian governorship. The people "snared in holes" are hiding from hostile bands (v. 22); the people in prison are captives waiting to be sold on as slaves.

5) The treatment of those in foreign lands does not fit the circumstances of the exiles. Those that ruled over them "made them howl" and they "blasphemed the name of Yahweh" (Isa 52:5). They were being shown no mercy and made to do hard labour (Isa 47:6). These details better fit the treatment of the larger numbers of Judahites involved in the eighth century Assyrian deportation of 701. Blaspheming the name of Yahweh suggests the hostility of local nations such as Moab, Ammon and Edom rather than Babylonians.

6) Parts of the south of Judah were still occupied by destroyers who had made cities waste (Isa 44:26; 49:17); they would "go forth". This is the language of the aftermath of invasion; there were no destroyers to go forth from the Jewish community in Judah or Babylon. Faithful Jews would have wanted to enlarge "their tent" by driving out occupying armies and liberating cities (Isa 54:2-3). This kind of language does not fit the aspirations of the exiles whose goal was to return to a land.

7) The address is to Zion/Jerusalem (Isa 40:2, 9; 41:27; 44:26, 28; 51:17; 52:1-2, 9), the physical city and its condition rather than to any group of exiles. The message delivered by the prophet has urgency and immediacy; Jerusalem is to be a herald to the cities of Judah (Isa 40:9). The force behind the prophetic injunction requires the prophet to be present in Jerusalem or Judah as a visible source of authority to the people of Jerusalem. This comes out clearly in the visual metaphor, "Behold, your God" (Isa 40:9) which requires the gesture of the prophet directing the cities of Judah to look and see their God coming with a strong hand.

8) Yahweh pleads with Judah to be unafraid of the nations (Isa 40:15-17), but the example nation is Lebanon. This does not suggest a Mesopotamian perspective on "the nations", but rather the Syro-Judean land-bridge. The nations are commanded to sing the praises of Yahweh (Isa 42:10) and the examples given are Kedar and Sela (Isa 42:11, RSV), which are neighbours

immediately to the east of Judah. This is not the end of the Exile; it is the chaotic conditions in 700 and afterwards.

9) The geomorphology of the oracles' metaphors is that of rivers, valleys, and mountains (Isa 40:3-5; 41:18), which suggests the topography of Judah rather than Lower Mesopotamia which is a flat plain. The "mountains" are to be threshed by Judah (Isa 41:15), which implies the presence of a prophet urging this policy upon the people in Judah; again 700 and afterwards, not 538.

10) The flora and fauna of Isaiah 40-55 is Judean. The cedar tree used for idols (Isa 44:14) is native to Judea rather than Babylonia; other trees mentioned are more naturally occurring in Judea than Babylonia (Isa 41:19; 55:13). The main tree found in Mesopotamia, the Palm, is not mentioned.

11) Yahweh states that he has "sent" to Babylon to achieve his purpose (Isa 43:14), and this implies that those he is addressing are not "in" Babylon but at some distance from Babylon. Isaiah is talking to his contemporaries about their concerns. Babylon featured in the politics of 700 as well as 538, and this remark fits 700 and after, not 538.

12) Egypt, Ethiopia and the Sabeans will make supplication to Jerusalem and affirm that God dwells in Zion (Isa 43:3; 45:15). This implies a "sphere of influence" for Judah and a perspective where the prophet is in Jerusalem and is looking south. In 700, Egypt and Ethiopia had just been defeated by Sennacherib; Hezekiah had used Arab mercenaries to reinforce Jerusalem according to Sennacherib's records. These nations are actively involved in the politics in the region in 700, but absent in 538.

13) The address to Babylon, "Go ye forth of Babylon, flee ye from the Chaldeans" (Isa 48:20, KJV), is spoken *from a distance*; the prophet does not say "flee from here" or "let us go from here"; the prophet is not among the exiles as one who expects to participate in an exodus from Babylon. This statement is consistent with a location of the prophet in Judah, and it is supported by the choice of the prophet to paint a picture of *returning to Zion* rather than *going from Babylon* (Isa 49:21; 51:11).[1] We may suppose that captives returned from Babylon in 700 and afterwards as well as 538, but this command fits the times around 700. The injunction to "flee" (ברח)

---

[1] R. Albertz, "Darius in Place of Cyrus: The First Edition of Deutero-Isaiah (Isaiah 40:1-52:12) in 521 BCE" *JSOT* 27 (2003): 371-383, (372); Barstad, *Babylonian Captivity*, 65; Coggins, "Deutero-Isaiah", 85.

does not fit with an orderly departure from Babylon under royal patronage (Cyrus); it suggests urgency in the need to take flight (cf. Isa 15:5; 22:3).[1]

14) The prophet records the words of Yahweh, "what have I here" (לִי פֹּה מַה, Isa 52:5)[2] and the demonstrative "here" is contextually defined as Jerusalem (v. 1), so that Yahweh is asking about the situation in Jerusalem (and the land). Similarly, Yahweh declares "Depart ye, depart ye, go ye out from thence" (v. 11), which has the same contextual definition and is an injunction for the people to go out from Jerusalem and engage in a holy war with the "armour of the Lord" (כְּלִי).[3]

15) The character of Yahweh's pleading with Zion and Jacob/Israel is dialogical; this suggests the presence of both Yahweh and the dialogue partner—Zion or Jacob/Israel. Thus, in Isa 40:27, Israel/Jacob says to Yahweh that his way is hidden to them, and in Isa 49:14, Zion addresses Yahweh complaining that Yahweh has abandoned them. This kind of material suggests that the prophet is present with the people in Jerusalem and engaged in dialogue with them on behalf of Yahweh. Again, Isaiah is not writing for an unborn generation 150 years in the future.

16) The prophet addresses a scattered people rather than one exiled group (Isa 41:9; 42:10-11; 43:5-6; 49:12; 54:7). The people are to be gathered from all points of the compass to the land of Judah and not just Babylon. The larger numbers involved in Sennacherib's deportation better fits this detail.

Yahweh is not "in" the north, south, east, or west; rather he is centred in Jerusalem and speaks to these places (Isa 43:5-6). The language of "gathering" is a gathering to a point from which the gatherer stands, and this is Jerusalem: the captives are "brought" to Jerusalem (Isa 42:16).

17) The First Temple exists. It is described as "our holy and beautiful house" (Isa 64:11), a description incompatible with the lament over the temple of the returnees (Hag 2:3). However, it is in a burnt state and in need of repair (Isa 64:11), and this prompts Yahweh's enquiry about the rebuilding of the house (Isa 66:1).[4]

---

[1] Torrey, *The Second Isaiah*, 49.

[2] Here we follow the marginal reading of the MT.

[3] Following Barstad, *Babylonian Captivity*, 67-69.

[4] Once the existence of the First Temple is admitted, a series of verses relating to the role of the house of the Lord come into view: Isa 56:5-7;

The temple and its sacrificial system is presupposed in Isa 43:23-24, "You have not bought me sweet cane with money, or satisfied me with the fat of your sacrifices. But you have burdened me with your sins; you have wearied me with your iniquities". This complaint would not have been made in Babylonia.

The sanctuary (Land, Jerusalem, or Temple?) was profaned because the "first father" sinned (Isa 43:27-28). Furthermore, Yahweh defers his anger (Isa 48:9) over some matter. How does this fit the end of the Exile, when the anger is meant to be over and the sanctuary is to be restored?

In addition to (1)-(17) we might ask: what should Isaiah have mentioned if he was talking in advance to the Babylonian exiles? The prophet does not address the living conditions of a group in exile; he does not show a detailed knowledge of Babylonian customs. In view of these indications, we cannot contextualise the application of Isaiah 40-48 to the end of the Exile except for the Cyrus oracles. The challenge for a conservative commentator is to construct a catalyst for the mention of Cyrus in 700; something that has not yet been done.

Conclusion

Of Whittaker or Walker and Walker, who is right? It would seem that Whittaker is right and Walker and Walker are wrong, but this may be too simplistic. There is the possibility of **secondary fulfilment** through typology; parts of Isaiah 40-48 could **in part** have a **typological application** to the end of the Exile and the return of the exiles.[1] And if there is this possibility there is also the possibility of tertiary fulfillment in the days of Christ. The mistake fostered upon the community of Christadelphian bible students by the German higher critics with their *exclusive* Babylonian reading of Isaiah 40-48 was a failure to distinguish the typological application of such oracles from their first and immediate fulfillment in Hezekiah's day.

60:7; 66:6. These texts do not fit with the image of the exiles' temple, to which Yahweh did not return.

[1] This is the mistake in the treatment of Walker and Walker in their *The Second Exodus*—of Isaiah's oracles, they say "their first, immediate fulfilment" is the Return from Exile (1, 10).

New Book from Willow:
Andrew Perry, **Isaiah 40-48**, (357 pages, ISBN 978-0-9563841-1-9). Available from www.lulu.com/willowpublications at £12.00 plus p&p.

The Rich Young Man
P. Wyns

Introduction

The gospel story of the Rich Young Man (Matt 19:16-26) has been chosen, in order to demonstrate the importance of an approach that utilizes "inner-biblical exegesis". The approach is not a purely academic exercise, but of relevance to anyone that studies or exhorts from the gospels (or for that matter the Bible in general). The charge is sometimes heard that *too much* can be *read into* (eisegesis) a text, but the truth is that ancient readers and listeners were often far more astute and 'tuned in' than their modern counterparts. Biblical texts often carry specific 'clues' (markings) – these are a few, but significant, words that form the dominant pattern of an allusion. R. L. Schultz observes:

> Yet **the comparative material suggests that minimal marking generally is the practice in literature** contemporary to the Old Testament and even later Jewish literature...One is forced to draw one of two conclusions: either the readers or listeners are not expected to identify the verbal parallel or they are considered competent to recognize it **despite only minimal marking.**[1]

B. D. Sommer notes that the key component is reader familiarity with the 'older text':

> Markers (usually borrowed vocabulary) point the reader to the older text, though only if the reader is familiar with them...In this formal category, the new text reuses vocabulary or imagery from the source...Probably the largest number of cases of what scholars have generally called 'inner-biblical exegesis' belongs to this category.[2]

---

[1] R. L. Schultz, *The Search for Quotation: Verbal Parallels in the Prophets* (JSOTSup 180; Sheffield: Sheffield Academic Press, 1999), 331.

[2] B. D. Sommer, *A Prophet Reads Scripture: Allusion in Isaiah 40-66* (Stanford: Stanford University Press, 1998), 21.

If these markings are missed then the theme that underlies the narrative is missed and the narrative is therefore subjected to a faulty interpretation. The markers will be 'special' vocabulary, but they may not be in the same 'pattern' as the original, although the words and phrases might not be organically related to the original they point to an underlying theme or topos. However, as Schultz (1999:228, 273) observes, a 'topos' is far more difficult to establish:

> These passages illustrate the problem of trying to distinguish between quotation and topos. In quotation one is looking for the repetition of significant words and syntactical structures; with topos one simply seeks the repetition of various terms conceptually related to a theme or topic.

Biblical authors allude to older texts (allusion differs from echo by the absence of the need for reference) in order to argue a specific point. Sommer (1998:15) states:

> In other words, allusion consists not only in the echoing of an earlier text but in the utilization of the marked material for some rhetorical or strategic end.

The Rich Young Man and the Rich Old Man

A casual reader of Matthew 19 will encounter a number of seemingly unrelated narratives. The chapter begins with a question about divorce (vv. 1-12), followed by the blessing of little children (vv. 13-15) and the encounter with the rich young man (vv. 16-30). However, once the 'markers' are identified the chapter's cohesiveness will become apparent.

The emphasis in vv. 16-30 is on the **wealth** of the young man – "he had great possessions" (κτήματα πολλά) and this prevented him following Jesus, who comments to his disciples; "Assuredly, I say to you that it is hard for a **rich** (πλούσιος) man to enter the kingdom of heaven" (v. 23). This astounded the disciples for if a man of such apparent moral integrity and wealth (a sign of God's blessings?) struggled to enter the kingdom, what hope for them?

It is at this juncture that the 'marker' points us in the right direction. The word **rich** is used **for the first time** in scripture to describe Abraham's circumstances; "And Abram *was* very **rich** (πλούσιος) in cattle, and silver, and gold" (Gen 13:2).[1] Further investigation discovers other lexical connections with the Abrahamic narrative.

> And , behold, one came and said unto him, Good **Master** (διδάσκαλε) , what good thing shall I do , that I may have eternal life ? Matt 19:16 (KJV)

> And he said, **Master** (δέσποτα) *and* Lord, how shall I know that I shall inherit it? Gen 15:8 (LXE[2])

Even though the KJV and LXE translate the word in question as "master" different Greek words are employed, the passages are syntactically similar and both pose questions about gaining/possessing/inheriting something. When investigating shared concepts and themes, A. Perry notes:

> The spread of words and/or phrases from the source text involve the reader/hearer in taking the whole of the source context as the background for the quoting narrative.[3]

Once the source text is identified (in this case the Abrahamic narrative) the markers become more readily identifiable:

> But Jesus looked at *them* and said to them, "With men this is **impossible**, (ἀδύνατόν) but with God all things are possible" Matt 19:26 (NKJV).

> Shall anything be **impossible** (ἀδυνατεῖ) with the Lord? At this time I will return to thee seasonably, and Sarrha shall have a son. Gen 18:14 (LXE).

Sometimes the texts employ different words but convey the same sense:

> Jesus said to him, "If you want to **be perfect,** (τέλειος) go, sell what you have and give to the poor, and you will have

---

[1] With the NT it is easier to use the Greek of the LXX as a, albeit imperfect, guide to correspondences rather than the Hebrew MT.

[2] The LXE is Brenton's translation of an LXX text.

[3] A. Perry, "Quotes, Allusions and Echoes" in *The Christadelphian eJournal of Biblical Interpretation Annual 2007* (Sunderland: Willow publications, 2007), 69-74, (72).

treasure in heaven; and come, follow Me." Matt 19:21 (NKJV)

And Abram was ninety-nine years old, and the Lord appeared to Abram and said to him, I am thy God, be well-pleasing before me, and **be blameless** (ἄμεμπτος). Gen 17:1 (LXE)

First century auditors would have recognised the connection with Abraham, and modern readers have also, as together with Matt 19:21, the Modern Greek Bible translates complete/perfect/whole from the Hebrew *tamim* (תָּמִים) of Gen 17:1 as *teleios* (τέλειος) instead of *amemptos* (ἄμεμπτος) used in the Greek Septuagint (LXX). Moreover, the injunction to "follow me" echoes the divine calling out of Abraham (Gen 12:1) and the **"treasure in heaven"** corresponds with God declaring "I *am* your shield, your **exceedingly great reward**"(Gen 15:1).

Jesus' advice to the rich young man draws on Yahweh's assessment of Abraham's faithfulness:

But if you want to enter into life, **keep the commandments** (τήρησον τὰς ἐντολάς) Matt 19:17 (NKJV)

Because Abraam thy father hearkened to my voice, and **kept** (ἐφύλαξεν) my injunctions, and **my commandments** (τὰς ἐντολάς), and my ordinances, and my statutes. Gen 26:5 (LXE).

Although there are only a few verbal correspondences, the theme for Matt 19:27, 29 also shares the topos of Abraham's calling:

Then Peter answered and said to Him, "See, we have left all and followed You. Therefore what shall we have?"Matt 19:27 (NKJV)

And everyone who has left houses or brothers or sisters or father or mother or wife or children or lands, for My name's sake, shall receive a **hundredfold**,[1] and inherit eternal life. Matt 19:29 (NKJV)

Now the Lord had said to Abram: "Get out of your country, From your family And from your father's house, To a land that I will show you". Gen 12:1 (NKJV).

Based on what has already been observed the last verse is probably a reference to the right of primogeniture, with the **first** being Ishmael (Abraham's seed after the flesh) and the **last** being Isaac (Abraham's seed after the spirit):

But many *who are* first will be last, and the last first. Matt 19:30 (NKJV)

As well as correspondences, we should also be aware of deliberate contrasts, such as the **sorrow** of the rich young man (Matt 19:22) contrasted with the **laughter** (and rejoicing; cf. John 8:56) of Sarah/Abraham (Gen 21:6), and the **everlasting possession** promised to Abraham in Gen 17:8 and **eternal life** of Matt 19:16, contrasted with the **great possessions** of the rich young man.

Interpretation and Application

Inner-biblical exegesis has identified connections with the Abrahamic narrative and the story of the rich young man is obviously deliberately referenced against Abraham. This should influence the way the narrative is interpreted.

Although riches form a key element in the narrative, the story is not *per se* a warning against the evils of materialism, for Abraham was extremely wealthy. The incident highlights the danger of a worldview prevalent in Judaism that understands entry into the kingdom as an act of human effort (works). Keeping the commandments (law) was of course critical but (here is the rub) **Abraham kept the law before it was even given.** The demands of Christian life seemed impossible to the disciples but (here is the rub) nothing is impossible with God because he is able to make the **barren bear fruit.** In fact he has given the means of redemption through

---

[1] There is probably a reference here to Isaac: "Then Isaac sowed in that land, and reaped in the same year a **hundredfold**; and the Lord **blessed him**" (Gen 26:12, NKJV).

the son promised to Abraham and therefore made the impossible, possible.

This does not mean that works are unnecessary, for Abraham was willing to give up his prize possession (his son) because he believed that God would provide. However, Abraham's work was an act of faith, not one of self assertion. He is justified by faith and he is "counted righteous" because **he believed that God is righteous.** Although he did not know how, his life experiences had taught him that God would keep covenant and therefore he believed that the promise through Isaac would (somehow) be honoured. Instead of Abraham giving up his prize possession, God sacrifices his beloved son. The purpose of the law was to emphasise the righteousness of God, not the (non-existent) righteousness of man.

In contrast with the rich old man, the rich young man was unwilling to give up his prize possessions and law keeping became therefore irrelevant. The rich young man failed to recognize that faith in the Messiah (who is the embodiment of the righteousness of God) was the only way to be justified. The conclusion of the story is to respond to the call of God/Jesus in faith (with rejoicing instead of sorrow), like Abraham, knowing that the reward held in store is disproportionate to the response – that it does not rely on human effort but on divine faithfulness which makes the impossible, possible.

The Cohesiveness of the Chapter

Do the connections with Abraham extend beyond the story of the rich young man? This becomes more difficult to establish as lexical and syntactic markers virtually disappear. Thematic connections remain, but they become a question of reader perception which can be subjective.

For example, the blessing of the "little children" (Abraham's seed) by Christ is probably meant to parallel the blessing of Abraham by Melchizedek. It also highlights that God keeps covenant and does the impossible – the evidence is simply that the descendants of barren Abraham/Sarah are being blessed by the Christ – who is the descendant of Abraham. The "little children"[1] become then a metaphor for all disciples who approach Jesus with the faith of Abraham.

---

[1] "Assuredly, I say to you, unless you are converted and become as little children, you will by no means enter the kingdom of heaven" (Matt 18:3, NKJV).

At first glance the question on divorce seems completely unrelated to the Abrahamic narrative, but rather the settling of a disputed question between different rabbinical schools of thought. The question was posed by the Pharisees as a "test" (v. 3) and raises suspicions that theological concerns were not the primary motivation. If we turn to the Abrahamic narrative we find that he "divorced" his maidservant Hagar at the behest of Sarah. This was done because Hagar encouraged her son to mock the legitimacy of the heir with the charge that he had been conceived in the tent of Abimelech (Gen 20:18-21:1). Obviously parallel questions existed around the legitimacy of Christ and rumours abounded about his unusual conception.

Relating the Abrahamic narrative to the question of divorce might seem far- fetched but not if the underlying question is one of adultery/legitimacy. This theory is lent support by John 8 which also commences with a question about adultery (John 8:3-11) and Jewish emphasis on Abrahamic status (John 8:33, 37) and the reply of Jesus which is based on the expulsion of Hagar and Ishmael (John 8:35). The true seed of Abraham has his legitimacy questioned and this is the subtext of divorce/adultery questions in the gospels that are directed at Christ.

Conclusion

Scripture interprets itself and ancient readers/hearers of the word deserve more credit than their modern counterparts for recognising complex patterns, allusions and echoes that lie below the surface of the narratives. Good biblical exhortation can only be achieved if inner-biblical exegesis is practised. If exhortation is based on a superficial surface reading then it usually misses the point completely.

Evangelicals and the Doctrine of the Trinity
T. Gaston

Introduction

In 2003, the *Evangelical Quarterly* published an article entitled "The Christadelphians and the Doctrine of the Trinity".[1] The article was written by J. Clementson, a former Christadelphian turned evangelical, with the expressed aim of finding "constructive alternatives" in language to aid Christadelphians in understanding and accepting the Trinity. In this present article I intend to explore the issues raised by Clementson.

---

[1] J. Clementson, "The Christadelphians and the Doctrine of the Trinity" *Evangelical Quarterly* 75.2 (2003): 157-176.

Evangelicalism

Clementson begins his article with a fair description of the origins of the Christadelphian movement, followed by summary of Christadelphian beliefs about Christ and the Holy Spirit.[1] A comparable analysis of the evangelical movement is not possible here, but a few general comments will be useful.

Evangelicalism may be defined as a theological system that puts emphasis of personal faith and conversion (being "born again") and the authority of the Bible. Nevertheless, the term carries a certain degree of ambiguity and can refer to a spectrum of beliefs. Belief in the tri-unity of God is one of the core tenets of the evangelical movements; it appears top of most evangelical statements of faith.[2] This emphasis on the doctrine of the Trinity may in part be explained as a reaction to apathy shown to the Trinity by the Protestant churches during the 18th and 19th centuries. It may also be a result of the significance placed on the doctrine of penal substitutionary atonement.

The evangelical emphasis on the authority of the Bible is something that they have in common with Christadelphians, in contrast to the authority given to tradition in the Catholic and High Anglican churches. It is ironic, then, that the evangelicals, including Clementson himself, often refer to the creeds and councils of Catholic Church to define and defend the doctrine of the Trinity.[3]

Sonship

Clementson writes, "The Christadelphian understanding of Jesus as the Son of God places much more emphasis on his virginal conception than does the New Testament" (p. 166). Whether or not this assessment is fair, it is nonetheless irrelevant since the issue of sonship is about ontology rather than an emphasis. The divine affirmations of Jesus' sonship at his baptism (Mark 1:9-11) and resurrection (Acts 13:33) do not explain how Jesus came to be the Son of God. It is the virginal conception of Jesus that explains both how he came to be and how he came to be the Son. The burden is upon evangelicals to find an understanding of sonship that coheres with their belief in the eternity and equality of the Father and the Son.

---

[1] Clementson, "The Christadelphians", 157-163.
[2] See the statements on the websites www.eauk.org, www.ifesworld.org and www.theevangelicalchurch.org [cited 15/01/10].
[3] Clementson, "The Christadelphians", 168, 170-1, 175.

Clementson puts much emphasis of the Johannine presentation of a pre-existent relationship between the Father and the Son (pp. 166, 169), arguing that Christadelphians did not give full significance to the Son. Yet he undermines his own argument in his attempt to argue that "Jesus does not speak on behalf of the Father" (p. 169). This is exactly what Jesus claimed to do: "I have not spoken on my own authority, but the Father who sent me gave me a command, what I should say and what I should speak" (John 12:49). Though we can agree that the Son should be distinguished from the angels and prophets who previously spoke on God's behalf, it is no denial of the Son to give preeminence to the Father.

The next argument is patristic, not Biblical: "the early church fathers concluded in the process of opposing Arius, if Jesus came to reveal the Fatherhood of God, then that Fatherhood must be intrinsic to God himself. And if God has always been Father, then he has always had a Son" (p. 170). This argument rests on the assumption that the content of temporal revelation is to be equated with ontological necessity; i.e. if God is a father, then to be God is to be father, therefore God was eternally father. The fallacy of the argument is demonstrated if we replace the concept of fatherhood with that of creation. If God is a creator, then (by this argument) to be God is to be creator, therefore God was eternally creating. Yet it is the teaching of the Bible, and generally accepted by Christians, that the world was created in time. Whilst God always had the power to create, there was not always a creation. Whilst God always had the power to "father" a child, there was not always a Son.

Pre-existence

Clementson notes the Christadelphian interpretation of Phil 2:6-8, that it refers to decisions made by a human Jesus not a pre-existent Son. He acknowledges that this opinion is shared by J. D. G. Dunn,[1] but gives preference to N. T. Wright, who argues that here is a non-human choosing to become human.[2] Thus, Clementson concludes, "the Christadelphian interpretation fails adequately to explain the reference to becoming human" (p. 167). However, it should be acknowledged that Paul does not say that Jesus took on the "form of a man" but the "form of a servant" – this was his choice. The "becoming in the likeness of men" is unlikely to refer to a change in nature since Paul refers only to "likeness" (*homoiomati*), not to form or nature. This being the case, it is likely that here Paul talking

---

[1] J. D. G. Dunn, *Christology in the Making* (2nd ed.; London SCM Press, 1989), 113-121.

[2] N. T. Wright, 'Adam in Pauline Christology', *SBL Seminar Papers* 22 (1983): 373-84.

about the outward appearance (clothes, mannerisms, etc.). No pre-existence need be implied.

Regarding Col 1:15-20, Clementson chastises Christadelphians for missing the allusion to Wisdom 7:25-26 due to "an unwillingness to consult any non-canonical sources" (p. 166). In fairness, most Christadelphians are probably ignorant of the views of modern biblical scholarship regarding the influence of Wisdom literature in early Christology. Even if we concede that possibly Paul, and certainly John, identified Jesus with a personified attribute of God,[1] it is not clear how this furthers the doctrine of Trinity. A personified attribute cannot make conscious choices to become human (see above).

Three Christadelphian objections to the concept of the pre-existent Son are noted, though the commonest is not mentioned – that Christadelphians do not find the pre-existent Son in the Bible. The first objection is "that God cannot be two (or three) persons because he is one" – more on this later. The second is "that a truly human person cannot pre-exist", to which Clementson responds that this is based upon a misunderstanding of Trinitarian doctrine: the human being called Jesus did not pre-exist, only the divine Son pre-existed. Clementson blames "popular Trinitarian language" for leaving itself open to such misunderstanding (p. 170). This clarification does not help much, because it does not explain how a divine person can become truly human. This is the third objection. Clementson acknowledges the problem of maintaining a personal continuity between the pre-existent Son and the human Jesus: "If, by personal continuity, we mean continuity of individual conscious existence and memory, then this must surely be rejected as interference in his ordinary humanity and, in modern terms, physiologically impossible" (p. 171). Clementson thus proposes an alternative understanding of the incarnation, "not the continuity of an individual being, but the embodiment in a new human individual of the parent-child relationship eternally present in the Godhead" (p. 171). Before evaluating this understanding of the incarnation it is important describe Clementson's view of personhood.

Personhood

The Trinity is traditionally defined as three persons (Gk: *hypostasis*) in one substance (Gk: *ousia*). It is Clementson's proposition that this language is of little value for discussion with Christadelphians because the term

---

[1] T. E. Gaston, 'Wisdom and the Goddess', *Christadelphian Ejournal of Biblical Interpretation*, 2:1 (2008): 53-60.

'person' is open to misunderstanding (p. 174). 'Person' in modern usage carries the connotation of a distinct individual being; Clementson acknowledges "on these terms, God is clearly one person, not three" (p. 175). He proposes, therefore, that what the church fathers expressed in *hypostasis* could be expressed to modern ears as "distinguishable centres of personhood" (p. 175) and as "relational qualities" (p. 171).

It is not entirely clear what is being expressed in these terms. Are these "centres of personhood" conceived of separate and distinct minds, or as aspects of the same mind? Are they self-conscious identities, or clusters of qualities? Clementson has already rejected the idea that the Son had an individual consciousness continuous from his divine state to his incarnation, proposing instead that Jesus was a new individual that embodied pre-existing relational qualities. This tends towards the concept that Father, Son and Spirit are not self-conscious minds but clusters of qualities. Such a doctrine would seem to tend towards a form of modalism, which is generally regarded as heresy.

Moreover, it seems to create numerous inconsistencies with common Trinitarian belief and practice. For instance, contrary to common evangelical dogma, Jesus apparently did not have a conscious pre-existence prior to his birth, at least not in any conventional sense, but his consciousness was created at his birth to include a cluster of qualities. Does this consciousness continue to exist? Clementson is unclear on this point. He insists that the human Jesus did not cease to exist and he ascended to the Godhead with his humanity "intact" (p. 172). Does this mean that there are now two consciousnesses within the Godhead, or has the Jesus-consciousness been subsumed into the consciousness of God? Furthermore, if the Trinity is not three consciousnesses but three clusters of qualities then in what sense is it meaningful to worship or pray to the Father, the Son and the Spirit? How can one have a personal relationship with a cluster of qualities? Surely, if God is a single conscious being then one can only have a relationship with God as unity. Such a tendency would seem to make the concept of the Trinity meaningless.

Despite the noble intention of the author of attempting to identify the right language for discussion with Christadelphians, it seems to me, at least, that he has failed. Neither *hypostasis* nor "distinguishable centres of personhood" are Biblical expressions for talking about the Father, the Son or the Spirit, and so are unlikely to appeal to Christadelphians.

Divine Identity

With regards to positive reasons for identifying Jesus as God (or the incarnation of a cluster of divine qualities, if you prefer), Clementson presents three. The first is R. Bauckham's concept of divine identity as presented in *God Crucified* (p. 167).[1] Bauckham asserts that Second Temple Judaism was "characterized by a 'strict' monotheism that made it impossible to attribute real divinity to any figure other than the one God",[2] thus any ascription of divine qualities to Jesus by the New Testament writers should be interpreted as including Jesus in "the unique divine identity as Jewish monotheism understood it".[3] Instances of Jesus sharing God's throne, having sovereignty over all things, being given the divine name, and being worshipped (see below) should, according to Bauckham, be taken as including Jesus in the divine identity.

The flaw in Bauckham's argument is the assertion of a strict monotheism in Second Temple Judaism. In reality the strict monotheism of Rabbinic Judaism that precludes "semi-divine" beings arose as a response to Christianity, and was not characteristic of Second Temple Judaism, which was heterogeneous. I have argued elsewhere,

> Jews of Jesus' day did not operate under a two-category system … but a multi-categorical system with God at its head. Nothing preached by Jesus or the early apostles implied that Jesus belonged in the God-category.[4]

In any case, in the NT believers are promised to sit on the divine throne (Rev 3:21), to have sovereignty over the nations (Rev 2:26), to bear the divine name (Rev 3:12), and to be worshipped (*proskuneo;* Rev 3:9). This argument fails to do justice to explicit statements in the NT that distinguish Jesus from the unique divine identity, that is from the one God (1 Cor 8:6; 1 Tim 2: 5; John 17:3; Jude 1:4; Eph 4:5-6).

---

[1] R. Bauckham, *God Crucified: Monotheism and Christology in New Testament* (Carlisle: Paternoster, 1998). [Ed. AP: Bauckham is aware of Christadelphian views, via personal conversations with me when he was at Manchester University and through his reading of A. Eyre, *The Protestors* (Birmingham: CMPA, 1976).]

[2] Bauckham, *God Crucified*, 2.

[3] Bauckham, *God Crucified*, 26.

[4] T. E. Gaston, *Proto-Trinity: The Development of the Doctrine of the Trinity in the First and Second Christian Centuries* (MPhil diss., University of Birmingham, 2008), 67.

Worship of Jesus

Clementson gives special emphasis to the worship of Jesus. He recognizes two ways in which Jesus may be worshipped, either because God specifically commands it or of one who is within the Godhead. The former alternative, which he identifies as the Christadelphian position, Clementson describes as coming "dangerously close to the polytheism that Christadelphians claim to reject" (p. 171). It is only the latter alternative that can be properly exercised within monotheism and thus is the only alternative that can explain the worship of Jesus by early Christians (p. 172).

The assumption that underpins this argument is that all worship is of the same sort and thus any form of worship carries with it an implicit recognition of divinity. This is simply not the case. The word used in the NT to describe the worship of Jesus is *proskuneo,* which can be used both of the worship of God and the reverence of worthy men (cf. Matt 18:26; Rev 3:9). An act of *proskuneo* implies only respect and honour, not the worship of a deity. The word used for the exclusive worship of God is *sebomai* and its cognates (cf. Rom 1:25). This is not applied to Jesus in the NT.[1]

Jesus and the Spirit

The third reason Clementson gives for identifying Jesus with God is his privilege of outpouring the Holy Spirit. Acts 2 records that Jesus poured out the Holy Spirit on the disciples. "But", Clementson reasons, "in Old Testament terms, the Spirit is not an independent power, but part of God's own identity; there is no place for the Spirit being owned or controlled by anyone other than God". Thus the outpouring of the Spirit by Jesus signifies that he is God. This, he says, is "perhaps the strongest argument of all for placing the exalted Jesus within the Godhead" (p. 169).

Clementson anticipates the Christadelphian response, that God granted Jesus control of this power. However, in fairness, it is not a Christadelphian argument at all but *ad verbim* quotation from the text:

> Therefore being exalted to the right hand of God, and having received from the Father the promise of the Holy Spirit, he poured out this which you now see and hear (Acts 2:33 [NKJV])

---

[1] T. E. Gaston, "Worship of Jesus" *Christadelphian EJournal of Biblical Interpretation* 3:2 (2009): 69-72.

One can hardly argue that Jesus was not given the Holy Spirit when the text itself states that he received it. Also, since there are ample references to the Holy Spirit being given and received by believers in the NT (John 7:39; Acts 8:15-9, 10:47, 19:6), it seems impossible to argue that one should need to be God to do either. Clementson baldy asserts that the Holy Spirit in the OT is part of God's identity without citing any biblical text or any scholarly authority.[1] Yet elsewhere in his article he acknowledges that the Holy Spirit in the OT "can be understood simply as God's power" (p. 172).

Holy Spirit

Clementson's comments regarding the Holy Spirit are somewhat reserved. He acknowledges that the Spirit can be understood as the power of God and that personification of the Spirit in the NT is not sufficient evidence of real personhood (p. 172). He even goes so far as state that if the Son is not regarded as being in the Godhead then "it is sufficient to discuss the relationship between the Father and the Spirit in terms of a person and his power" (p. 174). His argument for the "distinct identity" or "personhood" of the Spirit is taken from those NT passages that speak of the Spirit of Jesus (citing Rom 8:9; Gal 4:6; Phil 1:19): "we are forced to consider that the Spirit must in some sense be distinguishable from both Father and Son in order to be sent by either" (p. 173).

This argument fails to establish the personhood of the Spirit. If I project my voice from one room to another I can claim a certain independence for my voice (it can be in one room while I am in another); this does not mean my voice has personhood distinct from my own. That God can send his Spirit signifies some level of independence but not personhood. Further that the Spirit is often sent, but never sends itself, would seem to deny personhood. Those passages which speak of the spirit of Jesus deserve further evaluation since it is far from clear that the spirit of Jesus is the Holy Spirit.

Threefold Experience of God

Clementson avers, "The ultimate test of orthodoxy is not adherence to the ancient creeds but a faith that naturally expresses itself in the same way as the New Testament" (p. 175). Clementson believes that this natural

---

[1] [Ed. AP: This is also the principal argument of M. M. B. Turner (London School of Theology Professor), "Towards Trinitarian Pneumatology – Perspectives from Pentecost" in his *The Holy Spirit and Spiritual Gifts: Then and Now* (Carlisle: Paternoster, 1996), 166-176.]

expression is the threefold experience of God, which he claims the first believers knew. For all this, he can only provide two NT expressions of the threefold experience of God, each of which betrays his purpose: i) 2 Cor 13:14 speaks not of three divine persons but one "God", one "Lord Jesus" and the Holy Spirit. This does not appear to be a threefold experience of God, but a singular experience of God, accompanied by his Son and his power. Comparison with the close of Paul's other letters demonstrates that he did not experience God in Trinity; his usual benediction is "the grace of our Lord Jesus Christ be with you" (Rom 16:24; 1 Cor 16:23; Phil 4:23; 1 Thess 5:28; 2 Thess 3:18; cf. Gal 6:18); and ii) the baptismal formula of Matt 28:19 also does not speak of three divine persons, but is rather an early form of baptismal confession centred on a shared name.[1] This threefold formula must be contrasted with the early Christian practice of baptizing "in the name of Jesus Christ" (Acts 2:38, 8:16, 10:48, and 19:5).

Conclusion

In conclusion we can say that while Clementson has tried to be sympathetic to Christadelphians, his logic and arguments break down. The Christadelphian understanding and experience of God is based upon the Bible. There they encounter one God, the Son of God and the power of God.

El Shadday
P. Wyns

Introduction

This article originated as an exegesis of Ex 6:3, a verse that employs the epithet *El Shadday* (translated as "God Almighty") and the *Yahweh* name. It was realised that in order to do the subject justice the epithet required separate treatment. The problem is that no academic consensus[2] has been

---

[1] Cf. U. Luz, *Matthew 21-28: A Commentary* (Philadelphia: Fortress Press, 2003) 632.

[2] A brief survey of scholarship demonstrates a lack of consensus on the meaning and origin of this title. W. F. Albright offers the suggestion that *Shaddai* comes from the Babylonian *"Sadda'u,"* the gentilic of *Sadu,* noting that *Saddu* is the regular word for mountain; see *From the Stone Age to Christianity* (The Johns Hopkins press, 1940), 180 ff. G. F. Oehler avers that it is from the root *sadad* "to be strong" or "powerful" in his *Theology of the Old Testament,* (Zondervan Publishing House, 1962). , C. I. Scofield said that it was from *sad* which has primary reference to the female breast signifying nourishment, *Scofield Reference Bible,* (Oxford: Oxford University Press, 1917), 26. Recent studies also emphasise the feminine aspect: see D.

reached on the meaning of the title therefore philological and etymological approaches alone are not sufficient to reach a decisive conclusion. Indeed J. Barr has been critical of the traditional emphasis on comparative and etymological study because of its unfortunate semantic effects and admits (using rare Hebrew words as case examples) that "literary questions are relevant and one cannot proceed purely linguistically".[1] The case put forward here is therefore largely associative and contextually based, although some supporting philological and etymological evidence will be provided from recent studies.

Survey of OT usage

Shadday occurs 48 times in the Hebrew Bible the distribution is as follows:

Book			Form		Description
Gen-Num	Genesis 28.3; 43.14; 48.3	3	אל שדי	ʾēl šadday	Compound form (God Almighty)
	Genesis 17.1; 35.11	2	אל שדי	ʾēl šadday	Compound form: self-introductory formula - ʾănî-ʾēl šadday (I *am* God Almighty)

Biale, "The God with Breasts: *El Shaddai* in the Bible", *History of Religions* XXI.3 (Feb/1982): 240-256 and H. Lutzky, *Shadday as a Goddess Epithet* (Leiden: E. J. Brill, 1998).
[1] J. Barr, *Comparative Philology and the Text of the Old Testament*, (Eisenbrauns, 2001), 423; see also his *Semantics of Biblical Language* (London: Oxford University Press, 1961).

	Book		Form	Description
Gen-Num	Genesis 49.25	1	שׁדי šadday	Note paronomasia: šadday... šāḏáyim (Almighty... breast)
	Exodus 6.3	1	אל שׁדי ʾēl šadday	Compound form (God Almighty)
	Numbers 24.4,16	2	שׁדי šadday	Simple form
Writings	Ruth 1.20,21	2	שׁדי šadday	Simple form
	Job 5.17; 6.4,14; 8.3,5; 11.7; 13.3; 15.25; 21.15,20; 22.3, 17,23,25,26; 23.16; 24.1; 27.2,10,11,13; 29.5; 31.2,35; 32.8; 33.4; 34.10,12; 35.13; 37.23; 40:2	3 1	שׁדי šadday	Simple form
	Psalms 68.14; 91.1	2	שׁדי šadday	Simple form
Prophets	Ezekiel 1.24	1	שׁדי šadday	Simple form
	Ezekiel 10.5	1	אל שׁדי ʾēl šadday	Compound form (God Almighty)

	Book	Form		Description
Prophets	Isaiah 13.6	1	שׁדַּי šadday	Simple form Note paronomasia: šōḏ miššadday destruction from the Almighty
	Joel 1.15	1	שׁדַּי šadday	Simple form Note paronomasia: šōḏ miššadday destruction from the Almighty

In addition to the above table,[1] there are theophoric names to note:

- **Zurishaddai**[2] (my rock is *Shadday* - Num 1:6; 2:12; 7:36, 41; 10:19).

- **Ammishaddai** (the people of *Shadday*, or *Shadday* is my kinsman - Num 1:12; 2:25; 7:66, 71; 10:25).

- One name is pre-fixed with *Shadday*, which is **Shedeur** (*Shadday* shines, or light of *Shadday* - Num 1:5; 2:10; 7:30, 35; 10:18).

Shadday in Genesis

The first use of the epithet is also the self-introductory formula, "I *am* God Almighty" found in Genesis 17:1,

> And when Abram was ninety years old and nine, the Lord appeared to Abram, and said unto him: "I am God Almighty; walk before Me, and be thou wholehearted.

---

[1] For English readers, we include the full pointed transliteration of the MT, and for Hebraists we follow the convention of presenting just the consonantal text.

[2] Sarasadai (Judith 8.1 (RSV)) may be a variant of Zurishaddai.

And I will make My covenant between Me and you, and
will multiply you exceedingly. Gen 17:1-2 (JPS[1])

The title is linked with the promise to multiply Abram exceedingly indeed
he will become Abraham the father of a nation. The combination "fruitful
and multiply" is found *a further three times* in Genesis (28:3; 35:11; 48:4) in
the context of the blessings of *El Shadday*. This is similar to the pre-
patriarchal blessing formula "God blessed...be fruitful and multiply" found
in Gen 1:22, 28; 9:1. The patriarchal *El Shadday* is therefore a further
development of the creation and antediluvian blessing formula but with
added emphasis on feminine aspects as becomes apparent from the
paronomasia in Gen 49:25,

> By the God of your father who will help you, And by the
> Almighty (šadday) who will bless you *With* blessings of
> heaven above, Blessings of the deep that lies beneath,
> Blessings of the breasts (šādáyim) and of the womb. Gen
> 49:25[2]

Shadday seems to be related to the Hebrew *shad* (breast). Biale (1982:248)
states that, "given the persistent fertility traditions in which El Shaddai
appears in Genesis, the association is contextually and phonetically
reasonable, if not scientifically persuasive"—to be understood as "El with
breasts" or the "breasted El" by the author (s) of the various fertility
blessings. However, Baile himself admits that it is "a poetic
association...not a scientific etymology" and he (1982:253) attempts to link
the epithet to the wider ANE fertility cults.

---

[1] I have chosen the Jewish Publication Society OT (1917) version because
this translation renders the Hebrew syntax correctly as, "I am God
Almighty" instead of "I am Almighty God" (the NKJV and most other
translations).
[2] We should note that in Gen 49:25 *El* and *Shadday* are separated but the
association of the two terms elsewhere and a copulative sense for 'and' (i.e.
'even') allows us to apply the paronomasia to *El Shadday*. We could render
Gen 49:25 as, "~~By~~ From the God (ʾēl) of your father who will help you,
~~And by~~ even the Almighty (šadday) who will bless you *With* blessings of
heaven above, Blessings of the deep that lies beneath, Blessings of the
breasts (šādáyim) and of the womb".

However rather than the noun *shad* coming from a triconsonantal root *sh-d-y*, K. and K. Massey argue[1] for a derivation from the closely related Arabic word for breast (*th-d-y*) which in the singular form (*th-d*) also means "udder". This explains the presence of the final yod (*y*) in *Shadday* and is confirmed by its appearing in the dual/plural form *shadayim*. According to the Masseys the unpointed *sh-d-y* has the same spelling as the Hebrew for "udder" (2000:94). They conclude; "Blessings of the udder meant an ample food supply to an ancient pastoral people. Blessings of the udder meant assurance that the flocks and herds would grow. Thus "God of the Udder" would best be understood as a "prosperity" God rather than as a fertility God" (2000:95).

All the occurrences of *Shadday* in Genesis are associated with blessing or covenant formulas indicating prosperity and fecundity with the exception of Gen 43:14 where it is deliberately contrasted by Jacob with "bereavement of children".

Shadday in Exodus

Along with many other scholars, Biale (2000:247) dismisses the singular occurrence of *El Shadday* in Exod 6:3, "The Exodus text may be dismissed from the discussion because it is most probably a late editorial note explaining the change in God's name from El Shaddai to Yahweh". Although Biale is keen to stress "the biblical context in which expressions are used" (1982:242), he has neglected to apply this to Exod 6:3 because there is no immediate reference point. However, this is only true if the wider context of Genesis/Exodus is ignored. The first chapter of Exodus employs many of the same markers as the blessing formulas found in Genesis:

> But the children of Israel were <u>fruitful and increased abundantly</u>, <u>multiplied and grew exceedingly mighty</u>; and the land was filled with them. Exod 1:7 (KJV)

The markers are repeated in Exod 1:10, 12 and 20—the irony of the situation is that the divine *El Shadday* blessing of Genesis is so abundant that it causes problems for the descendants of Abraham. The epithet of Exod 6.3 must therefore be understood within the wider context.

---

[1] K. and K. Massey, "God of the Udder: Another Look at El Shaddai" (Mysteries of History!! Solved!; Massey Electronic Publishing, 2000). Online at <u>home.att.net/~phaistosdisk/mystery.pdf</u> [Cited 12 Feb 2009].

Shadday in Numbers

Both occurrences of *Shadday* in Numbers 24:4, 16 are in the context of the "blessing" of the people by Balaam/God which stresses the fecundity and supremacy of Jacob (Num 23:10; 24:6, 7). The theophoric names are of interest, particularly Zurishaddai (my rock is *Shadday*) which suggests "bringing water for them out of the rock" (Num 20:8)—a rock that provides nourishment in a fashion similar to a breast/udder (cf. the poetic - "He made him draw honey from the rock, And oil from the flinty rock") but the nation that suckled on the rock grew fat and kicked (Deut 32:13-15).[1]

Shadday in Ruth

The use of the epithet in Ruth is by way of contrast as Naomi "went out full and returned empty" thus implying that the *Shadday* epithet had not lived up to the promised blessing of fecundity and prosperity as she was returning without children and therefore without a means to redeem her deceased husband's name and estate. This is the first use of *Shadday* in a negative context. It is possible to posit that we are dealing with an inversion of the meaning as from this point onwards *Shadday* is predominantly used in a context of destruction rather than blessing. However, rather than inversion or broadening of the semantic range of the epithet the new development can be explained by changing literary conventions with *Shadday* used in an antonymic manner—deliberately contrasting the epithet with the context for literary effect.

Shadday in the Psalms

> When the Almighty scattered kings in it, It was *white* as snow in Zalmon. Ps 68:14 (KJV)

The first occurrence in the Psalms is enigmatic and the context in the early part of the psalm (vv. 1-18) is probably a reminiscence of Israel's wilderness journey. If this is the case then Zalmon is the Zalmonah of Num. 33:41, and the "kings" is a reference to Num 21:1-3 or to Num 21:33-35 where Bashan is also mentioned (cf. Ps 68:15). The Septuagint (LXX) translators struggled with this verse and instead of the usual "Almighty" - *pantokrator* (παντοκράτωρ) they opted for "heavenly

---

[1] Compare the context of *Shadday* in Job 29:3-6 "the rock poured out rivers of oil for me" (Zurishaddai) and "by His light I walked" and note that Job is reminiscing of the time when his "children" were still with him.

(ἐπουράνιον) [One]".[1] This suggests the possibility that the LXX translators either read the Hebrew *shadday* as *shamayim* (heavens) or that they were working from a Hebrew original that varied from the MT. In any case it is difficult to reach any conclusion from the context.

> He who dwells in the secret place of the Most High Shall
> abide under the shadow of the Almighty. Ps 91:1 (NKJV)

Similar to Psalm 90 this is probably also a "Psalm of Moses" reflecting the wilderness experience. References to the "secret place" and the "shadow of the Almighty" imply protection in the inner sanctum under the overspreading wings of the cherubim (cf. Ps 61:4). Psalm 27:5 likens this to being "set high upon a rock" and is reminiscent of Moses being hidden in the cleft of the rock when the Yahweh name was declared (Ex 33:22).

The love poem, Song 2:14, is based on the same experience; "O my dove, in the clefts of the rock, In the secret places of the cliff, Let me see your face, Let me hear your voice; For your voice is sweet, And your face is lovely". The suggestion here is that the "cleft of the rock" is euphemistic for the "bosom" and this is picked up by the Evangelist: "No one has seen God at any time. The only begotten Son, who is in the bosom of the Father, He has declared Him" (John 1:18, NKJV). *Shadday* in Psalm 91:1 is therefore linked with protection and intimacy, a fitting prospect for the younger generation that survived the wilderness and were about to enter the land.

---

[1] LXT Psalm 67:15 ἐν τῷ διαστέλλειν τὸν ἐπουράνιον βασιλεῖς ἐπ' αὐτῆς χιονωθήσονται ἐν Σελμων   Even the English translation struggles to make sense of the Greek: LXE Psalm 68:14 When the heavenly One scatters kings upon it, they shall be made snow-white in Selmon. There is an obvious poetic play between the white snow and the dark/shady Selmon (Zalmonah) – an alternative suggestion could be; "When the heavenly king commands the dark one becomes white as snow". J. Adey has suggested to me that the translator simply introduced a current inter-testamental period formula for God - see 2 Macc 3:39; 3 Macc 6:28; 7:6; Ps 67:15; Odes 14:11-12 and Tobit 5:16-17 where *pantokrator* (Almighty) is juxtaposed with 'heavenly one'.

Shadday in Job

Shadday occurs 31x in Job,[1] *El* some 50x, a dozen in parallel with *Shadday*. Equally interesting, **Yahweh is hardly ever used in the dialogues of Job**, only in the prologue and epilogue apart from the introduction to the Speeches of Yahweh (Job 38:1; 40:1), and one isolated reference in the poetic dialogue (Job 12:9) which is disputed.[2] The presence of the title in Job is thought "to serve archaizing purposes" as the book of Job is consider to be postexilic. H. Niehr and G. Steins,[3] for example, believe that *Shadday* is a late epithet and assert that "advocates of an early dating must deal with the observation that although this divine name was already familiar in Israel during a very early period, its use then completely receded for about five hundred years (!), the name then re-emerging during the Exile and becoming common again especially during the postexilic period". They consider that this "unexplainable lacuna....disappears" with the view that "the divine name was not picked up before the Exile and that more recent scholarship accords a late date to the disputed passages even though he acknowledges "explicit historical-theological association with the patriarchal period (Ex 6:3)".

This conclusion only stands if one accords a late (postexilic) date to Job and the prophetic books Isaiah/Joel. However, the consensus on the late dating of these books is not certain and A. Perry has presented compelling inter-textual evidence for an eighth century dating of Isaiah/Joel, moreover he presents a parabolic reading of Job as coming from the same period – a dramatization of Hezekiah's situation.[4] If Perry's approach is correct (and I

---

[1] The speakers employ *Shadday* with the following frequency: Eliphaz (7x), Bildad (2x), Zophar (1x), Job (14x), Elihu (6x), Yahweh (1x)(as self-reference).

[2] E. Dhorme draws attention to Eloah in a few Hebrew MSS, and claims that the original text was changed to YHWH due to the reminiscence of Isa.41:20. He notes that, "the entire book excludes the name Yahweh, accepts only very rarely and as if reluctantly that of Elohim, uses in the main only three names, El, Eloah, Shaddai, and subjects its use of these names to certain laws, the most obvious of which is the parallelism of Shaddai with one or other of the two other names". See E. Dhorme, *A Commentary on the Book of Job* (trans. by Harold Knight; London: Thomas Nelson and Sons Ltd., 1967), lxx, 174.

[3] H. Niehr and G. Steins, "Šadday" in *Theological Dictionary of the Old Testament* (Grand Rapids: Eerdmans, 2004), 14:418-446,(445).

[4] A. Perry, *Job* (2nd ed.; Sunderland: Willow Publications, 2009); A. Perry, *Joel* (Sunderland: Willow Publications, 2009).

believe it is) then Job reflects a situation where the reforming king Hezekiah is about to die without an heir to the throne. The Abrahamic and Davidic covenants would therefore be disannulled. This dire situation is worsened by the Assyrian invasion of Sennacherib with his burnt earth policy. The blessings of *Shadday* which include prosperity and children are therefore reversed:

> Have You not made a hedge around him, around his household, and around all that he has on every side? You have blessed the work of his hands, and his possessions have increased in the land. But now, stretch out Your hand and touch all that he has, and he will surely curse You to Your face! Job 1:10-11 (NKJV)

Hezekiah faces the loss of possessions and "children" (the 200,000 captives taken by Sennacherib) and the end of the Davidic dynasty. This explains why the central portion of Job exclusively employs *Shadday* instead of Yahweh. If the nation is destitute and depopulated then the promise implicit in the Yahweh name cannot be fulfilled. Our argument is that *Shadday* is employed ironically for literary effect. The *Shadday* blessing had implicitly promised not only prosperity and fecundity but kingship - the Davidic monarchy is anticipated in two of the patriarchal *El Shadday* sayings to Abraham and Jacob; "kings shall come from your body" (Gen 36:11; cf. Gen 17:6 with 17:1).[1] For Job/Hezekiah the failure of the *Shadday* blessing was unfathomable and undeserved after his efforts to court the northern tribes and reform the Yahweh cult. Fittingly, Job/Hezekiah is restored and his blessing is doubled but this time not by *Shadday* **but by Yahweh** (Job 42:12).

The usage of *Shadday* in Job is significant - particularly considering that Yahweh is absent in the dialogues. If Job is a parabolic dramatization of the suffering of Hezekiah set in the patriarchal period, then the use of *Shadday* (fecundity/blessing/kings/children etc) promised to the patriarchs is in direct contrast with Job's situation. This is not just an "archaizing" feature (which it is) but also a deliberate reminder that the patriarchal blessing has been reversed.

---

[1] The mention of "kings" so early in Genesis anticipates the Davidic monarchy (not the kings of Israel): "The sceptre shall not depart from Judah..." (Gen 49:10). This was most definitely in the mind of Hezekiah/Job....."Look to Abraham your father, And to Sarah who bore you; for I called him alone, and blessed him and increased him."(Isa 51:2).

Shadday in Isaiah/Joel

Isaiah and Joel are to extant contemporaries and both employ the title (Isa 13:6; Joel 1:15) as a paronomasia: "Wail, for the day of the Lord *is* at hand! It will come as <u>destruction from the Almighty</u>" (šōd, miššadday are the Hebrew for "destruction" and "from the Almighty"). The context is similar to that of Job and the suggestion is that the title is used ironically— the God who showers his people with blessings of fecundity and prosperity now rains down destruction. The background of Joel is the destruction of the agricultural infrastructure and the threat to Ahaz of the removal of the Davidic dynasty[1] - the opposite of what *Shadday* implies.

Shadday in Ezekiel

Ezekiel associates the simple and compound forms with the "wings of the cherubim" (Ezek 1:24; 10:5) and the "living creatures". The glory residing among the "living creatures" is symbolic of divine creative work in both a natural and spiritual sense. The withdrawal of the *Shekinah* from between the cherubim wings on the Ark of the Covenant symbolised the reversal of the *Shadday* blessing of prosperity and fecundity for the nation. Only the poorest people would be left and the neglected land would degenerate into a wilderness.

Conclusion

The Septuagint (LXX) translators struggled to translate *Shadday* into Greek and settled for *pantokrator* (παντοκράτωρ) which sentiment the Latin Vulgate translators followed with their choice of *omnipotens* rendered by the King James translators as Almighty. None of these translations is correct and philological and etymological approaches alone have proved inconclusive. However, when philological and etymological methodologies are combined with literary and contextual exegesis, new understandings can be reached. Recent studies have highlighted fertility as a common factor, and to the Higher Critics' "History of Religions" school of thought, this has suggested a syncretism with Canaanite fertility cults. While recognising that the epithet has definite feminine overtones this article rejects the view that its origins should be sought in native fertility cults[2] and hesitates to

---

[1] "If you will not believe, surely you shall not be established" (Isa 7:9) and the promise of "Immanuel" (Isa 7:14).

[2] H. A. Whittaker suggests that Ps 106:37 is a deliberate play on *Shadday* in opposition to the Canaanite fertility cults "……. in an allusion to Israel's apostasy in the time of the Judges: "They sacrificed their sons and daughters to devils (*shedim*, gods of destruction) (Ps 106:37). Their God-

translate the epithet as "God of the breasts (or udder)" as some suggest. However, the ideas of prosperity/nourishment/fertility are all present – and these related ideas are difficult to sum up in one phrase, therefore a tentative translation for *El Shadday* would be the "God who blesses{with offspring}and nourishes."

Should 'was' be 'became' in Genesis 1:2a?

"And the earth was without form and void"
wh'rṣ   hyth   thw   wbhw¹

J. W. Adey

PART 1

Introduction

My aim in this article is to show that the usual translation of the Hebrew היתה/*hyth* as 'was' in Gen 1:2a (as above) is correct and that 'became' is not justified either for certain Gap theorists or for any other reason. A 'Gap Theory'[2] that requires 'became' assumes a gap of countless millennia between vv. 1 and 2, in which there was a pre-Adamic habitation of the earth.[3] This era is said to have ended in a catastrophe which produced the

---

given fertility was laid waste to false gods". H. A. Whittaker, *Bible Studies: An Anthology* (Cannock: Biblia, 1987), 362-3.

[1] Hebrew וְהָאָרֶץ הָיְתָה תֹהוּ וָבֹהוּ vocalised: *wəhā'āreṣ hāy'ṯāʰ ṯōhû wāḇōhû*.

[2] See R. L. Numbers, *The Creationists: The Evolution of Scientific Creationism* (Berkeley: University of California Press, 1992), 446, and the index for many references to "gap theory".

[3] J. Thomas, *Elpis Israel* (Birmingham: CMPA, 1966), 10-12, held the view that there was a pre-Adamic habitation of the planet, citing 2 Pet 2:4's "the angels that sinned" as "pre-Adamic inhabitants of the earth", and affirming that "in the period between the wreck of the globe as the habitation of the rebel angels and the epoch of the first day, the earth was as described in Gen 1:2". He therefore believed that "Fragments . . . of the wreck of this pre-Adamic world have been brought to light by geological research" and

state of the earth as *thw wbhw* (vocalised: *ṭōhû wāḇōhû*), interpreted as 'chaos'.

My interest, here, is solely linguistic. Hence, although I report some of the history and reaction to the Gap Theory, I do not debate whether the earth is young or old. The gap view idea and 'became' surfaces from time to time. For example, M. Rooker (2003)[1] approvingly draws on B. K. Waltke's (1974) grammatical treatment of Gen 1:2 against the restitution or gap theory.[2]

I identify usage within the Hebrew Bible (HB) that differentiates היתה/*hyth* as 'was' from 'became', and draw on parallel language and quotational evidence in the GNT. This inter-textual arena is sufficient in itself, but mostly Greek translations in antiquity support 'was' in Gen 1:2a, and other linguistic aspects treated. Only Symmachus has the Greek term ἐγένετο/egéneto which tends to have a progressive 'became' sense, but I have not been able to discover the reasons for his deviation from 'was' of the Septuagint (LXX), Aquila, and Theodotion.[3]

In the beginning

The beginning of the linguistic life of the Hebrew term היתה/*hyth* (KJV's 'was') is in Gen 1:2. It is set in a context that presents, in a non-sensational matter-of-fact narrative style, a *'this is how it was'* account of creation. This following comment, from a paper attempting to interpret Genesis 1:1 in the light of near eastern archaeology adds:

> The literary genre of Genesis 1:1-2:4a is that of a report.
> In this unit we find no tension and no resolution of a

---

that "the scriptures reveal no length of time during which the terrene angels dwelt upon our globe".

[1] M. F. Rooker, *Studies in Hebrew Language, Intertextuality, and Theology.* (New York: The Edwin Mellen Press, 2003), 138-140.

[2] B. K. Waltke, *Creation and Chaos* (Portland, Oregon: Western Conservative Baptist Seminary, 1974).

[3] Symmachus has ἡ δὲ γῆ ἐγένετο ἀργὸν καὶ ἀδιάκριτον. "And the earth became inactive [idle] and undifferentiated [mixed]." But it is not clear what lies behind this choice. However, LXX, Aquila, and Theodotion all have ἦν/'was'. 4QGen^b, frg. 1i, and 4QGen^g, frg. 1, are both missing different parts of Gen 1:2 including the word *hyth* (Cf. E. Ulrich, ed., *The Biblical Qumran Scrolls: Transcriptions and Textual Variants* (*VTS* 134; Leiden: E. J. Brill, 2010), 1, 3.

crisis; what we encounter is doctrine which is not set out philosophically but under the guise of history.[1]

In Gen 1:1, God is both before and behind 'in the beginning'. This is the context for a first encounter with transcendence; comprehending the Creator starts here. Causally, creation, "the heavens and all their host" (Gen 2:4; Ps 33:6) "became" (וַיְהִי/wyhy Ps 33:9) "by the word of Yahweh", "[made] by the spirit of his mouth" (Ps 33:6; Heb 11:3).[2] In the beginning, therefore, was the word, and the word was with/towards God (John 1:1-2).

'(In) the beginning' (e.g., Matt 19:4; Mark 10:6; Heb 1:10; 2 Pet 3:4) terminates the time 'before the earth was' (Prov 8:23).[3] Genealogically (Gen 2:4; Ps 90:2)[4], the earth's primal condition is תהו ובהו/thw wbhw (KJV's) 'without form and void', read not as chaos but as a preparatory consequence of God's creative initiative recounted in Gen 1:1,[5] which

---

[1] A. J. Frendo, "Genesis 1:1, an Archaeological Approach" in *Michael: Historical, Epigraphical and Biblical Studies In Honor of Prof. Michael Heltzer* (eds. Y. Avishur and R. Deutsch; Tel Aviv-Jaffa: Archaeological Center Publications, 1999), 162.

[2] (i) Divine speech-act creation is the relevant sense of *creatio ex deo* 'creation out of God'. It compares with: ἐξ οὗ τὰ πάντα "out of whom are all things" (1 Cor 8:6). Cf. A. Gibson, "The Word-Creation Scheme" *The Testimony*, Vol. 48, No. 573, (Sept 1978): 312-313.

(ii) See D. Tsumura, *Creation and Destruction: A Reappraisal of the Chaoskampf Theory in the Old Testament* (Winona Lake, Indiana: Eisenbrauns, 2005), 74-76, re 'Exegetical Problems of *rûaḥ ʾĕlōhîm*', and his corrective of T. C. Vriezen's "view that *rûaḥ ʾĕlōhîm* (1:2) had no creative function, and 'this function is taken over completely by the word of God'."

[3] Cf. P. T. Geach, *God and the Soul* (London: RKP, 1969), 74.

[4] This can imply that each successive bringing into being over six days required the creative outcome that preceded it, as with human descent or genealogy. According to Gen 2:4, God's creation is presented as תּוֹלְדוֹת *tôlḏôt* 'generations' (cf. 'brought forth' in Ps 90:2; Isaiah 66:8). This *tôlḏôt* 'begetting' pattern next features in Gen 5:1ff.

[5] The initial state of the earth as *tōhû* is not in conflict with "he [Yahweh] created it not *tōhû*" in Isa 45:18 (KJV: "he created it not **in vain**"). How it was in Gen 1:2, was not how God intended it to remain. The Isaiah perspective contrasting with the initial geophysical *tōhû* reveals God's intention as a necessary presupposition of Gen 1:2. Eventually all would

included, we learn later, God's having "laid the foundations of the earth" (cf. Job 38:4-7; Ps 104:5; Prov 8:29; Isa 40:21; 51:13, 16).

In Gen 1:1 the earth is introduced created with the heavens and then the story of the earth is taken up in v. 2, as the Hebrew syntax positions the opening with ('*wāw*' = 'and'): "'and' the earth" (*wh'rṣ*). In fact, narratively, the *w[h'rṣ]* 'and' could carry the sense of 'now [the earth]'.[1] Gesenius states that "the noun-clause connected by a *wāw* copulative to a verbal-clause, or its equivalent, always describes a state contemporaneous with the principle action. . . ."[2] So, neither the principle action of Gen 1:1, nor 1:2's opening noun-clause, offers any scope for a 'gap' of time. It is in this grammatical and syntactical area that M. Rooker believes that "Waltke's critique of the gap theory is devastating."[3]

W. W. Fields, whom I cite more below, puts it like this:

> The grammar of verse two forces us to say that the earth was *created* unformed and unfilled, while the Gap Theory alleges that it should say the earth *became* unformed and unfilled *after* (perhaps centuries after) it was created! It is grammatically impossible.[4]

D. Kidner (1967) observes:

> If verse 2 were intended to tell of a catastrophe ('And the earth *became* . . .'), as some have suggested, it would use the Hebrew narrative construction, not the circumstantial construction as here.[5]

---

not be *ṭōhû* but 'good'. See Rooker, *Studies in Hebrew Language, Intertextuality, and Theology*, 138-149.

[1] Cf. Jonah 3:3, 'Now Nineveh was [היתה/ *hyth*] a great city to God' (my rendering and LXX are as the Hebrew).

[2] W. Gesenius, *Hebrew Grammar* (28th Edition;. Edited by E. Kautzsch; Translated by A. E. Cowley; Oxford: Clarendon Press, 1910/1970), 453, sect. 141e. Cf. the Hebrew structure of Hos 2:21, 22.

[3] Rooker, *Studies in Hebrew Language, Intertextuality, and Theology*, 139.

[4] W. W. Fields, *Unformed and Unfilled-A Critique of the Gap Theory* (Collinsville Il: Burgener Enterprises, 1976), 81-86.

[5] D. Kidner, *Genesis: An Introduction and Commentary* (London: The Tyndale Press, 1967), 44.

Likewise, E. A. Speiser (1964) has these two different constructions in mind and how v. 2 figures in relation to v. 1:

> The parenthetic character of this verse [Gen 1:2] is confirmed by the syntax of Hebrew. A normal consecutive statement would have begun with *wattəhî hā'āreṣ*, not *wəhā'āreṣ hāyᵊṭāʰ*.[1]

It is the case, however, that even if *wattəhî hā'āreṣ* had opened v. 2, without specific information favourable to 'became', that sense could not be sustained unambiguously; 'was' would still have been an acceptable sense.[2]

'Was' for היתה/*hyth* in Gen 1:2a is featured relating the earth to its first description: תהו ובה/*thw wbhw* (KJV's 'without form and void'). Therefore, היתה/*hyth* has a copula (connecting) and temporal (past time deictic) function.[3] I retain these two identifying features of the functional identity of this '(it/there/she) was' as a way of defining its job description.

---

[1] E. A. Speiser. *Genesis–Introduction, Translation, and Notes* (The Anchor Yale Bible; New Haven: Yale University Press, 1964), 5.

[2] This construction is purely hypothetical, as it is not used to open Gen 1:2. However, 'and *became*' would not be certain for *wattəhî*, anyway. In some similar cases it would be inappropriate. One such case is Gen 11:30, which, like Gen 1:2, is parenthetical to the introductory preceding verse: "And [tonally: 'but' or 'now'] Sarai **was** barren . . ." (וַתְּהִי שָׂרַי עֲקָרָה / *wattəhî śāray ʿăqārāʰ*. She did not 'become' barren this is how she **was**. (LXX concurs with: καὶ ἦν Σαρα στεῖρα).

[3] It is important not to be misled by conventional or elementary grammars' talk of 'Perfect' (a category applied to היתה/*hyth*) and it's opposite 'Imperfect'. Both terms are applied to Aspectual (complete or incomplete) actions of verbs, as if this adequately described all uses, or had priority over Tense (time). The verb 'to be' may initiate action (e.g., in 'Let there be...') but it is not an action verb; rather its main function is temporal, time marking. היתה/*hyth* as 'was' is about past time. In any case, broadly speaking, Perfect forms tend to be about "complete events or facts that often can be translated with the past tense." In practice, though, and this can easily be overlooked, the terms 'Perfect' and 'Imperfect' are about identifying the inflexional (prefix v suffix conjugation) "*forms* of the verb, not their *functions*." Cf. C. H. J. van der Merwe, et al, eds. *A Biblical Hebrew Reference Grammar* (Sheffield: Sheffield Academic Press, 1999), 142-143.

In sum: תהו ובהו/*thw wbhw* interpreted as chaos[1] is said to be evidence of a pre-Adamic habitation of the planet that ended in cataclysm in a supposed 'gap' between Gen 1:1 and 1:2. This changes Genesis 1's causal account of *how it was*. As A. Gibson (1983) cogently countered:

> Verse 2 does *not* mention that it includes the creation of the *planet* Earth. Verse 2 seems to rely on verse 1 for the record of the creation of the Earth. Thus verse 1 is about the creation of the planet; verse 2 tells us about God's creative activity on the planet . . . this interconnects the two verses quite closely. No time-gap is cited in either verse. Hence it is an assumption, not a present piece of information, which supports an appeal to the time-gap.[2]

The 'Gap Theory' context for 'became'

Gen 1:1-2 and texts like Exod 20:11; 31:17 and Neh 9:6 feature God's creation of the heavens (always plural in the HB) and the earth, providing for life on earth, within a symbolically-adapted chronological framework of

---

[1] Fields, *Unformed and Unfilled-A Critique of the Gap Theory*, 7-8. The Gap View's 'chaos' concept rates as a piece of modern mythology, particularly where some Gap theorists believe Satan's rebellion produced chaos. B. Thompson opposes this satanic view in *The Bible and the Age of the* Earth (Montgomery, Alabama: Apologetics Press, Inc, 1999), 61-64. 'Chaos', as the state of the earth in Gen 1:2, has long been read for *ṭōhû wāḇōhû* assuming an ancient near eastern mythic cosmogony background. However, in relation to possible ancient perspectives with Genesis, D. T. Tsumura (approvingly reviewed by H. G. M. Williamson in *VT* 42 [1992]: 423-424) argues against a view of primordial 'chaos'; see D. T. Tsumura, *The Earth and Waters in Genesis 1 and 2. A Linguistic Investigation* (JSOT Sup 83; Sheffield: JSOT Press, 1989). Importantly, also, in his *Creation and Destruction: A Reappraisal of the Chaoskampf Theory in the Old Testament*. Winona Lake, Indiana: Eisenbrauns, 2005), 75, Tsumura shows that the phrase *tohu wabohu* has nothing to do with a chaos concept at all. It simply refers to the "desolate and empty" state of the earth. It describes the initial state of the earth as "not yet" normal, as we know it; see his "Conclusions" p. 196. On p. 148, n. 33, he talks of the need to exercise interpretative control, especially across cognate languages where there is talk of 'the sameness' of two items, and he pertinently draws on A. Gibson, *Biblical Semantic Logic* (Oxford: Blackwell, 1981), 24 and 140.

[2] A. Gibson, 'Creation versus Evolution' *The Testimony*, Vol. 53, No. 631 (July 1983): 226.

six days, rather than, say, as an instantaneous[1] event. Modern science has projected different timescales for the start of the universe or the age of earth, and this has led to views, like the Gap Theory, that seek to accommodate Scripture to science.[2]

The origin of the Gap Theory is usually identified with Dr. Thomas Chalmers of Edinburgh University in 1814. Chalmers, who lived concurrently with Lyell and Darwin, deemed it necessary to harmonize the Scriptures and science in order to save Christianity from the onslaught of atheism.[3] W. W. Fields (1976) puts Chalmers' concern thus:

> [Chalmers felt the need to] make room for the vast expanse of time which the geologists of his day were demanding and at the same time maintain a literal interpretation of the creation account.[4]

Fields mentions that 'Gap', or 'Ruin and Restoration' theorists want the Hebrew term היתה/*hyth* of Gen 1:2a, usually translated 'was' here in English versions, to be a progressive 'became'(or, even 'had become').[5]

So, this view, centre-staging 'became', did not arise in a neutral interpretative context or through agenda-free exegesis. The following has been put to me by some who resort to 'became' and believe that God speaks to us both through Scripture and the fossil record:

> The way forward is for the Christian to accept that the planet on which God created Adam and Eve is an extremely old creation. Next, that God produced many,

---

[1] Compare the Greek of 1 Cor 15:52 for its expression of (infinitesimal, 'atomic') instantaneity (ἐν ἀτόμῳ, ἐν ῥιπῇ ὀφθαλμοῦ). KJV has "in a moment [ἐν ἀτόμῳ], in the twinkling of an eye." I assume no limitation on God's power (Jer 32:17), as He is 'power' (τῆς δυνάμεως Matt 26:64; Rom 1:20). *ʾĒl*, basically 'power'/'might', is the singular term for 'God'. In Ps 90:2, *ʾēl* is presented in the same way that *ʾĕlōhîm* is in Gen 1:1, there before creation. Isa 42:5 combines *hāʾēl*—'the God'—with Yahweh as the creator of the heavens.

[2] See A. Gibson, 'Creation versus Evolution'. *The Testimony*, Vol. 53, No. 631 (July 1983).

[3] Fields, *Unformed and Unfilled–A Critique of the Gap Theory*, 40.

[4] Fields, *Unformed and Unfilled–A Critique of the Gap Theory*, ix.

[5] Fields, *Unformed and Unfilled–A Critique of the Gap Theory*, 87.

many creations on this ancient planet, of which the fossils bear record. Next, that all life on this planet was extinguished, exterminated, and remained so up until God spoke at the start of Day One.

In 1970, A. C. Custance (1910-1985) published *Without Form and Void*, which according to Fields is the lengthiest defense of the Gap Theory any man has attempted in print.[1] Custance feels that the translation of *hyth* is the pivotal point in the controversy and he argues for (the pluperfect) 'had become' (translating Gen. 1:2a: "But the earth had become a desolation"), whereas previous gap theorists, along with the *New Scofield Reference Bible* (OUP, 1967), supposed that "the word rendered 'was' may also be translated 'became'".[2]

For Fields, as no gap is suggested between Gen 1:1 and 2, "the *only* sense in which the pluperfect could be understood, is as a description of the state of the earth as it had been created". That is, 'was' explained as implying: "Now the earth *had come into being* (been created) void and without form".[3] I quote Fields because in my view he contends clearly and fairly against a gap view. He argues against 'became' and rightly claims that the "pluperfect ['had become'] translation of Genesis 1:2 is better rejected."[4]

It is true that forms of the Hebrew verb *hyh*—'to be'—like *hyth* and cognates, which give 'was' and 'were', occur in (structuring) certain 'became' expressions. However, comparing usage soon shows when היתה/*hyth* is 'was' and how some of its 116 instances are configured to provide (the need for) the sense: 'became'.

There is Tense (and other grammatical or functional characteristics) in Hebrew verbs.[5] As noted already, a prominent feature of the behaviour of

---

[1] Fields, *Unformed and Unfilled-A Critique of the Gap Theory*, 44.

[2] Fields, *Unformed and Unfilled-A Critique of the Gap Theory*, 88.

[3] Fields, *Unformed and Unfilled-A Critique of the Gap Theory*, 107.

[4] Fields, *Unformed and Unfilled-A Critique of the Gap Theory*, 108.

[5] Regarding the Hebrew Verbal System (HVS), the interwovenness of 'time' (Tense) and 'kind of action' (Aspect: as in 'Perfect' = complete, 'Imperfect' = not complete) is a distinct verb feature of many languages (cf. van der Merwe et al, *A Biblical Hebrew Reference Grammar*, 143); Hebrew is no exception. See T. O. Lambdin, *Introduction to Biblical Hebrew* (London: Darton, Longman and Todd, 1973), 100, and J. F. A. Sawyer, *A Modern Introduction to Biblical Hebrew* (London: Oriel Press, 1976), 78-82, who

Hebrew 'be' verbs is as *temporal* indicators! Differently, 'became' (cf. '*be*came'/'*be*come') has a temporal contour that implies some duration, or marks 'happening', and it can also be suggestive of a result (as in 'come to *be*').[1]

Finally, J. Barr (1961), in his ground-breaking and now classic work *Semantics of Biblical Language*, and in a chapter exposing some scholars' theological or theory-laden approaches to the Hebrew verb, makes reference to the *be*-verb היה/ *hyh (hayah)*. In this context he mentions its third person feminine singular form היתה/ *hyth* in Gen. 1:2 (Field also cites Barr here).[2] Barr states:

> [A] statement like 'the earth is waste' will have the nominal sentence and no verb; but if we put it in the past and say 'the earth was waste (and is no longer)', then the verb *hayah* is used, as in Gen. 1:2. It would be quite perverse to insist on the meaning 'became' here.[3]

Reviews

W. Dever, Who Were the Early Israelites and Where Did They Come From? (Grand Rapids: Eerdmans, 2003)

Dever argues that the Israelites were not external conquerors, but ethnic Canaanites who at some point separated themselves from the larger Canaanite population to distinguish themselves as a separate ethnic, social, and religious group.

To commence, Dever provides a detailed examination of the history of Biblical archaeology, from its earliest apparent 'successes' to its later unfortunate 'failures' and confrontations with contradictory evidence. The

---

implements a neutralising 'prefix/suffix conjugational' approach, but has examples of tense, aspect and mood. Theoretical tensions can give the impression that the HVS is an enigma yet to be unravelled. Cf. L. McFall, *The Enigma of the Hebrew Verbal System: Solutions from Ewald to the Present Day* (Sheffield: The Almond Press, 1982).

[1] Cf. van der Merwe, et al, eds. *A Biblical Hebrew Reference Grammar,* §44.5, d., 331-333.

[2] Fields, *Unformed and Unfilled-A Critique of the Gap Theory*, 91.

[3] J. Barr, *Semantics of Biblical Language* (Oxford: Oxford University Press, 1961), 59, and n.1.

succeeding years are then described, during which various alternative readings of the Biblical text were proposed with no one model able to demonstrate sufficient support to establish a new scholarly consensus. By the end of this section it is apparent that no traditional readings of the Exodus-Conquest narrative can survive a confrontation with the evidence, and most of the post-traditional readings are also without any meaningful support.

Historic theories of Israelite origin are then discussed briefly, and their weaknesses exposed. Dever next moves to the core of his own model, which is that the Israelites were indigenous to Canaan. Taking issue with the interpretation of I. Finkelstein,[1] he provides a useful critique of Finkelstein's views (which have become popular with Minimalists).

Dever's primary argument against the Conquest narrative is that there is no substantial discontinuity of material culture within Canaan at the time of the Israelite invasion. However, Dever must also provide sufficient evidence to substantiate a significant discontinuity of material culture illustrating eventual Israelite emergence as a distinct group.

Providing an abundance of archaeological evidence for a discontinuity of Israelite culture from Canaanite culture, Dever acknowledges that this break in continuity took place during the very era that the Biblical record indicates Israel was conquering Canaan. In fact, Dever provides substantially more than that they were an indigenous Canaanite group.

Most striking of the evidence for discontinuity is that which is clearly religious in nature:

- Absence of pig bones from settlement sites: evidence for a radical departure from existing Canaanite food practices, and the emergence of a new ethnic group.

- Massive abandonment (and in some cases physical destruction) of Canaanite temples, cult sites and idols: evidence that these areas had now been taken by a new ethnic group which eschewed the religious beliefs and practices of the Canaanites.

---

[1] I. Finkelstein and N. A. Silberman, *The Bible Unearthed: Archaeology's New Vision of Ancient Israel and the Origin of its Sacred Texts* (New York: Touchstone, 2001).

Finally, Dever attempts to harmonize the evidence within a scheme which interprets the early Israelites as an indigenous Canaanite group. It is telling that this last section is the shortest of all and that Dever himself acknowledges 'my theory is speculative' and has 'little archaeological evidence to support it'.

Dever's work is an extremely useful survey of archaeological data and commentary concerning the early conquest, and the interpretation of Joshua and Judges. However, readers are advised of alternative readings of the evidence which are more sympathetic to the Biblical account:

- I. Provan, V. Philips Long and T. Longman *A Biblical History of Israel* (Louisville: WJK Press, 2003).
- J. K. Hoffmeier *Ancient Israel in Sinai* (Oxford: Oxford University Press, 2005).
- K. Kitchen, *On the Reliability of the Old Testament* (Grand Rapids: Eerdmans, 2006).

J. Burke

J. D. G. Dunn, Did the first Christians worship Jesus? (London: SPCK, 2010)

This book is worth having on the shelf because it brings together in one convenient volume the "worship" texts that an orthodox Christian is likely to use when arguing for the deity of Christ. Dunn himself says in the conclusion to the "Introduction",

> What I hope will become apparent is that the first Christians did not see worship of Jesus as an alternative to worship of God. Rather, it was a way of worshipping God. That is to say, worship of Jesus is only possible or acceptable within what is now understood to be a Trinitarian framework. Worship of Jesus that is not worship of God through Jesus, or, more completely, worship of God through Jesus and in the Spirit, is not Christian worship.[1]

---

[1] J. D. G. Dunn, *Did the first Christians worship Jesus?* (London: SPCK, 2010), 6.

This conclusion is astonishing for its dogmatism, especially since Dunn is a careful NT scholar. It condemns all Christadelphian worship of Jesus as non-Christian, but more significantly, it arbitrarily drops in the Trinitarian framework as the only acceptable framework for such worship. Even if the book were to prove that the first Christians worshipped Jesus as God, this would not be enough to establish a Trinitarian metaphysics. Dunn is unable to think outside his western Christian background and ask the question: is Christianity astray in its thinking about Christ. Scholars take for granted what they have received in their church traditions and "build" on this basis.

The problem that Dunn faces is illustrated in the conclusions for his first chapter, which is an examination of "worship" vocabulary in the NT. He says,

> 'Worship' as such is a term rarely used in reference to Christ…Cultic worship or service (*latreuein, latreia*) as such is never offered to Christ, and other worship terms are used only in relation to God. In the case of the most common words for praise and thanksgiving (*eucharistein*), they too are never offered to Christ.[1]

Dunn is not misrepresenting his discussion but he is creating a black hole of credibility in his argument because he has said in his "Introduction" that Christians "must" worship Jesus in a Trinitarian framework. The simple question is: given the paucity of evidence, why is there this "must"? To establish a "must" like this, you really need something systematic and structural in doctrine and practise in the NT letters. And of course this is what you do not have in the historical data.

Dunn goes on,

> All the same, the fact that such worship language is used in reference to Jesus, even if only occasionally, is very striking. This would have been entirely unusual and without precedent in the Judaism of the time.

Again the problem for Dunn is the "very occasionally" as this is not enough to generate the "must" of Trinitarian worship that he is seeking in order to validate his own faith. Still, there is a point here: devotion to Jesus and the "lordship" of Jesus are distinctive in the Judaism of the day.

---

[1] Dunn, *Did the first Christians worship Jesus?*, 27.

Christadelphians explain this in terms of the exaltation of Jesus by God the Father. Such exaltation is incompatible with the notion of Jesus as the incarnation of God the Son.

The reader is suitable warned by Dunn's careful hedging, "only occasionally"; s/he is warned to look carefully at the examples of worship language applied to Jesus; some or all may not be what Dunn claims. For example, Dunn regards Stephen's calling upon the name of Jesus as an example of the language of calling upon a deity (Acts 7:59, NASB). He admits that such language could be an illustration of calling upon a heavenly being, but prefers to link the language to the practise of calling upon the God of Israel in order to secure a comparison of deity for Jesus.[1] What is lacking in Dunn's analysis is the careful intertextual work that *explains* the visionary context for Stephen's address.

The argument, "Jesus was worshipped and only God should be worshipped, therefore Jesus is God", is popular. Dunn's book brings the texts together that are used in this argument. His cautiousness undermines his Trinitarian goal; nevertheless, his book has value as a source book of texts for constructing a correct understanding of such worship.

A. Perry

Letters

Dear Editor,

There were two main census carried out for the express purpose of consecrating God's army. The first occurred after two years in the wilderness and the second, after the Baal-Peor incident, where it was necessary to consecrate the army, as all those of the first census, apart from Caleb and Joshua, had perished in the wilderness.

> Now the Lord spoke to Moses in the Wilderness of Sinai, in the tabernacle of meeting, on the first [day] of the second month, in the second year after they had come out of the land of Egypt, saying: Take a census of all the congregation of the children of Israel, by their families, by their fathers' houses, according to the number of names, every male individually, from twenty years old and above—all who [are able to] go to war in Israel. **You and**

---

[1] Dunn, *Did the first Christians worship Jesus?*, 16.

Aaron shall number them by their armies. And with you there shall be a man from every tribe, each one the head of his father's house. Num 1:1-4 (NKJV)

The highlighted text clearly defines those involved in conducting the census. The NASB margin notes that the word 'number' is literally 'muster' and the half shekel is described as an 'heave' offering. The second census, as we have observed above, was made to consecrate the army before they crossed Jordan. There, as God's army, they were to inflict God's judgments on Canaan as the cup of their iniquity was now full.

David had led the army of Israel into battle many times. He might possibly have had concerns that the army was not consecrated and the census was a belated attempt to rectify this. If this was the case, then like the occasion of Uzziah, David had not consulted God's law before embarking on this census. For a legitimate census to be conducted, David and the High Priest together with twelve elders representing the twelve tribes were required. As each eligible man passed over to the 'mustered' group he would offer his half shekel for the atonement of his soul. None of these requirements were complied with and thus David was at fault.

The plague on Israel was one of the three explicit judgments that God warned he would use for unfaithfulness (Lev 26:25-27; Jer 24:10, 29:17-18). These judgments are only used against Israel. David saw the sword in the hand of the angel; pestilence was ravaging Israel and although famine is not mentioned here it can reasonably be concluded that these judgments were as a result of **Israel's** unfaithfulness.

Trevor Evans

Marginal Notes

1 Cor 11:3—J. Burke

The meaning of the Greek word *kephalē* (most commonly translated 'head'), in 1 Cor 11:3 has been debated extensively among evangelical commentators for years. However, among professional lexicographers there is no debate. Standard professional lexicons do not include the meaning 'source, origin' for *kephalē* here as understood by some egalitarians, nor do recognized authoritative lexicographers debate whether the word carries a fundamental meaning of 'source, origin' or 'chief, ruler'.

Despite the years of egalitarian arguments and claims of new evidence, none of the standard lexicons has accepted the egalitarian definition of the word *kephalē*,[1] although a number of the standard professional lexicons have been updated recently with additional lexicographical information derived from additional lexical studies or the discovery of new sources.[2] Furthermore, standard lexicons and dictionaries specifically identify *kephalē* as having meanings such as 'first, superior rank, pre-eminent status, leader, master, head' in the very passage under discussion, 1 Cor 11:3.

Postscript
Christadelphian Writing
A. Perry

It is well known that Christadelphian books cannot be bought in Christian bookshops or in mainstream bookshops. In the 1980s, a Christadelphian imprint, Aletheia Books, tried to break into this market in the UK, but success was limited to only one or two volumes. Compared to Christian publishing houses, of which there are many, Christadelphians have only one or two organizations that run as a business.

In the world, a tiny number of popular authors make a living from religious book writing. The writing of books on biblical topics offers less opportunity for money-making to an author. Generally, the authors of these books are making their living in academia or the church; their writing offers some royalties as a bonus to their salary. We might ask whether royalties or commission fees should be paid to Christadelphian writers who have their work accepted in the main magazines or who have works published by CMPA. The principle is that a labourer is worthy of his hire.

The Christadelphian community is a more or less completely lay community; it has no professional clergy. It supports missionary work through private and charitable donations; it supports many other good works through such means, for example Meal-a-Day and various care homes. The same endeavours can be seen in the churches. That area of human endeavour which we call writing receives virtually no support

---

[1] An entry in LSJ9 has been cited by egalitarians as evidence for their understanding of *kephalē*, but the editor of the lexicon has explained that this was not the intended meaning of the entry (which has been misinterpreted), that the entry was badly worded, and that the meaning 'source' for *kephalē* as asserted by egalitarians does not exist.

[2] BDAG, 541; L&N, 1:738; Balz & Schneider, 1:285; Friberg & Miller, 4:229; Kittel, Bromiley & Friedrich, 3:679.

financially in the Christadelphian community unless it is writing directed towards preaching.

A "giving of your time freely to the Lord" is the model that dominates Christadelphian writing. The same is true of Christadelphian preaching, except here there may be living expenses for foreign missionaries, for travel, or sundry expenses incurred in campaigns, *and so on*. The difference between the lack of financial support for writing compared to preaching is plain to see, but does it matter? Are there costs involved in writing which should be borne by the community; has the community suffered from its lack of support for writing? What are the problem conditions that arise from the lack of support for writing in the community? We could list several:

1) **Quality**: there are different qualities in different types of writing. In Biblical Studies, the best quality writing is based on careful research and thinking. The benchmark in method would be the doctoral writing that comes off the conveyor belt of the church seminaries and universities. This kind of writing is wholly lacking in the community. Other types of writing are also rare or scarce; writing that is overtly theological or philosophical in relation to biblical matters.

2) **False Doctrine**: When ecclesial magazines and those who publish books in the community neglect advanced writing, whether in biblical studies or in doctrine, there is a danger of false doctrine and error. Unless there is a counter-balance to the advanced writing that takes place in the churches, people will only have the one source to consult for such writing. The truths and the mistakes in advanced biblical studies are subtle, and readers imbibe each in equal measure. There is therefore a need for such writing in the community to counter the subtle falsehoods that exist in church writing.

3) **Problem Solving**: Hoary old chestnuts bedevil the community; they have a life of their own and they live on in each new generation. However, there is a need for advanced writing on such problems. One way to measure the lack of such writing is to ask: to which Christadelphian writers do I look for a solution to this or that problem? Is s/he a person who wrote over a hundred years ago, over fifty years ago, or in the last twenty years in the pages of an ecclesial magazine? Another question to ask is this: do the solutions being offered to biblical and doctrinal problems seem stuck in a time warp? This is another way in which the lack of advanced writing is felt. Again, people can go to the advanced writing in the churches for solutions to hoary old chestnuts and be misled.

4) **Doctrinal Development**: the Bible is a deep book and the believer can plumb to ever increasing depths. Doctrine can be developed to deeper levels. This is a form of advanced writing that is neglected in the community. It is a kind of writing that is required if Christadelphians are to combat the sophisticated false doctrines that are abroad in Christendom. Two pieces of evidence that show that we have neglected advanced writing on doctrine are: i) the extent to which pioneer writings are used; and ii) the temerity with which doctrine is handled; safe formulations are used from the past stock of writing (e.g. in the area of the Atonement).

We could, perhaps, add to (1)-(4), but this is a short opinion piece. The types of writing that predominate in the community are "devotional", "preaching", "proverbial back page sentiment" and "introduction". With these types of writing, there can be no complaint about quality; each has their own rationale and value. We can say, however, that the neglect of more advanced types of writing is a **strategic mistake** within the community. This applies not only to what we might call scholarly writing but also to deeper analysis of the biblical text without scholarly engagement. The evidence that this mistake has been made is simply what has been published by the mainstream ecclesial magazines since the late 1980s. The problem that is created is that there is virtually nothing to read from the community once the offered forms of writing have been read.

Time is a problem. If a person only has time to read one advanced book on a topic, by a Pentecostal or a Baptist, say, they will inevitably be in danger of a one sided view. If that view is then transcribed to an article in a Christadelphian magazine, then it is duplicated a hundredfold. What's required is: more time for personal research and/or a stock of Christadelphian writings that have written up such research, thereby offering a guide through topics.

The neglect of advanced writing in ecclesial magazines is a strategic mistake. For the last twenty years, magazines and those who publish books have not been building the stock of such writing for people to draw upon. This is not to say that false doctrine has crept into the magazines and books, although there are some obvious examples of scholarly mistakes that have migrated from scholarship into magazine and book materials. Rather, the conflict between true and false teaching has another battleground: the Internet. As opinions, viewpoints, and questions are posted on forums, Facebook, and mailing lists, it is here that the lack of advanced written material is felt, and the scholarly writing of the churches is quoted instead.

There are several ways to tackle this problem. Existing magazines could broaden their editorial policy to include advanced writing. Christadelphian publishing organizations could include the concept of an "academic series" in their portfolios, so that advanced biblical writing could be published. Christadelphian charitable foundations could broaden their articles of association to include research grants for the purpose of advanced writing and advertise this on their websites. These ideas are not new, but they would be a challenge. Perhaps the new generation of writers and editors (when they come) can undo the mistake of their forbears in this matter.

Supporting Biblical and Historical Research
A. Perry

The Christadelphian community does not support biblical and historical research that would be supportive to its ethos. Individuals may embark on post-graduate research and obtain secular funds for fees and maintenance and they may research topics of value to the community. Others may do such research part-time while holding down jobs and raising families. There is a great deal of research that can be done but none is currently supported by ecclesias.

For example, there are many inaccessible manuscripts from the renaissance and reformation eras supporting anti-Trinitarian points of view. Google Books and www.archive.org has some material, but there are other authors whose work is valuable, such as Samuel Clarke, Paul Best, or Johann Crell. Such works need transcribing and editing for storage and access online. Or again, another example of research that would be of value to the community would be to investigate the writings of the Restoration/Restitution Movement of the 1830s out of which came J. Thomas.

Biblical research topics that would be of value to the community are legion. However, one area of support that could be offered by ecclesias would be in the area of formal Greek and Hebrew Studies. There is a need for more expertise spread throughout the ecclesias in the original bible languages, and a good way to support young Christadelphians spend a gap year studying them would be through the a "Stewardship Account" registered with www.stewardship.org.uk. These are UK based accounts that attract gift aid status for repayment of tax for UK taxpayers. They function as an account that students draw upon while studying at a Bible College. A one year diploma would be one way in which Christadelphians could learn Greek and Hebrew as well as take modules in various areas of

Biblical Studies. This would then be a platform for further Biblical research.

```
┌─────────────────────────────────────┐
│      New Websites and Blogs          │
└─────────────────────────────────────┘
```

Anti-Trinitarian Studies Website

www.antitrinitarian-studies.sussex.ac.uk

A new site (in development) which includes Milton's *De doctrina Christiana* and a few other transcriptions.

Richard Bauckham

www.richardbaucckham.co.uk

This is a new website. He is a retired professor and an evangelical Trinitarian but a conservative biblical scholar that has interesting things to say about the Gospels. Some of his lectures are on the site and he is the sort of Trinitarian thinker whose work needs to be criticized when defending the Jewish monotheism of the NT writers.

Emanuel Tov

www.emanueltov.info

This old site is worth bookmarking for its series of studies on the LXX.

END

Editors: Andrew.Perry@christadelphian-ejbi.org
Paul.wyns@christadelphian-ejbi.org
T.Gaston@christadelphian-ejbi.org (Church history)
J.Adey@christadelphian-ejbi.org (Text and Language)

Contents

- Editorial
- Where the Vultures Gather
- A New Age
- Three Prophetic Utterances
- A Faithful and Wise Servant
- The Shema of Deut 6:4
- Marginal Notes: John 17:5
- Reviews: P. Pulman, The Good Man Jesus
- Report: The Great Trinity Debate
- Postscript

Editorial Policies: The Christadelphian EJournal of Biblical Interpretation seeks to fulfil the following objectives: offer analytical and expositional articles on biblical texts; engage with academic biblical studies that originate in other Christian confessions; defend the biblical principles summarised in the common Christadelphian statement of faith; and subject the published articles to retrospective peer review and amendment.
Submission of Articles: Authors should submit articles to the editors. Presentation should follow *Society of Biblical Literature* guidelines (www.sbl.org).
Publication: E-mailed quarterly on the last Thursday of January, April, July, and October. Published as a collected annual paper-back obtainable from: www.lulu.com/willowpublications.
Subscriptions: This is a "free" EJournal to communities and individuals whose statement of faith is broadly consistent with the Christadelphian common statement.

Christadelphian EJournal of Biblical Interpretation

Editorial

This issue of the EJournal is a "special" devoted to analysis of biblical texts and without any scholarship; there are no footnotes or quotations of scholars. The articles have been written with nothing more than a lexicon, a concordance, a creed, and the Bible. If feedback is supportive, we may repeat the exercise again next year, God-willing. Even though we may cite scholars and engage them, our only concern is the understanding of the text, and in particular a deeper understanding. We are passionate about intertextual analysis and the illumination of Scripture with Scripture. We do however finish up with some news about a debate on the Trinity.

The aim of the EJournal is to eventually extend the editorial panel to cover other specialisms like the Bible and Science, Apologetics, and Intertextual Analysis. This issue is an example of the sort of material we hope to publish under the rubric of "Intertextual Analysis". I don't know the exact number of years ago, but there was once a section in the UK Testimony magazine that was called "Analysis", and I remember good material being published during the 1980s in that section. The aim of the EJournal is to co-opt more section editors to take care of this kind of material.

Where the Vultures Gather
P. Wyns

> And when the vultures (ὄρνεα/LXX) came down on the carcasses (σώματα/LXX), Abram drove them away. Gen 15:11 (NKJV).

> Then they asked him, "Where, Lord?" He said to them, "Where the corpse (σῶμα) is, there the vultures (ἀετοὶ) will gather". Luke 17:37 (NRSV)

In the first instance, Jesus' reply to his disciples seems to be a complete *non sequitur*—we expect a location not an event as the answer to the question, "Where, Lord?" We might expect 'Jerusalem' or 'Sinai' or 'caught up to heaven', but not an answer that refers to vultures and corpses. It is here that intertextual connections with the land-covenant (Genesis 15) come to our aid —however, the interpretation is complicated by the use of Hebrew and Greek across the Testaments, and with different Greek words in the LXX that denote the birds, birds of prey, eagles or vultures.

Of course, eagles and vultures are birds and both eagles and vultures are birds of prey—however, one would expect carrion to be associated with vultures. The modern English translations prefer 'vulture' for Luke 17:37 (NIB/NLT/NRSV) rather than 'eagle' (NKJV/KJV/RSV), but Gen 15:11 is always translated with either the more neutral 'birds of prey', or with 'vultures', but never with 'eagles'.

This is of course a translational judgement call and the NT translators were no doubt influenced by the fact that the Roman 'eagle' had destroyed Jerusalem. There are many countries that use the eagle in an emblematic fashion (including the USA) and one would hardly expect a country to adopt the vulture as a national symbol (more on this *anon*). Nevertheless, a translation should be influenced by inner biblical exegesis rather than perceived historical correspondence. The situation is further complicated by the use of the saying in a different context—when Jesus offers it as the visible sign of his return;

> Therefore if they say to you, 'Look, He is in the desert!' do not go out; *or* 'Look, *He is* in the inner rooms!' do not believe *it*. For as the lightning comes from the east and flashes to the west, so also will the coming of the Son of Man be. For wherever the carcass (πτῶμα) is, there the eagles (ἀετοί) will be gathered together. Matt 24:26-28

Once again NT translators have chosen 'eagles' in preference over 'vultures' but it is the griffon-vulture that is really envisaged here – the 'unclean' vulture is fulfilling the divine will and serves as a signifier of the slaughter.

> Doth the vulture mount up at thy command, and make her nest on high? She dwelleth and abideth on the rock, upon the crag of the rock, and the stronghold. From thence she spieth out the prey; her eyes behold it afar off. Her young ones also suck up blood; and where the slain are, there is she. Job 39:27-30 (JPS)

Against all other translations the Jewish Publication Society OT (1917) translates the underlying Hebrew as 'vulture' in Job 39:27.[1] The idea in the Matthew passage seems to be the visibility of the slaughter—it can be seen from a great distance because it is marked by the circling vultures.

---

[1] [ED. AP]: The argument in favour of 'eagle' is the seeing from a far distance; eagles have excellent eyesight.

The saying concerning "vultures circling the corpse" is difficult to understand but in both NT instances it is associated with the Lord's advent—as a visible sign of his (imminent?) return (Matthew) and as the location (?) where the disciples will be taken (Luke). The setting seems to be the judgement of the Jewish nation and the connection with Genesis 15 requires us to re-examine the land-covenant.

Genesis 15

It is proposed that the 'cutting' of the covenant in Genesis 15 forms the basis of the 'vulture sayings' found in the gospels. Usually a covenant was 'cut' for reasons of ratification and/or imprecation. By that we mean that both parties walked between the cut-pieces of a sacrifice in order to establish the agreement, with the implicit understanding that whoever broke the covenant ought to be cut in pieces like the sacrifice. The covenant in Genesis 15 is unusual on two accounts - firstly, only God ratified the covenant; secondly, any imprecation is not applicable to God who is immortal. The covenant is therefore unconditional and unbreakable because God has sworn it by himself. However, the word 'unconditional' must be qualified—for although it was not conditional on the obedience of Abram's descendants (God would accomplish it despite disobedience), nevertheless, the disobedient would not inherit the land/kingdom. Abram (not yet Abraham the father of a multitude) was told that his descendants would be liberated from slavery in Egypt (Gen 15:14-15) and would inherit the land—indeed this occurred under Joshua, but only after a generation perished in the wilderness because of disobedience. The covenant is therefore unconditional, and will surely come to pass (despite disobedience), but God will not be mocked.

The other important aspect is that Abram was figuratively 'dead' when the covenant was ratified and therefore **Abram could not keep the vultures at bay** (only God could). The covenant was specifically about **inheriting the land** ("to give you this land to inherit it", v. 7) despite having no heir. Finally, it is often not realised, but the covenant of Genesis 15 was made on the night of the Passover.

Genesis 15 and the Passover

The covenant of Genesis 15 was ratified at night. The time of day is stated as being between the period when *"the sun was going down"* (v. 12) and *"when the sun went down"* (v. 17). This would be equivalent to the time specified in later years for the offering of the Passover lambs, i.e. *"between the two evenings"* (Exod 12:6, RSV mg.), a phrase that apparently means 'between mid-afternoon and sunset'. The Exodus account uses the expression *"the selfsame day"* (the Jewish day commences at sunset) making it clear that

Abram's descendants left Egypt exactly 430 years after the giving of the covenant (Exod 12:40, 41; Gal 3:17). So, Abram is given the land-covenant on the Passover night and 430 years later the Israelites are liberated from Egyptian slavery on the Passover night. On a Passover more than 2,000 years after Abraham another unconditional covenant (the new covenant) was ratified by God.

In Exodus, the Israelites, having departed from the land of death and slavery, passed through the sea—metaphorically, they were "resurrected" through the Abrahamic covenant. When they entered the land, they were baptized again, before re-establishing **the rite of circumcision covenanted to Abraham**; clearly, the Sinaiatic covenant should be understood as a subset to the Abrahamic covenant and certainly limited in what it could achieve. By obeying the law the Israelites made a choice for life, but that life was only made possible through the Abrahamic covenant. They were saved because of the Abrahamic covenant and **entered the land under the Abrahamic covenant**—ultimately the law could only bring death.

Egypt was known for its elaborate cult of the dead and preparations for the afterlife. Israel's emergence from the land of death and slavery was similar to Abram awakening from the "horror of great darkness". Moreover, the griffon-vulture, portrayed as the goddess Nekhbet, was also the symbol of upper-Egypt; her northern counterpart was the cobra goddess (cf. Exod 7:9-15). The unification of Upper and Lower Egypt was represented by the double crown bearing a prominent vulture and cobra. Over time Nekhbet was transformed from the personal protector of the Pharaoh and from the giver of the white crown to the Pharaoh; she became the symbol of sovereignty in ancient Egypt. Significantly, Nekhbet, who was the "wet nurse" of Pharaoh, became **the guardian of mothers and infants** (contrast the genocide of Hebrew male infants in Exod 1:6) and she took on the role of protector; she moved from being Pharaoh's own goddess to one who looked after **mothers and children** through the whole land. Egypt's oldest oracle was the shrine of Nekhbet at Nekheb, the original necropolis or city of the dead. A mamissi (**birth house**) can be found at the ancient city of Nekheb dedicated to Nekhbet. The temple was built around 2700 BC, and enlarged by later Pharaohs of the 18th through 30th dynasties, (1539-1069 BC) including Tuthmosis III, Amenophis II, and the Ramessids.

The Covenant in Abeyance

> The corpses of this people will be food for the birds of the heaven and for the beasts of the earth. <u>And no one will frighten *them away*</u>. Jer 7:33 (NKJV)

The incident that provoked this response was the blatant reversal of the promise that the ruling elite had made to liberate their fellow Hebrew slaves in accordance with the Jubilee laws. Yahweh reminded them that he had, "made a covenant with your fathers (the Sinai covenant) in the day that I brought them out of the land of Egypt, <u>out of the house of bondage</u>" (Jer 34:13). The Jews had once been a slave people in Egypt and the Jubilee law ensured that fellow Hebrews would not endure perpetual slavery or loss of property rights. The Jubilee enshrined the principle of liberty and restoration of land rights among the people of God.

However, although the Judean rulers imitated the Abrahamic covenant "when they cut the calf in two and passed between the parts of it" (Jer 34:18), and released their Hebrew slaves, afterwards they changed their minds and enslaved them again. This was an abomination to God and therefore the Abrahamic land-covenant was put in abeyance and the people were exiled to Babylon.

The Land Covenant in Matthew

It has already been suggested that the 'vulture saying' echoes the land covenant made with Abram. Other points of contact establish a connection between the narratives:

Matthew 24	Genesis 15
Vultures (v. 28)	Vultures (v. 11)
Carcass (v. 28)	Carcasses (v. 11)
The sun will be darkened (v. 29)	The sun went down and it was dark (v. 17) Horror *and* great darkness (v. 15)
The sign of the Son of Man will appear (v. 30)	There appeared a smoking oven and a burning torch (v. 17)

The signs of "the end" in Matthew's gospel are an allusion to the land-covenant that God made with Abram. The events of AD 70 saw Christ coming in judgement against the Jewish nation and the land-covenant was again put in abeyance – however, this does not diminish the eschatological significance of the prophecy, as it clearly remains unfulfilled until the Second Advent. Forms of the Greek verb συνάγω (gather together) which describe the congregation of the birds of prey in the 'vulture saying' in Matt 24:28 are also used to describe the assembly of the enemies of Christ:

> Then I saw an angel standing in the sun; and he cried with a loud voice, saying to all the birds (ὀρνέοις) that fly in the midst of heaven, 'Come and gather together (συνάχθητε)for the supper of the great God'. Rev 19:17 (NKJV).

> And I saw the beast, the kings of the earth, and their armies, gathered together (συνηγμένα) to make war against Him who sat on the horse and against His army. Rev 19:19 (NKJV).

The supper of the great God consists of the enemies of Christ—the 'banquet' that has been laid on for all the birds (vultures) is a recasting of the land-covenant and the 'supper' is also probably meant to contrast with the 'last supper' covenant meal. Intertextual links with Ezekiel demonstrates shared themes based on the land-covenant (note the mention of the mountains of Israel):

And as for you, son of man, thus says the Lord God, 'Speak to every sort of <u>bird</u> and to every beast of the field': "<u>Assemble</u> (συνάχθητε) yourselves and come; <u>Gather together</u> (συνάχθητε) from all sides to My sacrificial meal Which I am sacrificing for you, A great sacrificial meal on the mountains of Israel, That you may eat flesh and drink blood... Ezek 39:17 (NKJV)

The assembly of the wicked gathered together against Christ in Revelation 19 mirrors first century opposition to the preaching of the apostles:

And it came to pass, on the next day, that their rulers, elders, and scribes, as well as Annas the high priest, Caiaphas, John, and Alexander, and as many as were of the family of the high priest, were <u>gathered together</u> (συναχθῆναι) at Jerusalem. Acts 4:5-6 (NKJV)

In Acts 4:26 Peter addressed these rulers with the words of Ps 2:2,

The kings of the earth took their stand, and the rulers were <u>gathered together</u> (συνήχθησαν) against the Lord and against His Christ. For truly against Your holy Servant Jesus, whom You anointed, both Herod and Pontius Pilate, with the Gentiles and the people of Israel, were <u>gathered together</u> (συνήχθησαν). Acts 4:26-27

Finally, it should be noted that instead of the more usual 'body' (σῶμα, sōma) used in Luke's version of the 'vulture saying', Matthew employed the less frequently used 'carcase' (πτῶμα, ptōma) in order to describe the dead body. The usual Greek word for body (σῶμα) can denote a living or a dead body (the word is sometimes used metaphorically to describe the church as the 'body of Christ'); however, πτῶμα is only ever used of a dead body or carcass. This is significant because besides the 'vulture saying' in Matt 24:28, πτῶμα is only used five times in the NT. The word is twice used to describe the corpse of John the Baptist (Matt 14:12; Mark 6:29) and it is used three times for the corpse(s) of the witnesses (Rev 11:8-9). This is significant because John the Baptist pre-figured the eschatological witnessing.

Conclusion

The 'vulture saying' is based on the land-covenant made with Abraham. The 'cutting' (decapitation) of the body of John the Baptist heralded the establishment of the unconditional New Covenant in Christ. The Jewish and Gentile authorities who gathered together to oppose Christ and his Church were like the vultures swooping down to devour the pieces of the covenant sacrifice. The Judaist attempt to corrupt the Church and lead the nation back to slavery and death was therefore not allowed and the land-covenant was put in abeyance as it had been during the Babylonian Exile. Once again God did not frighten the vultures away and the carcasses of the people in AD 70 were a poignant reminder that God cannot be mocked—nevertheless, the covenant is unconditional and therefore after a 2,000 year *Diaspora* Yahweh has restored his people to their land.

However, the 'vulture saying' is intimately associated with the Second Advent and we should therefore expect an eschatological purging of Israel. The period of tribulation will be accompanied by a final witness to the nation and will conclude with the introduction of the Kingdom. This time the vultures are not frightened away, instead they are invited to dine on the enemies of Christ—as in the first century, this will consist of Gentile opposition and Jews who still reject him and his witnesses.

A New Age

A. Perry

Introduction

It is said that a new age in the purpose of God began with Jesus Christ. This age has been called various things, for instance, "The Christian Dispensation". People have identified various starting points for this new age including, in chronological order, the birth of John the Baptist, the birth of Jesus (or both); the baptism of Jesus (and/or the beginning of his ministry); Jesus' death and/or his resurrection; Pentecost; and finally, the end of the Jewish Commonwealth in AD70. The purpose of this article is twofold: first, to think about what it means to say that a new age began; and secondly, to show that if there is such an age, it did not begin with the baptism of Jesus.

Baptism of Jesus

What begins a new age in God's purpose? Is the "baptism" of Jesus by the Spirit just such a beginning? If there was such a beginning, is the new age properly called "the messianic age"? What arguments could be made for there being such an age and for it beginning with the descent of the Spirit upon Jesus?

Anointing with the Spirit

The characterization of a period of time as an "age" could be based upon the reign of a king, although a messiah is not necessarily a king. The work of deliverance that a messiah executes could constitute the beginning of a new age. This analogy could be the basis for identifying the **coming of Jesus** to Jordan as the beginning of a new age that is defined by him—the messianic age—the age of the Anointed One.[1]

> John answered, saying unto *them* all, I indeed baptize you with water; but one mightier than I <u>cometh</u>, the latchet of whose shoes I am not worthy to unloose: he shall baptize you with the Holy Ghost and with fire: Luke 3:16 (KJV)

On this interpretation, the old age ended with John the Baptist, and the new age is defined by Jesus, who would baptize with the Spirit and with fire. Jesus was "anointed" as messiah by the Spirit (Luke 4:18). This messianic age is characterized as one of spirit and fire.

This argument is fair enough, but it is inconclusive. Whether an age began in the purpose of God with the baptism of Jesus **depends on what subsequently happened**. The argument begs the question if the bestowal of the Spirit ceased at some point and/or Jesus ceased to baptize with the Spirit after his resurrection. The declaration that Jesus was coming and that he would baptize with the holy Spirit and fire does not of itself show that a new age was now beginning.

Instead, we should consider the work of a messiah: his first work is that of deliverance of the people from the enemy; subsequent to his victory, there is the beginning of a new age for the people. The proposal that the baptism of Jesus begins the messianic age overlooks this structure in the concept of "messiah": properly speaking, the messianic age does not begin until the victory has been won and the people thus delivered can enjoy the peace and security of the new age.

The Law and the Prophets were until John

It is said that John belongs to the age of the Law and the Prophets:

---

[1] The bestowal of the Spirit upon Jesus at Jordan is not an anointing as a king. Jesus was the Davidic king by dint of his birth; he did not need to be anointed as a king—such anointings take place in the purpose of God when there is a change of dynasty. The birth narratives identify the basis of Jesus' claims to the dynastic succession.

The law and the prophets *were* until John: since that time the kingdom of God is preached, and every man presseth into it. Luke 16:16 (KJV)

This would characterize the new age is one of "the kingdom", one in which the Law of Moses was no longer operative. The text has been taken as saying that a new age began after John and with the ministry of Jesus; thus, it is said that the baptism of Jesus began the new age.

There are problems with this proposal: first, the text excludes John from the old age—the putative new age begins with him because the Law and the Prophets were *until* John; secondly, the argument begs the question as to what then happened—an age has a beginning if, retrospectively, we can identify an age. The "preaching of the kingdom" happened in the ministry of both John and Jesus, but did it continue in the decades and centuries that followed?

If the new age began with John, it didn't begin with the baptism of Jesus. We could say that the new age began with the birth of John and Jesus. This would be a more plausible interpretation if we saw continuity between John and Jesus in their respective ministries. However, does the "end" of the Law and the Prophets mean that there is now a new age in the preaching of John and Jesus?

Since Jesus did not come to abolish the Law or the Prophets (Matt 5:17) but to fulfil their terms, the meaning of the saying 'the Law and the Prophets were until John' must be consistent with this idea of fulfillment. Thus, we can say that what Jesus means is that the teaching of the Law and the prophets in the synagogues were until John, but now there was the work of preaching the kingdom of God. He is drawing a contrast between the daily *teaching* of the Law and the Prophets and the *preaching* of the kingdom. We could make this difference the marker for a new age, but the new age so defined is then limited by this characterization: it is the age of the preaching of John, Jesus and their disciples. We do not have in this idea of a new age, a description of the messianic age, or the age of the kingdom, or the age of a restored Israel, or even "the age of the church".

The Kingdom of God is at Hand

Since the concept of an "age" is one to do with time, any reference to "the times" is critical evidence.

> And saying, The time is fulfilled, and the kingdom of God
> is at hand: repent ye, and believe the gospel. Mark 1:15
> (KJV)

This declaration takes place as Jesus returns to Galilee after his wilderness temptations. The kingdom is said to be "**at hand**" which implies that a new age had not yet begun: it was being preached. The reference to the "time is fulfilled" is therefore prospective and means a new age is about to begin. This line of interpretation suggests that the baptism of Jesus does not represent the beginning of the new age and it also excludes the birth of John and Jesus as the beginning of the new age if we take "the kingdom" to be the characterization of the new age.

This observation is important: if we take the new age to be the age of the kingdom, we would say that it did not begin with John or Jesus. If we take the new age to be instead the proclamation of the kingdom, we might say that it began with the births of John and/or Jesus or even the announcements to Zacharias and Mary. In this case, the baptism of Jesus does not look the obvious candidate for the beginning of a new age of preaching.

The Kingdom of God is in your Midst

John preached that the kingdom of God was "at hand" (Matt 3:2), but this message changed to some extent with Jesus because he says that the kingdom of God is in some sense present:

> But if I cast out devils by the Spirit of God, then the
> kingdom of God is come unto you. Matt 12:28 (KJV)

> Now having been questioned by the Pharisees as to when
> the kingdom of God was coming, He answered them and
> said, "The kingdom of God is not coming with signs to
> be observed; nor will they say, 'Look, here *it is!*' or, 'There
> *it is!*' For behold, the kingdom of God is in your midst."
> Luke 17:20-21 (NASB)

If we are going to date the beginning of the kingdom age, we should do so to the ministry of Jesus and this began with his baptism. Jesus' baptism by the Spirit is as good a starting point as any for the new age.

This argument is ambiguous at just the crucial point: it relies on the premise that the kingdom of God is in *some sense* present. But is this sense

the relevant sense that allows us to say that a new kingdom age has begun with the baptism of Jesus (or even the beginning of the gospel story)?

The kingdom of God was present in the sense that the powers associated with the kingdom age were being shown in the ministry of Jesus, but the kingdom age itself had not yet begun; it was still **at hand**. Hence, we cannot say that the new age had begun with the baptism of Jesus. This line of interpretation is clear from the link Jesus makes between his exorcisms and the kingdom of God:

> But if I cast out devils by the Spirit of God, then the kingdom of God is come unto you. Matt 12:28 (KJV)

> But if I with the finger of God cast out devils, no doubt the kingdom of God is come upon you. Luke 11:20 (KJV)

Insofar as Jesus cast out demons, the kingdom of God had "come upon" them, but it was not present as an "age" unless we define the "new age" to include the ministry of Jesus. Jesus' anointing with the Spirit at his baptism was an empowerment for his ministry but it was not the beginning of the new age which was still "at hand".

Battling the Kingdom of Satan

In Luke's account, Jesus is empowered by the Spirit (Luke 4:14) and he engages and resists Satan in the wilderness. His exorcisms throughout his ministry were an extension of this initial engagement, and in them he was continually defeating Satan (Mark 3:22-30). Although Jesus had possessed the Spirit since his childhood (Luke 2:40), it was only after his baptism by the Spirit that the clash between the kingdom of God and the kingdom of Satan began. The beginning of the new kingdom age is, therefore, his baptism.

This argument does not work for the reason that it begs the question as to whether Jesus' ministry is the new kingdom age in the purpose of God. The counter-argument is that his ministry was in the **last days** of a dying age and that the new age was **at hand**. In this case, Jesus' baptism does not have the significance of inaugurating a new age. In typological terms, a cosmic battle with Satan is a figure for the defeat of an enemy before the restoration of Israel and the beginning of new age. (It is beyond the scope of this article to explore the meaning of this narrative parable of the cosmic battle.)

The Descent of the Dove

The mention of the dove at Jesus' baptism may allude to the account of the Flood and the dove/homing pigeon sent out by Noah. The connection of the Spirit with a dove may also allude to the Genesis creation and the Spirit hovering as a bird over the waters. In either case, the symbology is of a new beginning at the baptism of Jesus and we could characterize this as the beginning of a new age.

The problem with this argument is that the two allusions are "new creation" types rather than types that signal a new age; they **relate to creation** rather than the structure of God's purpose in the working out of the history of Israel. We can accept the symbology of a new creation in the baptism of Jesus as that relates to him, but this does not make his baptism the beginning of a new age. The concept of a new kingdom age **relates to God's dealings with Israel**.

Messianic Anointing

Jesus' quotation of Isa 61:1-2a in his Nazareth address links his baptism by the Spirit at Jordan with the "anointing" of Isaiah's anonymous conqueror. This is a messianic anointing rather than an anointing associated with the Davidic dynasty. We could say therefore that the messianic age began with the baptism of Jesus (Acts 10:38).

This argument does not work. The anointing of an individual and the beginning of an age associated with that individual do not necessarily coincide. For example, the anointing of Saul or David did not coincide with the beginnings of their reigns; similarly with the dynasty of Jehu. The question is whether we take the beginning of the messianic age to coincide with Jesus' Davidic enthronement or his anointing at Jordan.

Given the conflict that Jesus engages upon and prophesies in his ministry, it is better to place the beginning of the messianic age after this conflict and tribulation—and place it at the beginning of the era of peace and good governance. We might want to speak of a new *stage* in God's dealings with Israel with the ministry of John and Jesus, but this is not the beginning of a new age, a kingdom age, or a Christian dispensation.

Beloved Son

The words spoken to Jesus at his baptism were,

> And the Holy Ghost descended in a bodily shape like a dove upon him, and a voice came from heaven, which

said, Thou art my beloved Son; in thee I am well pleased.
Luke 3:22 (KJV)

The words quote elements of Ps 2:7 and Isa 42:1,

> I will declare the decree: the Lord hath said unto me,
> <u>Thou art my Son</u>; this day have I begotten thee. Ps 2:7
> (KJV)

> Behold my servant, whom I uphold; mine elect, in whom
> my soul <u>delighteth</u>; I have put my spirit upon him: he
> shall bring forth judgment to the Gentiles. Isa 42:1 (KJV)

The elements being quoted are 'Thou art my...son', 'delight/well-pleased',
'with thee/in whom' and 'I/my soul'. The question is whether these OT
texts indicate the beginning of a new age.

The Isaiah source refers to God's Servant, Hezekiah in its primary
application. The catalyst for the oracle is Hezekiah's return from the east
of Jordan and a victory over Ammon and/or Moab;[1] he has liberated
Judahites recently deported to this region during Sennacherib's invasion in
701. It is this action of which God is well pleased, but there are yet further
enemies around Judah for Hezekiah to subdue. The quotation of these
words by the divine voice identifies Jesus as God's servant.

The psalm source shares thematic elements with Isaiah and it is an
appropriate text with which Isaiah can be combined in a quotation. The
declaration in the psalm is in favour of David and Zion; God announces
that he will subdue his enemies. The use of the quotation at the baptism of
Jesus is an announcement of Jesus' rights as the Davidic king.

The two OT contexts do not lend a typological basis for seeing the
beginning of a new age in the baptism of Jesus. We are in the middle of
Hezekiah's reign in Isaiah 42; furthermore, while there is a new beginning
in his reign after 701, and the times can be characterized as a time of
restoration, this does not allow us to say that it was a new age. What
happened in just over a hundred years was the dissolution of Judah as an
independent kingdom and exile for the upper and middle classes.
Moreover, God was shortly to announce the deportation of the royal
house to Babylon (Isa 39:6) which is a prophecy that would be fulfilled in
the Babylonian Exile.

---

[1] See A. Perry, *Isaiah 40-48* (Sunderland: Willow Publications, 2010).

Similarly, the Psalm is not from the beginning of David's reign, but from some time during his reign at a time when Israel are dominant in the region (Ps 2:3). The declaration that God had begotten David is a metaphor for his *renewal* of the choice of David as his king upon Zion. The use of the quotation in the divine voice at Jesus' baptism is for the same purpose: it is a metaphorical avowal of Jesus as God's anointed.[1] The metaphor is used again by Paul in Acts 13:33 in relation to Jesus' resurrection: Jesus is raised from the dead and declared again to be the Son of God with power in this act (Rom 1:4).

The Last Adam

The sequence of events at the start of the synoptic gospels suggests that Jesus is being presented as an antitype to Adam:

- the Spirit descended into Jesus (εἰς αὐτόν, Mark 1:10)/God breathed into Adam the breath of life
- Jesus is tested by Satan/Adam is tempted through the Serpent

Luke's gospel confirms this comparison because he includes the genealogy of Jesus between the account of his baptism and his temptations in the wilderness. Jesus is presented as the descendent of Adam, the son of God (Luke 3:38) and declared to be a beloved son. The typology here is one of new creation—the creation of the "second man" and the "last Adam" (1 Cor 15:45, 47), but it is not a typology of a new age, unless we insist that a **new creation** is by definition a new age.

We could compare Jesus' conception by the holy Spirit to God breathing the breath of life into Adam. If we do so, we might then try and find a typical analogue to Jesus' receiving the holy Spirit at his baptism and construct a typological pattern with three elements:

- Jesus is born of the holy Spirit/Adam received the breath of life
- the Spirit descended into Jesus/compared to ??
- Jesus is tested by Satan/Adam is tempted through the Serpent

This would work if we paralleled the command to Adam in the garden (a spirit-word to not eat of the tree of knowledge) with the Spirit coming

---

[1] The declaration is not an "adoption" of Jesus as God's son at this time, but a characterization of his "anointing" as God's messiah of deliverance. There is only one literal sense in which Jesus is God's son, and this is described in the birth narratives.

upon Jesus at his baptism. This would make the new creation type begin with Jesus' birth and any new age would be seen to have begun at that time.

Once again, the argument here turns upon how we think of the concept of an age. Is this a concept that just describes **the history of Israel**; or is it a concept that also embraces creation as a whole?

Israel

There are typological links between Jesus and Israel's experience in the Book of Exodus. Since the exodus from Egypt and all that ensued at Sinai represents a new beginning in God's purpose, it is argued that the Gospel writers are presenting Jesus' baptism and wilderness experience as a new beginning, the beginning of a new age:

- Israel crossed the Red Sea/Jesus was baptised. The crossing of the Red Sea is a type of baptism (1 Cor 10:2).

- Jesus was led by the Spirit in the wilderness just as Israel/Moses were led through the wilderness (Luke 4:1, NASB; Exod 13:21; Isa 63:14).

- Israel was in the wilderness 40 years; Jesus was in the wilderness 40 days.

- Israel was tested in the wilderness (Deut 8:2-5); Jesus was tested in the wilderness and cited texts from Deuteronomy 6-8.

Israel was God's son (Hos 11:1) and this pattern reinforces the identity of Jesus as God's son. However, there are other types in the account:

1) The heavens were "rent" (σχίζω, Mark 1:10), which fulfils the hope expressed in Isa 64:1, 'Oh that thou wouldst rend the heavens'. This hope follows on from the remembrance of the exodus story (Isa 63:7-19) and it reflects that story: God had come down and delivered his people in their exodus from Egypt, and the prophet urges Yahweh to come down and deliver his people once again. This echo to the exodus through Isaiah configures the descent of the Spirit upon Jesus as a theophany and a type of deliverance.

2) The Spirit descended into Jesus (εἰς αὐτόν, Mark 1:10); the holy Spirit likewise was put within Moses (Isa 63:11). Jesus is a "new Moses" for the people—he will deliver them. This type should not be misconstrued as an

analogue to Sinai; the giving of the Spirit cannot parallel the giving of the Law because there is no corresponding element for the new covenant. The **new covenant sacrifice still lay in the future** with the death of Jesus (Matt 26:28; Mark 14:24; Luke 22:20). The covenant transaction had not yet been effected.

3) Jesus came up out of Jordan and after a wilderness period entered Galilee (cf. Josh 4:14). This typical comparison sees Jesus "coming up" out of Jordan, which echoes the crossing of Jordan under Joshua, even though Jesus does not then immediately enter Galilee. The prominence of the verb "to come up" in the Joshua account, particularly in relation to the ark, makes this echo likely (Josh 4:16-19, 5x), and the point being made is that after baptism, or in baptism, a person should then "enter" the kingdom of God (John 3:5). Jesus' own example is an enacted demonstration of the message he was preaching.

These various types in the baptism of Jesus are not designed to signal a change in the ages but the **nature of deliverance** through water and the spirit.

New Covenant

Jeremiah prophesied,

> Behold, the days come, saith the Lord, that I will make a new covenant with the house of Israel, and with the house of Judah... Jer 31:31 (KJV)

This is picked up in Hebrews,

> In that he saith, A new *covenant*, he hath made the first old. Now that which decayeth and waxeth old *is* ready to vanish away. Heb 8:13 (KJV)

> For this reason He is the mediator of a new covenant, so that, since a death has taken place for the redemption of the transgressions that were *committed* under the first covenant, those who have been called may receive the promise of the eternal inheritance. Heb 9:15 (KJV)

Jesus is the mediator of the new covenant insofar as he is its high priest and its sacrificial death. Individuals enter this covenant through water baptism since they are baptized into the death of Christ (Rom 6:3). Such individuals are then in the position of waiting for the Abrahamic promise of inheritance, an inheritance that would last forever, to be fulfilled. Jesus' baptism is different to the baptism of his followers because they are baptized **into him** and into his death.

We cannot say therefore that the new covenant began at Jesus' baptism or that he entered the new covenant when he was baptized of John or the Spirit. The old covenant was passing away and did so finally in the destruction of the temple in AD70. The new covenant was and is mediated by Christ and the critical event for that covenant is the death of Christ. The structure of the concept of "covenant-making" is: God-mediator-covenant-people; in this structure, Jesus is the mediator and not the people; it is a mistake to have Jesus *entering* a new covenant in his baptism.

We can exclude the baptism of Jesus as the beginning of a new age, but we could say that a new age began with the death of Christ, because this is the one sacrifice that did away with the Mosaic system. However, this raises the question as to what an age *is* from God's point of view. It is possible to mix up different "beginning and ending" motifs and get into a muddle. Thus, while we might say there is no evidence that the messianic age or the kingdom age began, because there is no evidence that Israel were restored, but the reverse—they were scattered among the nations in AD70, we could say that the mosaic order did come to end and a new covenant age began. Is this the correct analysis?

Conclusion

This has been a discursive essay. We haven't successfully argued that *any* new age began in the first century; we haven't shown that a Christian dispensation began. This is because while the Mosaic Age ended, we haven't shown that a new age based on the new covenant has **continued** since the first century; it may be that the introduction of the new covenant does not signal a new age from God's point of view. The subject is large and complicated, involving as it does, the interpretation of Revelation as well as Daniel and the Prophets. However, the subject is not just an arcane matter of prophetic interpretation; the doctrine of the Spirit is bound up with the correct understanding of the structure of the ages.[1]

---

[1] Although there is no scholarship cited in this article, it does engage a popular scholarly view of the last forty years in Lucan scholarship. Not citing scholars allows the textual reasoning to stand by itself (or not), and as such it is not tied to the passing and fading of scholars.

Three "Last Days" Prophetic Utterances
J. Adey

Numbers 24	Psalm 110	2 Samuel 23
vv. 3–4 'Said' = 'ne²um' (x3); incl. 'said the man' = Heb. nə²ūm haggéḇer. (Cf. Prov 30:1 'said the man').	v. 1 'Said Yahweh' = Heb. ne²um Yahweh	v. 1 'Said' = 'ne²um' (x2); incl. 'said the man' = Heb. nə²ūm haggéḇer. (Cf. Prov 30:1 'said the man').
v. 17 (subject) him x2	vv. 5–7 his/he (x 6)	v. 3 (subject) he
v. 17 star out of Jacob	v. 3 dawn/morning (Cf. Rev. 22:16)	v. 4 light of the morning
v. 17 sceptre	**vv. 2 & 4** rule . . . Melchizedec	v. 3 he . . . rules
v.17 shall rise	Theme of the Psalm (Cf. Acts 2:24, 32, 33; 5:31).	v.1 raised up
v. 17 shall smite	vv. 5–6 shall smite x 2	v. 6 [war/judgement . . .
v. 18 possession (of his enemies…) x 2	vv. 1–2, 5–7 acquiring enemies' dominion	Belial thrust away…fire]. vv. 10 and 12: Yahweh wrought a great victory.
v. 18 (subject) him x2	vv. 5–7 his/he (x 6)	v. 3 (subject) he
v. 18 enemies (Cf. Gen. 22:17–18)	v. 1 (thine) enemies	Cf. 2 Sam. 23:6–39

Numbers 24	Psalm 110	2 Samuel 23
v. 18 Israel	v. 3 thy people	vv. 1, 3 Israel (x2)
v. 18 Heb. ḥayil valiantly/powerfully	v. 3 Heb. ḥayil power	Heb. ḥayil cf. 2 Sam. 22:40 & 23: 6–39
v. 19 he…dominion	v. 2 rule thou (= he, vv. 5–7)	v. 3 he…rules
v. 19 [Amalek] first = head/chief	vv. 6–7 heads…head	vv. 8, 13, 18 head/chief
Cf. 24:7 his king shall be higher than Agag, and his kingdom shall be exalted.	v. 7 Lift up [the head]	v. 1 raised up

The Faithful and Wise Servant
P. Wyns

> Who then is a faithful and wise servant, whom his master
> made ruler over his household, to give them food in due
> season? Matt 24:45 (NKJV)

When we read a text like this a number of questions suggest themselves.
Does Jesus have a specific servant in mind? Is this text applicable to the
first century or 'the end' or both? What does it mean to give the household
food (literal/metaphoric…or both?) in due season? The wise and faithful
servant is contrasted with the servant who abuses his fellow servants and
eats and drinks with the drunken. How do we understand this?

The faithful and wise servant is <u>made ruler over</u> (κατέστησεν) the
household. The Greek implies delegated responsibility and is translated as
'put in charge', 'give the responsibility' or 'appointed'—the NLT renders
the sense of the verse as follows; "Who is a faithful, sensible servant, to
whom the master can <u>give the responsibility</u> of managing his household
and feeding his family?" The same word is used in Acts for the
appointment of the seven brethren (including Stephen) to oversee the
Greek widows;

> Therefore, brethren, seek out (ἐπισκέψασθε) from among
> you seven men of good reputation, full of the Holy Spirit
> and wisdom, whom we may appoint over (καταστήσομεν)
> this business (τῆς χρείας). Acts 6:3 (NKJV)

One of the criteria for choosing the seven is that they are "full of the Holy
Spirit and **wisdom**" and Stephen himself is described as a "man full of
faith and the Holy Spirit" (v. 6) and "full of **faith** and power" (v. 8) and
Stephen's opponents "were not able to resist the **wisdom** and the Spirit by
which he spoke" (v. 10).

Stephen forms the benchmark for the "faithful and wise servant" who is
appointed (made ruler over) "this business". Of course Stephen was
following in the footsteps of his Master, whose own appointment had
been foreshadowed by Moses—"[Jesus] who was faithful to Him who
appointed (ποιήσαντι) Him, as Moses also *was faithful in all his house*" (Heb
3:2, 5). During his trial Stephen reminded his accusers that the Hebrews
resented the fact that Moses had been made ruler over them (the parallel
with Jesus being implicit); "Who made you a ruler (κατέστησεν) and a judge
over us?" (Acts 7:27) The answer was, of course, that God had appointed
both Moses and his Son over his household – and now his Son had
appointed Stephen – and the Jews rejected all three appointments.

Food in Due Season

The apostles appointed Stephen over "this business" (τῆς χρείας), the same
word is used to describe the welfare requirements of first century
Christians in Acts 2:45—"and sold their possessions and goods, and
divided them among all, as anyone had need" (χρείαν). Stephen was
therefore put in charge of solving the problem of discrimination against
the Greek widows (Greek speaking Jewish widows from the *Diaspora*) in
the distribution of welfare (v. 1). The apostles gave the instruction to seek
out (ἐπισκέψασθε) seven men to resolve the problem. Interestingly, the
same word is used by James; "Pure and undefiled religion before God and
the Father is this: to visit (ἐπισκέπτεσθαι) **orphans and widows** in their
trouble, *and* to keep oneself unspotted from the world (i.e. 'of *good*
reputation')" (James 1:27).

Inner-biblical evidence from James supports an early dating of the epistle
and points to composition by James the brother of John (not James the
brother of the Lord) with the background shaped by the death of Stephen
and the persecution that followed. The trial of Stephen operated as a
catalyst in triggering a chain reaction that culminated in the conversion of

Paul and the inclusion of the Gentiles. No longer would the early Christian church be regarded as a Jewish sect within the Synagogue. The inclusion of the Gentiles hastened the "parting of the ways".

The way that James (a former disciple of John the Baptist) directs his invective against "adulterers and adulteresses" (James 4:4) and murderers (James 4:2) demonstrates that he has in mind the murder of John the Baptist (for condemning the adultery of Herod) and the murder of Stephen for "envy" (James 4:4-5; compare Num 11:26-29). James' comments are therefore directed at a mixed audience within the synagogue which was compromised of Judaists and Christian converts.

For James, Stephen was the paradigm of a Jew who practised "true religion" the perfect combination of faith and works (James 2:26). The twelve apostles, including James, did not want to "leave the word of God" in order to "serve tables" (Acts 6:2). Stephen demonstrated that it was possible to do both—to give the Greek widows organic *and* spiritual food. He was fulfilling the commission given to Peter in John 21:16—"feed my sheep" and he is the first Christian outside the apostolic group to perform "signs and wonders" (Acts 6:8). It was the trial and death of Stephen which forced a parting of the ways between Judaism and Christianity:

> Then there arose some from what is called the Synagogue of the Freedmen (Cyrenians, Alexandrians, and those from Cilicia and Asia), disputing with Stephen. Acts 6:9 (NKJV)

There is confusion regarding this synagogue. Some consider it a singular institution, others as referencing more than one synagogue. What does the term "Freedmen" ($\Lambda\iota\beta\epsilon\rho\tau\hat{\iota}\nu o\varsigma$) mean? Were they former Roman slaves and converts to Judaism who had their synagogue at Jerusalem? It is possible that they were Jews living in Rome who had been made slaves by the Romans under Pompey but afterward were set free, and had built a synagogue at Jerusalem. Others understand "Libertines" as denoting the location of Libertum (A Jewish community in Africa) rather than a descriptive term.

However, the mention of Cilicia is interesting, as the apostle Paul was a citizen of Tarsus, which lies within the region of Cilicia (Acts 21:39; 22:3). Paul was born a Roman citizen (from a father who was a freedman? cf. Acts 22:28) and was a Hellenistic Jew. Paul was also closely involved in the dispute with Stephen and was present at his sentencing (Acts 8:1; 22:20).

The tentative conclusion suggested here is that we are dealing with a singular synagogue in Jerusalem, home to well educated Hellenistic *Diaspora* Jews, who were Roman citizens by birth (like Paul). They resented the fact that Stephen cared for the Hellenistic widows (which they saw as their sphere of activity) and probably saw his concern as a drive to undermine the authority of their Synagogue. Moreover, they found that it was impossible to best Stephen in Scriptural proofs (even Saul of Tarsus?) demonstrating that Jesus Christ was the Messiah. It seems that the *Diaspora* Jews were more influential (and affluent) than we give them credit for and they wanted to stop the "contamination" of Christianity spreading beyond Jerusalem. Clearly the Sanhedrin was unable to halt the spread of the movement in Judea and therefore extreme measures were necessary to prevent dissemination to the *Diaspora* community.

Eating and Drinking with the Drunken

> **(45)** Who then is a faithful and wise servant, whom his master made ruler over his household, to give them food in due season? **(46)** Blessed *is* that servant whom his master, when he comes, will find so doing. **(47)** Assuredly, I say to you that he will make him ruler over all his goods. **(48)** But if that evil servant says in his heart, 'My master is delaying his coming', **(49)** and begins to beat *his* fellow servants, and to eat and drink with the <u>drunkards</u> (μεθυόντων), **(50)** the master of that servant will come on a day when he is not looking for *him* and at an hour that he is not aware of, **(51)** and will cut him in two and appoint *him* his portion with the hypocrites. There shall be weeping and gnashing of teeth.

If Stephen is the paradigm for the faithful and wise servant then who is the evil servant who abuses his fellows and eats and drinks with the drunken? The evil servant is the believer who loses faith in the return of Christ— "Where is the promise of His coming?" (2 Pet 3:4), expresses the same sentiment as Matt.24:48—"My master is delaying his coming". During his trial Stephen pointed out that the Israelites had reacted the same way when Moses was in the presence of Yahweh on Mount Sinai; "we do not know what has become of him" (Acts 7:40). On that occasion the Israelites used the absence of Moses to make an idol (a copy of the calf-cherubim?) and "the people sat down <u>to eat and drink</u>, and rose up to play" (Exod 32:6). The apostasy and the orgy were justified as a "feast to the Lord" (v. 5) and both the creation of the idol and the feast was (reluctantly?) supported by the priesthood.

In Hezekiah's day the "drunkards" were an element among from the northern tribes who had sought a new life in Judah and Jerusalem. Some within the capital acted as a fifth column[1] and betrayed Hezekiah by making an agreement with the Assyrians, which they celebrated with a feast. They were the "drunkards" of Ephraim –

> Woe to the crown (cf. LXX: Στέφανος, *Stephen*) of pride,
> to the drunkards of Ephraim... that are overcome with
> wine[2]... Isa 28:1 (KJV)

The priest and the prophet erred through intoxicating drink (Isa 28:7). The revolt extended beyond the northerners[3] as the traitors are described as "scornful men, Who rule this people who *are* in Jerusalem"(Isa 28:14). They boasted that they had made an agreement with death and hell (with the Assyrians) and therefore they were untouchable (Isa 28:15). The parallels with first century Judaism are obvious, as the rulers of Jerusalem (Jew and Gentile) agreed to crucify Christ (Acts 4:27). Moreover, the internal situation depicted by Isaiah during the Assyrian crisis is characterised by the factionalism, in-fighting and betrayal that occurred during the Roman crisis and siege of Jerusalem in 66-70 AD.

With Isaiah in mind, we can say that the evil servant in Jesus' parable would be one who defected to the party of the "drunken" and abused his fellow servants (beats them). The warning in Matthew also recalls the woman who made the inhabitants of the earth, "drunken with the wine of her fornication" (Rev 17:2) and who was "drunk with the blood of the saints and with the blood of the martyrs of Jesus" (Rev 17:6). In Matthew 24:30-36 Jesus accused the authorities of being the sons of those who murdered the prophets (v. 31) and warned that they would murder and persecute the prophets, wise men and scribes that he sent to them (v. 34). Stephen levels the same accusation against the Sanhedrin; "Which of the

---

[1] [Ed AP: They are possibly by now (some twenty years after the sack of Samaria) an established group in the political ruling class].

[2] The drunken are not necessarily intoxicated with wine but possibly just with exercising power (as suggested by the LXX interpretation).

[3] [Ed AP: It is also possible that the reference "drunkards of Ephraim" is sarcastic and used of southerners acting like the Ephraimites before the demise of Samaria].

prophets did your fathers not persecute? And they killed those who foretold the coming of the Just One, of whom you now have become the betrayers and murderers" (Acts 7:52).

I will give the nations for your inheritance

The trial of Stephen marked a turning point in the spread of the gospel. Instead of crushing the movement, the persecution contributed to the growth of the gospel to the *Diaspora* as Christians fled from Jerusalem. When the chief persecutor experienced his Damascus road conversion and became the apostle to the Gentiles, the growth-rate of Christianity increased exponentially. The trial of Stephen was therefore instrumental in a drastic change of direction:

> **(55)** But he, being full of the Holy Spirit, gazed into heaven and saw the glory of God, and Jesus standing at the right hand of God, **(56)** and said, "Look! I see the heavens opened and the Son of Man standing at the right hand of God!" **(57)** Then they cried out with a loud voice, stopped their ears, and ran at him with one accord; **(58)** and they cast *him* out of the city and stoned *him*. And the witnesses laid down their clothes at the feet of a young man named Saul. **(59)** And they stoned Stephen as he was calling on *God* and saying, "Lord Jesus, receive my spirit". **(60)** Then he knelt down and cried out with a loud voice, "Lord, do not charge them with this sin." And when he had said this, he fell asleep. Acts 7:55-60 (NKJV)

Acts 7 juxtaposes the judgement of the earthly council (Sanhedrin) on Stephen with the judgement of the heavenly council on the Sanhedrin. In an allusion to Ps 82:8, Jesus is depicted as standing instead of sitting (cf. Ps 110:1); "Arise, O God, judge the earth; for You shall inherit all nations". Significantly Psalm 82 is quoted by Jesus in his own dispute with the Sanhedrin (John 10:34-35) and the motif of inheriting all nations is also found in Psalm 2 which was extensively quoted by the apostles and applied to the rulers who had crucified Christ (Acts 4:25-29). Interestingly, Psalm 2 concludes with the following admonition;

> **(10)** Now therefore, be wise, O kings; Be instructed, you judges of the earth. **(11)** Serve the Lord with fear, And rejoice with trembling. **(12)** Kiss the Son, lest He be angry, And you perish *in* the way, When His wrath is

kindled but a little. Blessed *are* all those who put their trust in Him. Ps 2:10-12 (NKJV)

Saul was one of the judges that required instruction, he almost perished on the way to Damascus but he "kissed the Son" and preached justification by faith (those who put their trust in Him) **to the Gentiles.** The request by Stephen "not charge them with this sin" was therefore answered by the conversion of Saul—the judgement against the Sanhedrin was that, henceforth, the message would go forth to the Gentiles (Rom 11:12).

Conclusion

We can now attempt to answer the questions that were posed at the beginning of this article. The wise and faithful servant who is appointed to give the household food in due season is Stephen. The "food" that Stephen supplied was both literal (organic food) and Spiritual (the Word of God). He was the perfect example of faith and works operating in unison. The party of the "drunken" are those who are guilty of the blood of the saints (of all ages), those that make covenants with enemies of the gospel in order to save their own skin—the "evil servant" is the one who defects to this party (and who no longer eats and drinks with Christ).

The apostle Paul encountered a deliberate attempt to infiltrate the early church and turn believers back to Judaism. This included forged epistles and character assassination with the situation worsening to such an extent that Paul complained that "all those in Asia have turned away from me"(2 Tim 1:15). Paul may have had a particular individual in mind when he warned the Corinthians about "deceitful workers, transforming themselves into the apostles of Christ" (2 Cor. 11:13). In any case, the danger of defecting back to Judaism was very real—"But it has happened to them according to the true proverb: "A dog returns to his own vomit" and "a sow, having washed, to her wallowing in the mire" (2 Pet 2:22[1]).

Jesus warned that he would come unexpectedly and "will cut him (the evil servant) in two and appoint *him* his portion with the hypocrites. There shall be weeping and gnashing of teeth" (Matt 24:51). The cutting in two (διχοτομέω) is a reference to the land-covenant of Gen 15:10 which went into abeyance in AD 70. Those who had "gnashed their teeth (in anger)" at Stephen (Acts 7:54) would come to gnash their teeth in sorrow and weeping (Matt 24:51) when the nation was judged and scattered.

---

[1] Peter did not just have Gentile converts in mind as 2 Peter 3 warns of the coming judgement on Judaism.

The Shema of Deut 6:4
J. W. Adey

Abstract

Hebrew: יְהוָה אֱלֹהֵינוּ יְהוָה אֶחָד

Transliteration:	YHWH ʾĕlōhênû YHWH ʾeḥāḏ
Word-for-word translation:	Yahweh God of us, Yahweh one
King James' Version:	The LORD our God *is* one LORD

Aim: Is *ʾeḥāḏ* in this text about 'unity' or numerical 'one'? I argue that *ʾeḥāḏ*, an adjective qualifying 'Yahweh', is performing its normal quantitative role as the cardinal numeral 'one', and thus (the) 'unity' (of Yahweh) is not its intended sense. This presentation should also affirm that Scriptural revelation insists Yahweh is one, not a unity. That He, (with singular pronouns), is indivisible, the sole occupant of the category 'God'.

Introduction

Deut 6:4's *ʾeḥāḏ*, Trinitarians claim, is 'one' of 'unity', specifically "compound unity". However, they also cite Jesus' usage to insist that the numerical sense of 'one' applies:

> And the scribe said unto him, Well, Master, thou hast said the truth: for there is one God; and there is none other but he... Mark 12:32 (KJV)

For Trinitarians, Deut 6:4 is a gift proof text. It features, for example, in 'Article I: "I Believe in One God"' of the *Catechism of the Catholic Church* (1999), where "God is unique; there is only one God."[1] Maintaining this sense of 'one', having "faith in God, the only one",[2] aligns with Scriptural (unitarian) language about God, and thus the Shema text can be cited as if their creed were *totally* faithful to it.[3]

---

[1] *Catechism of the Catholic Church* (London: Geoffrey Chapman 1999): 49, paras 199-202.

[2] *Catechism*, 54-55, paras 222-227.

[3] Indeed, Deut 6:4//Mk 12:29ff. is cited in the *Catechism*, 55, para 227, with Tertullian's testimony: 'The supreme being must be unique, without equal...If God is not one, he is not God'.

Yet, mention of 'one' facilitates talk of '[tri]-unity'. Presupposing a 'tri-une' God, *eḥāḏ* is read as *more-than-one-as-one*; whence, "compound unity". A Hebrew abstract noun for 'unity', different in form from *eḥāḏ*, but a cognate of 'one', does not occur in the Hebrew Bible.[1] Had a term like *aḥdût* been used in Deut 6:4, then not only would 'unity' be the statement's sense, 'one' singular would not have been possible.

Conceptual clarification is necessary, here. Whilst 'one' can be transposed in sense (in the relevant usage and context) as the metaphoric 'one' = unity ('oneness'); the term 'unity' cannot be deconstructed (back) to 'one'; the composition of 'unity' requires *more than one*. So, on these terms, if 'unity' were the sense of *eḥāḏ* (though it is not the Hebrew for 'unity'), then numerical 'one' which Trinitarians rightly insist on, and Scripture's own commentary confirms, would not be a possible feature of this Deuteronomy text.

So, Deut 6:4, used in the Trinitarian's dual way, serves their purposes. But it should not be overlooked that the text is used by them to insist that *eḥāḏ* numbers a singular 'one (thing)' lest they should be charged with 'tri-theism' (that they believe in three Gods); thus *God as one being* means (their) monotheism is upheld. However, 'one' is being subtly used in two different ways, as is also the case with respect to (what it is to be) 'God'.

It is clear from the New Testament (NT) and Jesus' usage, that talk about 'Yahweh' qualified by *eḥāḏ* in Deut 6:4, is about the same referent as either 'God' or 'the Lord'. (Not for subordinationist reasons, but to avoid confounding the "three divine persons", Trinitarians distinguish Jesus as

---

[1] The KJV of Ps 133:1 has the only instance of the English word 'unity' in the OT. However, they give a three-word paraphrase of the (*eḥāḏ* – related) single word יָחַד / *yāḥaḏ* - 'together' as "together in unity". 'Together' does not, of itself, *require* an intimate togetherness like 'union' or ideal 'unity' suggests. The use of *yāḥaḏ* can simply mark unity of purpose, or expedient collaboration, as in Ps 2:2, "The kings of the earth set themselves, and the rulers take counsel **together**, against Yahweh, and against his anointed." The Greek of the Apostles' citation of Ps 2:2 in Acts 4:26 uses the idiom ἐπὶ τὸ αὐτὸ—lit. 'upon the same'—which also features in how the ecclesia should "come together" (Acts 1:15; 2:1, 44, 47; 4:26; 1 Cor 7:5; 11:20; 14:23; the KJV wrongly renders this idiom 'into one place' in 1 Cor 11:20; 14:23).

Lord from his Father as Lord). In the NT it is 'Lord' in the place of Old Testament (OT) 'Yahweh' that is qualified by 'one':

> And Jesus answered him, The first of all the commandments is, Hear, O Israel; The Lord our God is one Lord. Mark 12:29 (KJV)

Jesus maintained that "Scripture cannot be broken" (John 10:35), so these next two (eschatological) texts will share the same theological viewpoint about Yahweh/Lord as Jesus' use of Deut 6:4. None of the cited statements suggests 'unity' but rather 'one (thing)', as also intended in the limiting sense of 'alone'[1]:

> And Yahweh shall be king over all the earth: in that day shall there be **one** Yahweh, and his name **one**. Zech 14:9

> That men may know that thou, whose name **alone** is Yahweh, art the most high over all the earth. Ps 83:18. [My bold text.]

I adduce these texts and others in this article to show what 'one Yahweh' conceptualises for ancient Israel, about their relation to God by His name, for their Godly observance (Deut 12:29-32), and to prevent polytheistic compromise or confusion. Moreover, modern Christadelphian unitarians are conditioned by the same 'one' that associates with the Father only being God: "To us there is but one God, the Father" (1 Cor 8:6, cf. Mal 3:10). How could 'unity' apply to the self-complete, perfect, one-person, unchangeable God of the Bible? How important 'one' is (instead) to the doctrine of God as Yahweh.

I do not deny that unity *associates* with God or His name; Jesus' authority in John 17 teaches that. Indeed, *ʾĕlōhênû*—'our God'—in Deut 6:4 presents a relational God, one to whom the approved 'us' (Israel/saints) are united (cf. Exod 3:6, 12, 14-15; 6:7; Num 16:5; Rev 21:3, 7; 1 Cor 15:28). Even if 'Yahweh' is a class-name for the set of the redeemed (Rev 14:1), those kept in God's name (John 17:11-12) are not Yahweh; He remains Himself.

---

[1] The use of 'alone' (Hebrew בַּד *bad*) of Yahweh complements the restricting use of 'one' (cf. Deut 32:12; Neh 9:6; Isa 2:11, 17). 'Alone' marks the incomparable wholly other being that is Yahweh; He is in a set of one.

However, I take it that 'unity' presupposes the uniting or harmonious relation of at the least two parts or parties. Eve made for Adam has been expressed thus: "Each for the other—a unity in two".[1] In Biblical cases, as with our first parental pair, the sense of 'one' as unity is usually apparent. Man and woman are and typify "a communion of persons"[2]; "they two shall be one flesh" (Matt 19:5-6) cites what the original Divine joining facilitated (Gen 2:24; a type for Rev 21:2-10).[3] Divine joining is the presupposition in these cases, too: "I and my Father, we are one" (John 10:30),[4] or "that they may be one as we *are* one" (John 17:11, 21-22; 1 Cor 15:28).

These instances use the number 'one' to present 'one-ness'. This is not the concrete counting of objects as 'one (thing)' but a bonding measured by 'one' as a single qualitative property. 'Oneness', or the unity of a "multitude which no man can number" (Rev 7:9)[5], is transcendental, on a scale reckonable only by Yahweh who's "understanding is infinite" (Ps 147:5).[6]

In what follows, as my treatment's exposition is partly for apologetic purposes, I occasionally cite non-Biblical sources.

---

[1] Cf. 'III. "Male and female Created He them".' *Catechism*, 84, paras 369-372.

[2] 'III. "Male and female Created He them".' *Catechism*, 84, para 372.

[3] The NT reuse of Gen 2:24 inserts 'the two': καὶ ἔσονται οἱ δύο εἰς σάρκα μίαν. And (they) shall be the two into flesh one.

[4] Since "God was in Christ reconciling the world" (2 Cor 5:19), and He made His willing son strong for Himself (Ps 80:15 [HB 16]-17 [HB 18]), as previewed in Genesis 22, both 'Father and son went **together**' (used 3x in Gen 22:6, 8, 19) in this act of reconciliation. This ('parabolic': Heb 11:19) sacrificial context of Abraham and Isaac contains both the Hebrew adverb 'together' (יַחְדָּו *yaḥdāw*) and the related adjective "only *son*" or 'only one' (יָחִיד *yāḥîd*) also used three times (Gen 22:2, 12, 16). These two terms are related to both 'one' (*'eḥād*) and the verb 'unite' or 'join' (יָחַד *yāḥad* : Genesis 49:6; Ps 86:11; Isa 14:20). So, with 2 Cor 5:19, this OT background explains, or cannot be denied as relevant to, "I and my Father are one" in John 10:30.

[5] Cf. J. W. Adey, 'Accounting for Abraham' (1), *The Testimony* Vol. 72. No. 855, March 2002: 71-73; 'Accounting for Abraham' (2), Vol. 72. No. 856, April 2002: 108-112.

[6] 'Infinite' is from the Hebrew *'ên mispār*, lit. 'without number'.

[1] Terms of Reference

On YHWH and ʾĕlōhênû

My prime focus is how the use of the term ʾeḥāḏ in the Hebrew Bible (HB) can inform us of its meaning in the *Shema* of Deut 6:4. I develop this in section [2] and connect with the New Testament (NT) 'one' in relation to God. The KJV's italicised '*is*', in '*is* one', notes the absence of a verb. YHWH ʾeḥāḏ can be 'one Yahweh' as in Zech 14:9 (KJV), which also has "and his name one" (*ûšəmô ʾeḥāḏ*).

On YHWH

- The two KJV English non-name renderings 'The LORD' and 'LORD' are not representing the original Hebrew which has two instances of God's name 'Yahweh'.

- There are 'lord' terms in the HB, but the Holy Spirit has not used them in Deut 6:4.
- So, ʾeḥāḏ is not qualifying a 'Lord' form in Deut 6:4 but the Divine name.[1]

- Of course, the capitalised 'LORD' device perpetuates the Jewish practice of avoiding reading or pronouncing the 6828 instances of the Divine name in the HB.[2]

- In Mark 12:29-34, compliant with the NT's *mode of presentation*, the citation of this Deut 6:4 text is given with the Greek 'Lord' κύριος/kurios.

---

[1] This mode of presentation matches Joshua's conquest list in Jos 12. Each king and his place is given, followed by 'one': e.g., "king of Jericho one" —*melek yərîḥô ʾeḥāḏ*—אֶחָד יְרִיחוֹ מֶלֶךְ (Jos 12:9). See n. 2 on p. 39.

[2] From October 2010, the new *Holman Christian Standard Bible* (HCSB), a study Bible, will be available: http://www.hcsb.org/. Like the *Jerusalem Bible* (1966), and its updated version the *New Jerusalem Bible* (1985), the HCSB also drops the 'LORD' device and returns to God's name 'Yahweh' of the Hebrew text. They support this with the fact that names crossover into other languages, as within the Bible, by transliteration.

- It is anachronistic to treat the OT as if it were the NT, or to cite NT's *kurios* quotational replacement for OT 'Yahweh' to justify 'Lord' (or other) replacements of 'Yahweh' back in the OT.[1]

- God speaks solely to His son in rare moments in the NT, but there is no use of 'Yahweh' or His 'I'-speak as in the OT. This theological difference is marked by Jesus using His Father's 'I' (e.g., John's "I am" – egō eimi) and manifesting God's name.[2]

- The prophetic focus on God's name being again made known is presented in Ezek 38:23; 39:6-7 (cf. 48:35), **as well as** Zech 14:9 already cited (a text clearly linked to Deut 6:4), to be realised theophanically by Jesus' as he intimated: "And I have declared unto them thy name, and **will declare** *it*" (John 17:26).

On ʾĕlōhênû

I only draw attention, here, to the grammatical and semantic features of ʾĕlōhênû. I do not expound its meaning from comparative usage, as 'one Yahweh' is my focus. However, the relational 'God of us' or 'our God' (cf. ʾĕlōhîm) is about the kind of God 'one Yahweh' is.

- 'Our God', ʾĕlōhênû, is the plural ʾĕlōhîm shortened to (the genitive) ʾĕlōhê. 'God of'.

---

[1] In the OT God never says: 'I *am* the Lord', where that would be solely to combine 'I' and 'Lord' (some form of ʾadon) in Hebrew. So, to versions with "I *am* the LORD: that is my name" (Isa 42:8), or to those that have not yet realised that 'LORD' (or 'Lord') is not a name, a just challenge would be: "Yea, hath God said?" However, God utters 'I *am* ___ [ʾēl, ʾēl šadday and Yahweh]' many times in the HB (mostly: 'I *am* Yahweh', His only name, with or without something added, 220 times). "I am the Lord GOD" uses 'Lord' but it is followed by God's name: ʾny ʾdny yhwh (in Ezek 13:9; 23:49; 24:24; 28:24; 29:16).

[2] Jesus' composite theophoric name (cf. 'Joshua'), with a 'Yah' or 'Yeho[shuaʿ]' prefix, is to the NT what God's name 'Yahweh' is to the OT. Although there is no Graecised or transliterated 'YHWH'/'Yahweh' in the NT, 'Yah' occurs in 'Allelu**ia**' (Rev 19:1, 3-4), ready to be revealed in the last time.

- This form has the suffix *nû* meaning 'our(s)' or 'us' (cf. *nû* in 'Imma**nue**l').

- So, *'ĕlōhênû* stated in English is: 'God of us' or "our God".

- The plural *'ĕlōhîm*, rather than the singular terms for 'God' *'ĕl* and *'ĕlô^ah*, is used for the relating, through theophanic extending, of God to others.

- It is this functional differentiation (a *'value-addedness'*) between plural *'ĕlōhîm* and the singular 'God' terms, that in Deut 6:4 conditions, or reciprocally is conditioned by, "Yahweh *is* one".

[2] Term for 'One'

On *'eḥād* and 'one'

a) Compound unity versus counting

Trinitarians claim that the Hebrew word *'eḥād* translated 'one' in Deut 6:4, denotes a compound unity, not a simple unity. So, 'unity' is what 'one' means for them in this text. However, their idea of Divine 'unity' as "compound unity" is an interpretation regulated by preconception. It would help if there was a Biblical Hebrew term, a cognate of 'one' especially, which was the abstract noun 'unity'.[1]

An example of 'compound unity' often given is where 'one' is applied to 'day' (lit. 'day one') in Gen 1:5 (*yôm 'eḥād*: KJV "first day"), because 'day' is made-up of parts: morning and evening, or day and night. However, in Zech 14:7, mention is made of a future 'one day' which does not have, or is denied (such day and night) parts; another is Joshua's 'day'. This makes clear, as in 'day one of the first month' (Ezra 10:17), that the role of 'one' qualifying 'day' is simply numbering, or time-marking in Gen 1:5. 'Compound unity' is not a relevant functional feature of 'day one'. No explicit or implied consideration of the *uniting* of parts (two or more to make 'one') is taking place.

---

[1] Ezek 37:17 repeats 'one' to describe a uniting of each one, but a Hebrew term for 'unity' is not used (which would be, e.g., *'aḥdût*): And join (Heb *qrb*) them one to one into one stick for yourself; and they shall become one (literally or grammatically: 'ones'- *'ăḥādîm*) in your hand. Cf. n. 4 on p. 34 above.

In Genesis 1, following use of the cardinal 'one' in v. 5, subsequent numbering of days use ordinal numbers ('second' 1:8, 'third' 13, etc.). In Gen 2:10-14, this same sequential pattern, starting with 'one' (KJV "the first" *hāʾeḥāḏ*), then continuing with 'second . . . fourth' is repeated in relation to the four rivers. Taking *ʾeḥāḏ* or 'one' to be about 'unity' is governed by the notion of a compound that is 'three-in-one': unity as tri-unity. There are three related or united persons in their one God(head). The *Catholic Catechism* affirms,

– The Trinity is One (para 253).
– We do not confess three Gods but one God in three persons, the 'consubstantial Trinity' (para 253).
– The Divine Unity is Triune (para 254).
– God is one <u>but not solitary</u> (para 254).[1] (My <u>underlining</u>.)

b) <u>'Unity' is special pleading</u>

The analysis that follows shows "for 'one' read 'unity'", of the kind stated in the *Catechism*, above, is special pleading. Biblical proof is needed to show that *ʾeḥāḏ* should become 'unity' as a different order of 'one'. Of course, even if *ʾeḥāḏ* in Deut 6:4 were to do with 'unity', that does not of itself mean a unity comprised of three ('Gods'). Indeed, two human persons, or an innumerable redeemed "many becoming 'one'" (in Christ and in God, his Father) aligns with Biblical precedents. By contrast, 1 John 5:7's 'three are one' is notorious as a spurious trinitarian interpolation.

- In Hebrew idiom, as in Gen 11:6, whether masculine *ʾeḥāḏ* [of 'people'], or feminine *ʾaḥat* [of 'language'], 'one' always follows the noun it quantifies, whereas subsequent cardinal numbers (two, three, four, etc.) precede the noun to which they apply.

- Whatever the semantic or conceptual role of 'one'/*ʾeḥāḏ* in this Deut 6:4 formulation, it is positioned in the normal way so any *emphasis* or *nuance* is not obvious.[2]

---

[1] *Catechism*, 60-63.

[2] If the point being made is 'one of (something)', like אַחַד הָעָם / *ʾaḥaḏ hāʿām* : 'one of the people' (Gen 26:10), then 'one' precedes the noun ('the people'). See n. 1 on p. 36 above.

- Similarly, in Mal 2:10, both 'father' and 'God' (the singular form *ʾēl*) are qualified by *ʾeḥāḏ*: "Have we not all **one** father? Hath not **one** God created us?"

To sum up, what we have regarding Israel's God and *ʾeḥāḏ* / 'one' in the OT is a pattern of usage as follows,

> 'One Yahweh' ('Yahweh *is* one') in Deut 6:4 and Zech 14:9.
> 'One Father' and 'one God' in Mal 2:10.[1]
> 'One name' ('name one') in Zech 14:9.

c) <u>Greek NT 'one' corresponding to HB/OT *ʾeḥāḏ* in statements about God</u>

We have already seen that Jesus cites Deut 6:4 in reply to a question in Mark 12:29:

> And Jesus answered him, The first of all the commandments *is*, Hear, O Israel; The Lord our God is one Lord. (KJV) (NIV: ...the Lord our God, the Lord is one).

κύριος ὁ θεὸς ἡμῶν κύριος **εἷς** ἐστιν
Lord   the God of us Lord **one** (he/there) is

'One' (thing), as in a numbering sense, is explicit in Mark 12:32:

> And the scribe said unto him, Well, Master, thou hast said the truth: for **one** [STE God] there is; and not there is (an)other but he.

ὅτι **εἷς** [STE Θεὸς[2]]᾿ἐστιν   καὶ οὐκ ἔστιν   ἄλλος   πλὴν αὐτοῦ.

There are other NT texts that qualify God, or the Father, by 'one' (Gk. εἷς):

John 8:41   We have one Father, God.
1 Cor 8:4   An idol is nothing in the world, and that there is none other God but one.

---

[1] Mal 2:10 is reflected in 1 Cor 8:6.

[2] Stephanos' Greek text, i.e. the same text as the Textus Receptus, includes Θεὸς. The Majority Text and UBS/GNT agree in excluding the word.

1 Cor 8:6	But to us, one God, the Father, out of whom are all things.
Gal 3:20	Now a mediator is not of one, but God is one.
Eph 4:6	One God and Father of all, who is above all, and through all, and in you all.
1 Tim 2:5	For *there is* one God, and one mediator of God and of men, the man Christ Jesus.
Jas 2:19	You believe that there is one God; you do well.

In 1 Tim 2:5, 'men' and 'God' are distinct contrasting categories. 'Men' (ἀνθρώπων) is the plural of 'man' (ἄνθρωπος) which is used of Christ Jesus. God is one, and Jesus, who was a mediator of God[1] and of men as the messenger of the covenant in his ministry, is also one individual. God and his son act in concert or complementarily, but 'one' used of the mediator Christ Jesus is not a 'one' of 'unity'; this not the issue, here, although 'making one' was what his role achieved.[2] Likewise, 'one' is used of God because He is the sole occupant of the set '(Most High; Only Wise) God'.

It is of particular note that 'idol' in 1 Cor 8:4, a category-term for polytheism, is contrasted with there being only one (who is) God. In the Deuteronomy context, the 'one' qualifying 'Yahweh' would be a witness against any tendency to go after other named neighbouring gods. God's name, the vehicle by which He *made Himself known* (Exod 6:3) to His people, is identified in His acts the one who alone is Yahweh, the ʾēl/God with(in) Israel.

Elsewhere Jesus confirms his words to the scribe about the exclusive singularity (utter uniqueness) of God:

Matt 19:17; cf. Mark 10:18

Why me callest thou good? there is none good but **one**, that is, God.[3]
BYZ: Τί με λέγεις ἀγαθόν; Οὐδεὶς ἀγαθός, εἰ μὴ **εἷς**, ὁ θεός.
UBS 3/4: Τί με ἐρωτᾷς περὶ τοῦ ἀγαθοῦ; εἷς ἐστιν ὁ ἀγαθός [4]

---

[1] I make the genitive (or relational semantics) explicit with 'of God' and 'of men', as in 'of one' of Gal 3:20.

[2] Cf. n. 4 on p. 34.

[3] "Why do you ask me about what is good? There is only one who is good." (ESV)

[4] It is beyond the scope of this article to discuss the differences between the Majority Text (BYZ) and the critical text (UBS 3/4).

This "one that is God", who alone is good, is Jesus' God, his Father, to whom he prayed (Matt 26:39, 42, 53; 27:46; Mark 15:34), and ascended after his passion (John 14:28; 20:17. Cf. Rev 3:21).

d) NT quoting an OT text that connects with Jesus' words about God and 'good'

In Ps 14:2, Yahweh (God/ *ĕlōhîm* in the Ps 53:2[3]-3[4] parallel) "looked down from heaven upon the children of men, to see if there were any that did understand, that did seek God." In Ps 14:3, Yahweh/ *ĕlōhîm* observes:

ʾên   *ʿōśēʰ-ṭôḇ*   *ʾên*   *gam-ʾeḥāḏ*
there is not *one* doing good, there is not *one* even one.

So, here is a case of 'one' (*ʾeḥāḏ* ↔ ἑνός cf. εἷς), where that amount is denied. *Not one* of the children of men could be found doing good, or by implication *not one* sought God (*ĕlōhîm*). This is quoted in Rom 3:12:

not there is (the) doing good, not there is as far as/even/ much as one.

BYZ: οὐκ ἔστιν ποιῶν χρηστότητα,   οὐκ ἔστιν   ἕως ἑνός
UBS 3/4: οὐκ ἔστιν ὁ ποιῶν χρηστότητα, [οὐκ ἔστιν]   ἕως ἑνός

The OT and NT read that a count of the number 'doing good' gets nowhere, as not even one can be found. Also, why there is "not one doing good" is explained in Ps 14:3 by use of 'all' in the contrast: "They are all gone aside, they are *all* together (*yaḥdāw*)[1] become filthy."

This use of Hebrew *ʾeḥāḏ* and its Greek counterpart εἷς or ἑνός is about God's own numbering use of 'one', which cannot be ignored when we look at God's usage of *ʾeḥāḏ* in Deut 6:4. Here, in this quoted Psalm text, God's heavenly observation leads Him to (a quantitative) denial of 'one'. 'Not one (thing)' is equal to zero; an empty set.

So, Jesus says there is 'none good', which agrees with his Father's observation in the Ps 14:2-3 about the sons of Adam (*bənê-ʾāḏām*), and adds by contrast that only **one** is good, his Father, that is God (see the NT texts cited in (c) above). Jesus' understanding draws on Scripture; his followers do the same.

---

[1] Cf. nn. 1, p. 143 and 4, p. 145.

God's being in the category of 'one' respecting 'good', or His own just use of 'one' to deny that 'there is one' on earth who is good, encourages us to relate this quantifying sense of 'one' to God's revelation that 'Yahweh *is* one' in Deut 6:4.

(e) YHWH ʾĕlōhênû YHWH lōʾ ʾeḥād: 'Yahweh our God, Yahweh is not one'

Here is a test of whether 'one' can be 'unity'. I have inserted *lōʾ* the Hebrew for 'not'[1] in the Shema, thus negating *ʾeḥād*. What this does, as examples below show, is to make 'unity' irrelevant, and the only sense to be inferred for 'one' from *ʾeḥād* is a restricting or quantitative marking.

A few examples of 'not one' using lōʾ ʾeḥad in the HB[2]:

Job 14:4   Who can bring a clean thing out of an unclean? **not one.**

Exod 9:6   [but of the cattle of the children of Israel] died **not one.**

Exod 8:31   there remained **not one.**
Exod 10:19   there remained **not one** locust.
Exod 14:28   there remained **not** among them even **one.**

Observations

- The above texts show how 'not one' is expressed using *ʾeḥad* negated by *lōʾ*.
- This negation of *ʾeḥad* denies 'one' is there, or that that much can be counted.

---

[1] In section 2(d) the negation 'there is not', used twice in Ps 14:3, was the Hebrew אֵין / *ʾên*, not *lōʾ* as in my hypothetical insertion into Deut 6:4. The NT citation of Ps 14:3 has just 'not' (οὐκ) with 'there is' (ἔστιν). The term *lōʾ*, as 'not', will be familiar from English versions that transliterate the names in Hos 1:6 '**Lo**ruhamah' (*lōʾ ruḥāmāh*), and in v. 9 '**Lo**ammi' (*lōʾ ʿammî*). They deny, respectively, both God's mercy and Israel as His people.
[2] 'Not one' *lōʾ ʾeḥad* / לֹא אֶחָד in Hebrew is close in sense to 'there is not even one' in Ps 14:3—אֵין גַּם־אֶחָד / *ʾên gam-ʾeḥad*.

- 'Yahweh *is* not one' or 'not one Yahweh' is the logical opposite (negation) of 'Yahweh one'.
- This shows that אֶחָד / *ʾeḥāḏ* is not about 'unity' but a marker of 'one' (thing).
- Therefore, 'unity', in this hypothetical formulation, is not denied but 'one' is.
- This case of binary opposition is important for establishing the actual semantics of the non-negative form, as in Deut 6:4.

[3] Conclusion

Deut 6:4 is a foundational formula for the Israel of God, in which 'one' is the measure by which to recognise and differentiate (the wholly otherness of) Yahweh.

Biblical terms like 'alone' and 'solitary', or 'only' going in the direction of 'unique', 'without equal', 'incomparable', 'most high', etc., are true of God as they are of no other being. They complement or share some semantic symmetry with 'one'. The sense of 'unity' is not hidden within them.

When the Hebrew term *ʾeḥāḏ* comes into its NT equivalent εἷς it does so as 'one' and not as 'unity'.

Ephesians 4:3 and 13 are the only places in the NT where the word 'unity' is used. Paul speaks of the need to strive for unity; it is the end of a perfecting process in Christ. This defines a context for talk of 'unity' and the relevance of employing a word with that meaning, ἑνότητα, a developed form of 'one' (but not usable for the number or quantity 'one').

When Jesus cites Deut 6:4 in reply to a question in Mark 12:29, and the scribe attests to the truth of what Jesus said, the discussion of 'one' limits God to a single indivisible being, the Father only, as in 1 Cor 8:6 and elsewhere. Neither Jesus nor the scribe use 'one' to talk about (the) 'unity' of God as the Lord.

Deut 6:4's 'one Yahweh' or 'Yahweh one' corresponds to "one Yahweh and His name one" in Zech 14:9.

'One' of Yahweh should serve as a check against ecumenical infidelity, to go after other gods which are not God, or to pluralise the Deity in any way. After all there is no other God but the one with the exclusive name, as identifyingly self-referenced in these texts:

That they may know from the rising of the sun, and from the west, that *there is* none beside me. I *am* Yahweh, and *there is* none else (Isa 45:6).

For thus saith Yahweh that created the heavens; God himself that formed the earth and made it; He hath established it, He created it not in vain, He formed it to be inhabited: I *am* Yahweh; and there is none else (Isa 45:18).

Marginal Notes

John 17:5 – P. Heavyside

And now, O Father, <u>glorify</u> thou me with thine own self with the glory which I had with thee before the world was. John 17:5 (KJV)

The following points may be noted,

- "glorify [something]", an imperative expression used for appealing to God , is found only three times in scripture: John 12:28; 17:1, 5; so in his prayer Jesus is clearly, twice, referring back five days to something he said then;

- Jesus said then, "father, glorify your name" (John 12:28), language which clearly connects with Jesus' prayer, not only because of the expression "glorify" but also "father" and "name" (John 17:1, 6);

- in John 12's context, glorifying the father's name is presented as fulfilled in "the judgment of this world" and the Lord's being **lifted up**, signifying what death he should die (John 12:31-33);

- this is confirmed by John's later explanation that the things of which he spoke related to Isaiah's prophecy which he spoke "when he saw his glory and spoke of him" (John 12:41) – this speaks of Isaiah's vision of "the Lord sitting upon a throne, high and **lifted up**" (Isa 6:1);

- this set of connections shows that the "glory" (John 17:5) of which Jesus speaks in his prayer is the "glory" (John 12:41) which Isaiah saw in his vision;

- the same set of connections show that the "world" (John 17:5) before which the Lord had glory with the father was the "world" (John 12:31) which was to be judged and whose prince was to be cast out by the crucifixion of our Lord; that is, this world was that which was framed by distortions of the law of Moses through the traditions of the elders;

- thus, the glory which the Lord had with the father before the world was is typified by his glory prophetically portrayed in visions such as those seen in Isaiah 6;

- this is part of a comprehensive theme in John's gospel (and other scriptures such as Hebrews) that portrays Jesus' foreordination by the figures and prophetic visions of the Hebrew scriptures.

The following correspondences between Jesus' prayer and Genesis 22 support this approach:

John 17	Genesis 22
lifted up his eyes v. 1	lifted up his eyes vv. 4, 13
father vv. 1, 21, 24 holy father v. 11 righteous father v. 25	my father v. 7
the hour is come v. 1	they came to the place v. 9
your son v. 1	your son vv. 2, 12, 16
with your own self v. 5	by myself v. 16
I have manifested your name v. 6	Yahweh-yireh...it[1] shall be seen v. 14
one as we v. 11 even as we are one v. 22	together vv. 6, 8
as you have loved me v. 23 you loved me v. 24 the love wherewith you have loved me v. 26	whom you love v. 2
they may behold my glory v. 24	saw the place afar off v. 4

The "seeing" theme of Genesis 22, expounded in John 8:56-58, relates also to the glory which Isaiah "saw" (John 12:41; Isa 6:1). Another correspondence is found between John 12 and Genesis 22, reinforcing the themes that are being shared here: the "voice from heaven" (John 12:28)

---

[1] [Ed. JWA]: or 'he shall be seen'.

which some ascribed to "an angel" (John 12:29) relates to the angel of the Lord twice calling from heaven (Gen 22:11, 15).

Consideration of this and other themes shows the marvellous depths of meaning involved, and the burden borne, in our Lord's obedience to "the volume of the book" (Heb 10:7; Ps 40:7).

> Worthy is the lamb that was slain [from the foundation of the world (13:8)] to receive power, and riches, and wisdom, and strength, and honour, and glory, and blessing... Rev 5:12

Reviews

P. Pullman, The Good Man Jesus and the Scoundrel Christ, Edinburgh: Canongate, 2010. 245pp. (TG)

"This is a story". The words emblazoned across the back cover that attempt to pre-empt and placate any of the expected religious fervour. It is true that this is a work of fiction and, in one sense, makes no claims to historical veracity at all. However, in another sense this book is very much about history and how history in interpreted – in the words of the blurb "this book is about how stories become stories".

Pullman's central literary device is the idea that Mary bore twins; a proposition with no historical credentials but handy for explaining away that inconvenient resurrection story. The lives of these two sons are delineated along the familiar paradigm of the so-called "historical Jesus" and the "Christ of faith". The "Jesus" character is an ordinary child, who gets into mischief and shows no particular signs of greatness until, inspired by the teaching of John the Baptist, he becomes a wandering teacher preaching the coming of the Kingdom. The "Christ" character is an obsequious child, who studies in the synagogue, and who also responds to the teaching of John but with a vision of a worldwide church. "Christ" is visited on several occasions by a stranger who encourages his vision and instructs him to write down the sayings of Jesus, being careful not to confuse history with "the truth beyond time" (i.e. the truth that better serves the church). It is this stranger that persuades "Christ" to betray "Jesus" to the High Priest and later to stage the resurrection by pretending to be "Jesus" thereby providing a "miracle" that will inspire men. Pullman's agenda is clear.

Though the book is not intended as a historical study, it is clear that Pullman is attempting to present a "rationalist" view of the life of Jesus and his fairly amateurish attempt flags up some of the problems with this approach. Pullman's approach to the sources in eclectic and uncritical, drawing on the four canonical gospels and some apocryphal material. At some points, such the Sermon of the Mount, he pretty much paraphrases the gospel accounts; other instances, which do not suit his purposes, are reworked or omitted. The problem for Pullman is he wants to take some of the words of gospel accounts at face value and some as later fabrications but his only criteria for distinguishing between the two is what fits his conception of who Jesus was. This is a microcosm of the attempts of critical scholars to discover the "historical" Jesus; often their efforts, though steeped in academic language, amount to no more than Pullman's arbitrary methodology.

The events of Jesus' life are treated in a similar way. Miracles are created out of coincidence and rumour; the sick hear "Jesus" speak and feel better, the five thousand had some food really and "Jesus" encourages them to share, the wedding runs out of wine because the chief steward keeps back some to sell and "Jesus" shames him into bringing it out. Yet Pullman never attempts to explain why "Jesus" does not contradict the miracle-stories or turn away those seeking to be healed but instead seems to accept the fame that the miracle-stories bring. Pullman's explanation of the resurrection is a good example of this clumsy revisionism. The body of "Jesus" is stolen but Pullman never reveals who stole it – not the disciples who are surprised by the empty tomb. Mary, the mother of Jesus, present at the crucifixion, conveniently returns to Nazareth before the resurrection morn, and presumably is never consulted about her two sons. "Christ" makes a few appearances and then leaves for a new town to lead a quiet life; we are left to presume that the disciples just let him go without question. The book is full of apologetic phrases about "Christ", such as "he had the sort of face that few people remember" (!), in an effort to make the twin story stick. Even with the free-hand of artistic license, Pullman cannot create a plausible alternative to the resurrection event.

Viewed as a work of fiction, the book has few merits. It follows the gospel accounts rather slavishly. The characterisation of "Jesus" is poor; he is overlooked in favour of "Christ", whose character is also under-developed. The story struggles to get going and has no real drive impelling the reader forward. Perhaps the most interesting sections are where Pullman's own angst comes through clearest, particularly in Gethsemane where we find "Jesus" in prayer. Rather than "let this cup pass from me", we find "Jesus" complaining about God's absenteeism, espousing existentialist attitudes and predicting the corruption of the Catholic Church.

In sum, this book is neither a great literary work nor a significant challenge to Christianity.

The Great Trinity Debate
D. Burke

In November 2009, Robert M. Bowman proposed a debate on the Trinity between himself and any non-Trinitarian challenger at his blogsite (www.reclaimingthemind.org/blog). Bowman is a well known evangelical author in the USA who specialises in Christology and has written a number of books on the Trinity and the deity of Christ. He provided a list of criteria that all applicants were required to meet and said if more than one suitable candidate emerged, a vote would be held to determine his opponent. After a few weeks, readers were asked to vote for one of five candidates: myself, Anthony Buzzard (Unitarian), Michael Richardson (Mormon), David Barron (Seventh Day Adventist), and Kermit Zarley (Unitarian). In the poll which followed, I won the most votes and was selected to debate Bowman.

Brother Bill Farrar generously donated two reference books that I needed for research purposes, and purchased several others on my behalf. Brethren Jonathan Burke (my identical twin), Steve Cox, Andrew Perry and Steve Snobelen acted as my support team, proof-reading my arguments before they went online. Each of them spent many hours checking my work for errors, making suggestions, and discussing the progress of the debate. They also provided additional resources (such as commentaries, journal articles and word definitions) when required. I am deeply indebted to these brethren for the wealth of experience, expertise and academic resources they brought to the debate.

Two days before the debate began, Bowman attempted to change the rules, stating that philosophical and historical arguments would not be allowed on the grounds that they were "irrelevant". He also claimed that I had agreed to these restrictions. I challenged him on this and advised that I would be using both forms of argument regardless of whether or not he considered them to be relevant. Ultimately this proved to be a moot point, since Bowman himself ended up arguing from philosophy and history in response to my arguments.

The debate covered six weeks, with each week devoted to a specific subject:

- Week 1: God

- Week 2: Jesus Christ

- Week 3: Jesus Christ

- Week 4: Holy Spirit

- Week 5: Father, Son and Holy Spirit

- Week 6: Summary and conclusion

Readers were able to post general comments and criticisms throughout the debate, and at the end of Week 6 they were invited to pose questions directly to myself and Bowman.

The format of the debate required us to post a positive argument on each subject, and respond to the opposing argument in the form of rebuttal. Thus, on the first day of the first week, we both presented an opening argument which articulated our respective understanding of God (His identity, characteristics, etc.) and then posted rebuttals throughout the rest of the week. Bowman had originally proposed a limit of 10,000 words for each opening argument but changed this to 5,000 words at my request. There was no word limit for rebuttal. It was agreed that a vote would be held at the end of the debate, to determine a winner.

Bowman's arguments consisted almost entirely of material copy/pasted from his book (*Putting Jesus In His Place*). Having purchased a copy of this book in preparation for the debate, I was able to predict his approach to various passages and anticipate the nature of his responses.

The debate was followed by a number of bloggers, most notably Scott Lencke, a pastor at Cornerstone International Church[1] and Dale Tuggy, associate professor of philosophy at SUNY Fredonia.[2] Lencke criticized my arguments from an evangelical perspective, while Tuggy (who confesses a Unitarian Christology) provided a weekly commentary on both

---

[1] prodigalthought.net [Cited 14/7/2010].
[2] trinities.org/blog [Cited 14/7/2010].

sides of the debate and concluded with an analysis of the final outcome (.[1] At the Kingdom Ready website, participants offered commentary, discussion and counter-argument in equal measure.[2]

Responses to the debate at the Parchment & Pen blogsite were very encouraging. Despite a strong and persistent Trinitarian presence, a majority of readers came out in support of the Unitarian position. Some were Unitarians already; some said they were moving from a pro-Trinitarian view to a Unitarian Christology; others said they had no specific Christology prior to the debate, but now favoured Unitarianism over the alternatives. Several people expressed an interest in joining or studying with the Christadelphian community. I was touched by the robust support I received from Unitarians of various backgrounds, including Sir Anthony Buzzard *(The Doctrine of the Trinity: Christianity's Self-Inflicted Wound*, 1998*)*, Patrick Navas *(Divine Truth or Human Tradition?*, 2006) and Kermit Zarley *(The Restitution of Jesus Christ*, 2008).

The debate ended abruptly when Bowman locked all the threads without warning or consultation while I was still composing my last counter-rebuttal. He also removed my ability to post new threads or edit my posts, which prevented me from responding to his final arguments. When someone asked if readers would still be invited to vote for a winner, Bowman gave an oblique reply and closed the discussion. At the present writing (14.07.10) there has been no vote and no explanation.

I have now commenced writing a book on the Trinity, which will incorporate the material I used in the debate and further develop the arguments from reason, Scripture and history. Readers are welcome to contact me via email (evangelion@thechristadelphians.org) to discuss the debate and/or my upcoming work. I will be grateful for all submissions.

Postscript
A. Perry

Is there a distinctive Christadelphian method of interpretation? More broadly, is there a distinctive method of interpretation shared by groups that have a similar Biblical Unitarian and Abrahamic centred faith? This

---

[1] trinities.org/blog/archives/2046 [Cited 14/7/2010].
[2] kingdomready.org/blog/2010/02/02/another-trinitymonotheism-debate [Cited 14/7/2010].

second question partly answers the question: a Biblical Unitarian and Abrahamic faith is a distinctive characterization of a method of interpretation. We should therefore expect different results to other methods of interpretation practised in the churches.

There are other aspects of such a method, such as a belief in inspiration and integrity of Scripture, and a harmonic approach to the resolving of apparent conflicts in and with the text. These aspects are shared by other churches, as is recognition of typological patterns and a dense intertextual weave. Is there anything else that is distinctive to Christadelphian interpretation?

The Biblical Unitarian and Abrahamic faith produces (in some) an independent approach to the text. Because this faith is distinctive and isolated, shunned by the churches, its adherents often reciprocate and are open to independent thinking about Scripture, willing to support and develop original approaches to the text. But there is still more to be said on what is distinctive about the method of interpretation within this faith.

The practice of reading should and has led to a **perception** of how Scripture interprets Scripture; this perception has thus issued in an expositional method that mirrors how Scripture interprets itself. This is best seen in the original exposition that the faith has produced; exposition that has no counterpart in the writings of the churches. If we follow the best practise of the faith, we may hold fast to the faith.

END

Editors:

Andrew.Perry@christadelphian-ejbi.org
Paul.wyns@christadelphian-ejbi.org
T.Gaston@christadelphian-ejbi.org (Church history)
J.Adey@christadelphian-ejbi.org (Text and Language)

Christadelphian EJournal of Biblical Interpretation

Contents

- Editorial
- Galatians 3:28—An Equality Text?
- The Philippians Hymn and Pauline Theology
- Seals, Trumpets and Vials
- The Spirit of the Lord in the History Books
- Quirinius
- Pre-historic Genealogies
- Was the Ark a Practical Size?
- Marginal Notes: Isa 41:3
- Book Notice
- Letters to the Editors
- Web Resources and News
- Postscript
- Supplement: Dating Revelation

Editorial Policies: The *Christadelphian EJournal of Biblical Interpretation* seeks to fulfil the following objectives: offer analytical and expositional articles on biblical texts; engage with academic biblical studies that originate in other Christian confessions; defend the biblical principles summarised in the common Christadelphian statement of faith; and subject the published articles to retrospective peer review and amendment.

Submission of Articles: Authors should submit articles to the editors. Presentation should follow *Society of Biblical Literature* guidelines (www.sbl.org).

Publication: E-mailed quarterly on the last Thursday of January, April, July, and October; published as a collected annual paperback obtainable from: www.lulu.com/willowpublications.

Subscriptions: This is a "free" EJournal to communities and individuals whose statement of faith is broadly consistent with the Christadelphian common statement.

Editorial

This issue brings to a close the fourth year of the EJournal. As each year finishes, the editors ask themselves whether they can commit for another year, whether it is time to end the project, and/or if they should change anything. The justification for the journal is the same as in 2007, and so in 2011 we hope to continue fulfilling these objectives.

In the last issue we avoided any reference to Biblical scholarship. One of the objectives for the EJournal is to engage such scholarship. The reasons for this are several. First, we live in a world where there is a large body of scholarship and there is interesting and enlightening material in such writing. Secondly, there is a lot that is wrong in such scholarship; wrong because of the use of humanistic methods of interpretation of the Bible; wrong because of philosophy and theology; and wrong because it is judgmental and sceptical of the Bible. The prophets "engaged the wrong" and this is our precedent.

A final objective for engaging scholarship is this: anyone in the community preparing a talk or a piece of writing may pick up what is wrong from their own selective reading of scholarship, from commentaries, from Bible dictionaries, or any number of other works. So a vehicle in the community where there is explicit engagement of scholarship over what is wrong and what is right is therefore valuable as a place where there might be necessary and/or useful correction. We see through a glass darkly, and precision in exposition is difficult to achieve, in particular, balanced precision. While there is a an obvious need for general writing in the brotherhood, there is also a need for precise and detailed writing that tackles topics such as God's name; the two types of writing should trade off one another, with the general reflecting the detailed expositions, summarizing and simplifying what can be complex and complicated. In this way mistakes in general writing can be avoided.

We have produced another "Annual" of the year's issues (2010) which is now available from www.lulu.com/willowpublications. Although the quarterly issues remain on the password protected website, ecclesial librarians might like to consider purchasing the paperback Annuals for ecclesial libraries, as we do not know how long back issues will be available on the website..

Galatians 3:28: an 'equality text'?[1]
J. Burke

Introduction

A point raised by those egalitarians who do not see Gal 3:28 as an 'equality text' is the simple fact that the verse says nothing about equality. The subject is unity, 'all **one**', not equality, 'all **equal**', as has been pointed out by both egalitarians and complementarians.[2] This article reviews the points that are made by such scholars.

Equality or Unity?

Complementarian R. W. Hove notes that there are two key reasons why the 'all one' phrase does not mean 'all equal'. One reason is the fact that the Greek word for 'one' here simply does not mean 'equal':

> As noted in the previous chapter, there are two critical reasons why "you are all one" does not mean "you are all equal".
>
> I will review these two reasons briefly. The first reason is the **lexical range** of the word 'one'. **Lexically this word cannot mean "equal."** Our overview of BAGD confirmed this, as we found that **there is no known example of 'one' being used this way**.[3]

The other reason is the fact that uses in other Greek literature of this same 'all one' phrase indicates that it was not used to refer to equality, but unity; Hove states:

---

[1] The substance of this article was previously published on BTDF at www.thechristadelphians.org.

[2] Standard modern Bible translations render the text as a statement that those in Christ are all 'one', not that they are all 'equal'; readers are invited to test this themselves, and see if they can find any standard modern translation which renders the text as a statement that those in Christ are 'all equal' (of course all those in Christ are equal spiritually speaking, even if not socially, legally, physically or financially, but this passage is not denying that spiritual equality).

[3] R. W. Hove, *Equality in Christ? Galatians 3:28 and the Gender Dispute* (Wheaton: Crossway Books, 1999), 108; emphasis is added here and in all subsequent quotations from scholars.

The second reason "you are all one" does not mean "you are all equal" is that the phrase was not used in that way in the era of the New Testament. As we have seen, a study of every parallel use of the phrase "we/you/they are one" in the 300 years surrounding the New Testament reveals that this expression fails to express the concept of unqualified equality.

In fact, "you are all one" is used of diverse objects to denote one element they share in common; it is not used of similar objects to denote that they are the same.[1]

Likewise, egalitarian F. Watson argues that Paul is not addressing hierarchy and equality in this passage, but that the 'all one' phrase refers to unity in Christ:

In baptism, Jew, Greek, slave, free, male, female receive a new identity as they 'put on Christ' (3:27): **the emphasis lies not on their 'equality' but on their belonging together** as they participate in the new identity and the new practices and modes of interaction that this will entail.

Paul could have assumed that the three distinctions he mentions were hierarchical ones, and that in Christ these are replaced by an egalitarian oneness, **but there is nothing in the wording of his statement** (or in the hypothetical baptismal formula supposed to underlie it) **to suggest that he actually did so**. The polarity of hierarchy and equality is an exceedingly blunt instrument for interpreting this text.[2]

Hove provides several Biblical examples of the use of 'one' to denote unity rather than equality or the same roles:

In 1 Corinthians 3:8 Paul writes that the one who waters and the one who plants **are one**. Both of these individuals **have different roles and different rewards**, but Paul uses the expression "you are one" **to show that they**

---

[1] Hove, Equality in Christ?, 108.
[2] F. Watson, "The Authority of the Voice: A Theological Reading of 1 Cor 11.2–16" *NTS* 46 (2000): 520-536 (521).

share one thing in common— that they have a common purpose.

> In Romans 12:5 Paul writes that, **"We who are many form one body**, and each member belongs to all the others. We have different gifts..." Again, the expression **"we are one"** is an expression **that denotes what different people, with different gifts, have in common—one body in Christ.** The pattern is the same with the Father and Son (John 10:30) and the husband and wife (Mark 10:8). In both cases the expression "you are one" highlights an element that **diverse objects share in common.**[1]

He also notes that in such cases the roles of those who are 'one' are different:

> The New Testament examples of "we/you/they are one," where a plurality of people are called one, are: the planter and waterer (1 Cor. 3:8); Father and Son (John 10:30; 17:11, 21, 22 [2x], 23); husband and wife (Matt. 19:6; Mark 10:8); **and different believers with different gifts** (Rom. 12:5; 1 Cor. 10:17).

> **In every instance the groups of people in these pairs have different roles.** Given these expressions, which formally are directly parallel with Galatians 3:28, **it is difficult to see** how the meaning of "you are all one" can be "there are no distinctions of role between you".[2]

Watson argues against an egalitarian reading of Gal 3:28 on the basis that none of the three relationships referred to by Paul are hierarchical, so the passage cannot be arguing for their abolition on the basis of equality:

> In Gal 3.28, for example, the three distinctions (Jew/Greek, slave/free, male/female) **do not straightforwardly represent a series of hierarchical relationships.** The distinction between Jew and Greek

---

[1] Hove, Equality in Christ?, 108.
[2] Hove, Equality in Christ?, 119

does not constitute a hierarchical relationship, since each party regards itself **as superior to the other.**[1]

As for the second distinction, the terms 'slave' and 'free' refer **less clearly to a hierarchical relationship than if Paul had written 'slave or master'.** 'Male and female (ἄρσεν καὶ θῆλυ)' is an allusion to Gen 1:27, as the substitution of καὶ for οὐδὲ indicates, **and there is no suggestion in the Genesis text that this relationship is understood hierarchically.**[2]

This being the case, Watson points out, the purpose of Gal 3:28 is to identify unity, not to argue for egalitarianism:

If the distinctions of Gal 3.28a do not refer to 'hierarchical' relationships, then the 'oneness in Christ Jesus', in the face of which the distinctions are declared to be irrelevant, **is not to be understood as an 'egalitarian' oneness.**[3]

Egalitarian scholar N. T. Wright says the same:

The point Paul is making overall in this passage **is that God has one family, not two, and that this family consists of all those who believe in Jesus**; that this is the family God promised to Abraham, and that nothing in the Torah can stand in the way of this unity which is now revealed through the faithfulness of the Messiah. **This is not at all about how we relate to one another within this single family**; it is about the fact, as we often say, that the ground is even at the foot of the cross.[4]

---

[1] Watson, "The Authority of the Voice", 521.

[2] Watson, "The Authority of the Voice", 521; [Ed. AP]: Whether Gen 1:27 has an hierarchical overtone depends on how you read 1 Cor 11:7 which is also an allusion—Watson betrays his egalitarian preferences in this quote].

[3] Watson, "The Authority of the Voice", 521.

[4] N. T. Wright, "Women's Service in the Church: The Biblical Basis", which was a conference paper for the Symposium, 'Men, Women and the Church" held at St. John's College, Durham, 4 September, 2004; cited from the online copy at N. T. Wright's website, www.ntwrightpage.com, which has no pagination.

M. E. Glasswell further comments,

> The three pairs do not have precisely the same significance if one looks at other places where Paul discusses them separately. The differences within each pair are seen as being overcome in Christ but not abolished completely, though this is true of each pair differently.[1]

Hove quotes another commentator who demonstrates that Paul's treatment of certain relationships actually contradicts the egalitarian claim. Paul does not use Biblical arguments to support the Jew/Gentile and slave/master relationships of his era, but **does** use Biblical arguments to support other social relationships, such as male/female and husband/wife:

> Colin Kruse, investigating human relationships in the Pauline epistles, comes to a similar conclusion. Kruse examined Paul's treatment of six pairs of human relationships throughout the Pauline corpus: Jew/Gentile, master/slave, male/female, husband/wife, parent/child, and citizen/state. He concludes:

>> No common pattern emerges as far as the retention in principle of all six human relationships surveyed is concerned. On the one hand, theological support **was not offered for the retention in principle of Jew-Gentile and slave-master relationships**.
>> On the other hand, however, theological reasons **were provided** which imply the necessity of the retention in principle **of the male-female, husband-wife, parent-child and citizen-state relationships**.[2]

Wright insists that Gal 3:28 is being misread by other egalitarians, that it is not about the position women have in 'church ministry', nor does it speak

---

[1] M. E. Glasswell, "Some Issues of Church and Society in Light of Paul's Eschatology" in *Paul and Paulinism: Essays in Honour of C. K. Barrett*, (eds. M. D. Hooker and S. G. Wilson; London: SPCK, 1982), 315. Cited by Hove, *Equality in Christ?*, 94.

[2] Hove, *Equality in Christ?*, 94 citing Colin Kruse, "Human Relationships in the Pauline Corpus" in *The Fullness of Time: Biblical Studies in Honour of Archbishop Donald Robinson* (eds. David Peterson and John Pryor; Homebush West, NSW: Anzea Publishers, 1992), 180.

about the relationship of brothers and sisters within the ecclesia. He objects to misuse of this passage by his fellow egalitarians in strong terms:

> The first thing to say is fairly obvious but needs saying anyway. Galatians 3 is not about ministry. Nor is it the only word Paul says about being male and female, and instead of taking texts in a vacuum and then arranging them in a hierarchy, for instance by quoting this verse and then saying that it trumps every other verse in a kind of fight to be the senior bull in the herd (what a very masculine way of approaching exegesis, by the way!), we need to do justice to what Paul is actually saying at this point.[1]

Wright also identifies a common egalitarian straw man:

> I am surprised to see, in some of your literature, the insistence that women and men are equally saved and justified; **that is, I'm surprised because I've never heard anyone denying it**. Of course, there may well be some who do, but I just haven't met them.[2]

He also notes a mistranslation of the verse which is commonly used by egalitarians:

> First, a note about translation and exegesis. I **notice that on one of your leaflets you adopt what is actually a mistranslation of this verse**: neither Jew nor Greek, neither slave nor free, neither male nor female. That is precisely what Paul does *not* say; and as it's what we expect he's going to say, we should note quite carefully what he has said instead, since he presumably means to make a point by doing so, a point which is missed when the translation is flattened out as in that version. What he says is that there is neither Jew nor Greek, neither slave nor free, no '*male and female*'.[3]

G. P. Hugenberger (a moderate egalitarian who considers women are free to speak and teach in the ecclesia if the male eldership approves them),

---

[1] Wright, "Women's Service in the Church: The Biblical Basis".
[2] Wright, "Women's Service in the Church: The Biblical Basis".
[3] Wright, "Women's Service in the Church: The Biblical Basis".

objects to the typical egalitarian use of Gal 3:28 on several grounds. Most significantly, Hugenberger observes that the passage is simply being taken out of context (it has to do with salvation rather than roles in ecclesial organization), and points out that this is becoming recognized even by other egalitarians, such as B. Witherington III:

> Perhaps more compelling, however, is an objection being raised with increasing conviction: **Galatians 3:28 and the other so-called "equality texts" actually have less to do with ecclesiology than with soteriology** and are in fact concerned to assert **not equality but salvific unity** within the body of Christ.[1]

This is of course the same interpretation which complementarians have held all along. Another egalitarian who does not agree with the common egalitarian reading of this passage is E. L. Miller. He affirms that the passage teaches a union with Christ which is available to all, regardless of social, ethnic, and gender distinction:

> The good news is that this passage does indeed teach that at some level and in some sense such distinctions as Jew/Greek, bond/free, male/female, fall away and prove irrelevant from the standpoint of Christian faith. At this level, **the soteriological level**, all believers enjoy **a salvific union with Christ**.[2]

However, he points out that the distinctions referred to by Paul are not eliminated, despite the fact that they are no barrier to salvation. On the contrary, Miller insists that these distinctions are reinforced:

> The bad news is that there is another level presupposed by the passage, and it turns out that at this other level **such distinctions, far from being abrogated, are**

---

[1] G. Hugenberger, "Women in Church Office: Hermeneutics or Exegesis? A Survey Of Approaches To 1 Tim 2:8-15" *JETS* 35 (1992): 341-360 (347); Hugenberger cites the following articles in support: J. J. Davis, "Some Reflections on Gal 3:28, Sexual Roles, and Biblical Hermeneutics," *JETS* 19 (1976): 201-208 and B. Witherington III, "Rite and Rights for Women—Galatians 3.28," *NTS* 27 (1981): 593-604.

[2] E. L. Miller, "Is Galatians 3:28 the Great Egalitarian Text?" *ET* 114 (2002): 9-11 (9).

actually reinforced. This is the ordinary, everyday level of practical, social life.[1]

Miller recognizes that this conclusion will not be viewed favourably by other egalitarians:

> **This may be a disappointing interpretation of this celebrated 'egalitarian' passage**, for it turns out at one level to be only another proof-text for those very elements in Paul that many are struggling to get rid of - sexism and patriarchalism, for example.[2]

However, he insists that this reading of the passage is in agreement with its context, and with Paul's overall teaching:

> It must be admitted, though, for better or for worse, **that this view of Galatians 3:28 coheres both with its immediate context and with the rest of what we know of Paul**. This includes his notion of the priority of the true Israel over Gentile Christians who are merely grafted on to it, his implicit condoning of slavery, **and his hierarchical view of husband-wife relations**.[3]

Miller acknowledges that it is possible to extrapolate beyond what Paul wrote and apply the passage in an egalitarian manner, but he still declares that Christians must be honest about the fact that Paul's teaching in this passage did not have an egalitarian aim:

> That is not to say that we today, as others before us, cannot work that out and draw the implication on Paul's behalf. But it seems not to have been done in the Pauline texts themselves, and certainly **not the one before us**. We have **to try to be honest about that**.[4]

Conclusion

What would an 'egalitarian' Gal 3:28 look like? While observing that arguments should not be based on what **was not** written,[5] Hove notes that

---

[1] Miller, "Is Galatians 3:28 the Great Egalitarian Text?", 9.

[2] Miller, "Is Galatians 3:28 the Great Egalitarian Text?", 11.

[3] Miller, "Is Galatians 3:28 the Great Egalitarian Text?", 11.

[4] Miller, "Is Galatians 3:28 the Great Egalitarian Text?", 11.

[5] Hove, *Equality in Christ?*, 110.

it was entirely possible for Paul to have written such a passage which spoke of brothers and sisters as 'equal' in some way if that was the point of the passage, and provides a relevant 1ˢᵗ century parallel:

> Philo, **writing at about the same time as Paul,** uses the phrase πάντες ἐστὲ ἰσότιμοι ("you are **all entitled to equal honor**"), which is **almost directly parallel to Galatians 3:28** ὑμεῖς εἷς ἐστε ("you are all one").[1]

> Moses' argument here is much like Galatians 3:28. The parts (Jew/Greek, slave/free, male/female) **have inheritance only because of the whole** (being in Christ).[2]

However, Hove also notes that even such a term as Philo uses here would not necessarily mean that those referred to by it would have identical roles:

> But notice, while each tribe has equal honor, and each is treated the same way when it comes to fighting battles or settling land, **not all the tribes have the same roles** (e.g., Gen. 49:10, "the scepter will not depart from Judah," and Numbers 3, which details the unique role of the tribe of Levi). Thus, even if Paul had used an ἴσος ("equal") word in Galatians 3:28, **it would not follow that Jew/Greek, slave/free, male/female have the same roles.**

> In addition, the fact that Paul did not use an ἴσος root word, when it was available, is evidence, though admittedly not weighty, that his intent was not to emphasize the equality of Jew/Greek, slave/free, male/female."[3]

---

[1] Hove, *Equality in Christ?*, 110; the text is cited from Philo's *The Life of Moses*, 1.324.
[2] Hove, *Equality in Christ?*, 110.
[3] Hove, *Equality in Christ?*, 110.

The Philippians Hymn and Pauline Theology
P. Wyns

Introduction

The hymn[1] in Philippians 2 (vv. 6-11) is usually employed to establish both the pre-existence and incarnation of Christ. Scholars believe that the hymn is based either on Adam (Adam Christology) or on Isaiah's Suffering Servant. The following article suggests an incident that inspired Paul to write the hymn and examines whether the hymn draws on Servant Theology or Adam Christology.

The Setting

The NT background to the Philippians hymn can be found in John 13:3-7 a suggestion first noted by Hawthorne:[2]

> Jesus, knowing that the Father had given all things into His hands, and that He had come from God and was going to God, rose from supper and laid aside His garments, took a towel and girded Himself. After that, He poured water into a basin and began to wash the disciples' feet, and to wipe *them* with the towel with which He was girded. Then He came to Simon Peter. And *Peter* said to Him, "Lord, are You washing my feet?" Jesus answered and said to him, "What I am doing you do not understand now, but you will know after this" John 13:3-7 (NKJV)

The entire hymn in Philippians preserves the descent-ascent motif that is prominent in the Gospel story (John13:3-17//Luke 22:24-30). Moreover, the context is complementary, for the background to the gospel story is rivalry among the disciples. A struggle for leadership and pre-eminence had been a continuing cause of friction amongst the disciples (Mark 9:34; 10:37), so much so that Jesus warned against power struggles and the desire for prominence (Luke 14:7-11; cf. Mark 9:34, 35). And later this very incident is referred to by Peter (1 Pet 5:3, 5). It is suggested that Jesus washed the disciples' feet because they were arguing about the priority of the seating arrangements at the Last Supper. Unlike the selfish attitude of the disciples, fired as it was by personal ambition, Jesus voluntarily took the position of a servant. This is a key theme in Philippians and the context

---

[1] It is beyond the scope of this article to discuss whether the text is a hymn; we just assume this common designation.

[2] G. F. Hawthorne, *Philippians* (WBC 43; Waco: Word, 1983), 65.

of the hymn, "Look not every man on his own things, but every man also on the things of others. Let this mind be in you, which was also in Christ Jesus" (vv. 4, 5).

> You call me Teacher and Lord, and you say well, for [*so*] I am. If I then, *your* Lord and Teacher, have washed your feet, you also ought to wash one another's feet. For I have given you an example, that you should do as I have done to you. Most assuredly, I say to you, a servant is not greater than his master; nor is he who is sent greater than he who sent him. John 13:13-17 (NKJV)

The Greek of John 13:13 (λέγετε· εἰμὶ γάρ) does not contain the adverb *so* (placed here between parenthesis) and is the more emphatic *I am* – translated by Young's Literal Translation as, "ye call me, The Teacher and The Lord, and ye say well, for I am".[1] Significantly, Jesus does not rebuke them for calling him 'Teacher and Lord'. Is Jesus claiming to be God? Obviously not, because "A servant is not greater than his lord; neither he that is sent greater than he that sent him".

Jesus Christ is not claiming to be God, but rather he is the covenant manifestation and embodiment of the divine character revealed in <u>the name</u>. Hence, he can affirm 'I am' and confirm what is implicitly anticipated in Yahweh's use of 'I will be'—he is the present ('I am') and full manifestation (*phanerosis*) of the promised covenant self-revelation ("<u>I will</u> have mercy on whom <u>I will</u> have mercy, and <u>I will</u> have compassion on whom <u>I will</u> have compassion", Rom 9: 15).

Jesus' use of 'I am' in John is a circumlocution linked to the revelation of the divine name and Philippians expressly notes that, "at <u>the name</u> of Jesus every knee should bow...and confess that Jesus Christ *is* <u>Lord</u>" (Phil 2:10, 11). Jesus was the perfect embodiment of the name of *Yahweh* but both Philippians and John 13 stress his subordination to the Father.

It is this future manifestation that R. Bauckham latches onto and for which he coins the phrase 'eschatological monotheism':

> This means that it is often in scriptural texts that refer to the final and universal manifestation of the unique

---

[1] UBS/GNT places a full stop after λέγετε; the BYZ text has a comma. By this device, UBS/GNT are placing Jesus' saying within the scope of the other Johannine 'I am' sayings.

identity of the one God that Paul understands Jesus to be YHWH. Jesus himself is the eschatological manifestation of YHWH's unique identity[1] to the whole world, so that those who call on Jesus' name and confess Jesus as Lord are acknowledging YHWH the God of Israel to be the one and only true God.[2]

Bauckham has sensed something correct in his analysis of the application of the Yahweh name to Jesus (as the "eschatological manifestation of YHWH's unique identity"); however, he then proceeds to negate the implications of his analysis by forcing it into a Trinitarian paradigm:

It [the name] is given to Jesus in recognition of his identity as Lord of all creation, but at the same time it rebounds to the glory of God the Father ([Phil]2:11) because Jesus is not an alternative object of worship in competition with the one God but himself belongs to the unique identity of that one God. Thus the passage ([Phil]vv 9-11), to which we have so far confined our comments, refers to the incarnate and risen Christ exercising the divine sovereignty not simply as such, but as the eschatological role of achieving and receiving the recognition of that unique sovereignty by all creation. Rather only one who already belonged to the divine identity could occupy this position of eschatological supremacy. It is part of the function of the opening words of the passage ([Phil]2:6), which I understand, with the majority of scholars, as depicting the pre-existence of Christ, to make clear his identity with the one God from the beginning.[3,1]

---

[1] [Ed. AP]: R. Bauckham's popular book, God *Crucified: Monotheism and Christology in the New Testament* (Grand Rapids: Eerdmans, 1999) introduced the phrases 'unique identity' and 'include in the unique identity' for Jesus' relation to God. It is a lamentable failing of the book that he does not include an elementary discussion of his notion of identity; he entirely ignores the work of logicians.

[2] R. Bauckham, "Paul's Christology of Divine Identity" (paper presented at the annual meeting of the Society of Biblical Literature, Toronto, Canada, November 25, 2002), 1-26 (11). Available online [cited 21/03/2010]: www.forananswer.org/Top_JW/Richard_Bauckham.pdf.

[3] Bauckham, "Paul's Christology of Divine Identity", 12: However, some scholars (besides J. D. G. Dunn) do argue that pre-existence and

The reading of pre-existence into the hymn is caused by a failure to correctly recognise the typology that forms the basis of Pauline thought.

Is the Hymn based on the Suffering Servant or on Adam?

Both viewpoints are represented in scholarship but J. D. G. Dunn, who proposes an Adam Christology as the basis for the hymn, found that he had to defend his position[2] because the Adam paradigm challenges the notion of a pre-existent Christ. New Testament scholar N. T. Wright offers the following critique on 'Adam Christology':

> To begin with, this background [Adam Christology] depends heavily on a rejection of pre-existence in the hymn (see Hurst, 449). Therefore, if one accepts pre-existence, its appeal diminishes greatly. Even if one does not, there are still problems, such as why Adam's fall should prompt the idea of slavery in 2:7 (see Hurst, 451-52; Wanamaker, 181-83). Also, the language of 2:7-8a suggests something more comprehensive even than Adam's fall (Hurst, 451). Similarly, how would the general idea of Adam's disgrace prompt the particulars of Phil 2:9-11? For instance, what is the connection between Adam speculation and Isa 45:23, which Phil 2:9-11 clearly reflects? In the end, he [Dunn] seems almost to abandon Adam speculation by concluding that "the nearest

---

incarnation have no place here (for bibliography, see L. D. Hurst, "Re-enter the Pre-existent Christ in Philippians 2.5-11?" *NTS* 32 (1986): 449-57.

[1] [Ed. AP]: In this quote we have a formulation of the "worship argument" for the deity of Christ, one which has been popular in academic theology in the last two decades.

[2] J. D. G. Dunn comments, "The dialogue has probably been more fierce over the christological hymns, Phil 2.6-11 and Col 1.15-20, than anywhere else. It is clear from comment and conversation that some regard the questions I pose and suggestions I make in relation to these texts as insubstantial and wholly implausible, if not absurd, if not perverse". See his foreword to the second edition of *Christology in the Making* (2nd ed.; London: SCM Press, 1989), xviii-xix and xxxiii-xxxiv.

antecedents" to a Christology of pre-existence are
personifications of Wisdom or Torah". [1]

Dunn observes the following connections with Adam in Phil 2:6-11:

> **v.6a** – in the form of God (cf. Gen 1.27);
> **v.6b** – tempted to grasp equality with God (cf. Gen. 3.5);
> **v.7** – enslavement to corruption and sin – humanity as it now
> is (cf. Gen 2.19, 22-24; Ps 8.5a; Wisd 2.23; Rom 8.3; Gal 4.4;
> Heb 2.7a, 9a);
> **v.8** – submission to death (cf. Wisd 2.24; Rom 5.12-21; 7.7-
> 11: 1 Cor 15.21-22)
> **vv.9-11** – exalted and glorified (cf. Ps 8.5b-6; I Cor.15.27, 45;
> Heb.2.7b-8, 9b)

Dunn concludes that, "It is the Adamic significance of Christ which the
hymn brings out, of his life and death and exaltation (as in Rom. 5, I Cor.
15 and Heb. 2), not necessarily a chronological parallel phase by phase.
This is why it still seems to me an open question as to whether the hymn
carries any thought of pre-existence, other than the pre-existence involved
in the paradigm – that is, the metahistorical character of the Adam myth".

Other scholars contend that the basis of the hymn is not Adam
Christology but rather the Suffering Servant of Isaiah. They are no doubt
correct in this insight, but there is no reason why one paradigm should
preclude the other. In fact even Dunn recognizes the limitations of his
Adam Christology when he states that the "fit is not exact or precise", but
there is no reason why both models cannot operate in a complementary
fashion. It is therefore entirely plausible that Paul combined Adam
Christology with Suffering Servant theology. The following connections
are suggested:

Isaiah (NKJV)	Philippians 2 (KJV)
Thus says the LORD, the King of Israel, And his Redeemer, the LORD of hosts: 'I *am* the First and I *am* the Last; Besides Me *there is* no God' (44:6 cf. 40:18).	He did not count equality with God a thing to be grasped (v.6 RSV)

[1] N. T. Wright, *The Climax of the Covenant* (Minneapolis: Fortress, 1992), 91-
92, 97. See also P. O'Brien, *The Epistle to the Philippians* (NIGTC; Grand
Rapids: Eerdmans, 1991) 263-68.

Isaiah (NKJV)	Philippians 2 (KJV)
My righteous <u>servant</u> (53:11)… His visage was marred more than any man, And His <u>form</u> more than the sons of men (52:14 cf. 53:2)	But made himself of no reputation, and took upon him the <u>form of a servant</u>, and was made in the likeness of men (v.7)
…. <u>He poured out His soul unto death</u>, And He was numbered with the transgressors, and He bore the sin of many, And made intercession for the transgressors (53:12). I will ….give thee for <u>a covenant of the people</u>…. (49:8)	And being found in fashion as a man, he humbled himself, <u>and became obedient unto death</u>, even the <u>death of the cross</u>. (v.8)
Behold, My Servant shall deal prudently; He shall be <u>exalted and extolled</u> and be very high. (52: 13)	Wherefore God also hath <u>highly exalted him</u>, and given him a name which is above every name: (v.9)
I have sworn by Myself; The word has gone out of My mouth *in* righteousness, And shall not return, That to Me <u>every knee shall bow</u>, <u>Every tongue shall take an oath</u>. (45:23)	And that at the name of Jesus every knee should bow, of *things* in heaven, and *things* in earth, and *things* under the earth; (v.10) *that* <u>every tongue should confess</u> that Jesus Christ *is* Lord, to the glory of God the Father. (v. 11)

The connections with the Suffering Servant of Isaiah are obvious although there are different languages involved (Hebrew and Greek).

R. P. Martin detects a parallelism in the lines of verse 7 in which μορφὴν δούλου [form of a slave] is parallel with ἐν ὁμοιώματι ἀνθρώπων [in the likeness of a man].[1] This parallelism is a good example of how Adam Christology is subtly combined with Suffering Servant terminology. Genesis narrates how Adam, who was 'created in the likeness of God' (Gen 5:1) 'begat a son in his own likeness, after his image' (Gen 5:3). The son of Adam inherited the sin-prone nature of his father and became metaphorically a 'servant' to sin.

---

[1] R. P. Martin, *An Early Christian Confession* (Tyndale Press,1961), 57 fn. 48; see online at www.biblicalstudies.org.uk/pdf/confession_martin.pdf [cited 20/03/2010].

The phrase "made himself of no reputation" is literally "emptied (κενόω) himself" and has given rise to kenotic theology, now almost universally rejected. Martin comments that, "linguistically the self-emptying is related to the taking of the form of a servant and the verse teaches nothing about the abandonment of divine attributes". He also adds that, "the phrase...which is found nowhere else in Greek, and is grammatically harsh, may go back to a Semitic original in Isaiah 53:12, 'he poured his soul unto death (RV)'".[1]

Conclusion

Philippians 2 employs the Hebrew Scriptures in a characteristically Pauline manner which is complex, subtle and polyvalent **by combining Adam Christology with Suffering Servant theology.** L. D. Hurst and C. A. Wanamaker also favour a combined model as the basis of the hymn.[2] Paul deliberately contrasts the actions of Adam with the actions of the Suffering Servant. The Suffering Servant offered himself as an atoning sacrifice for the nation. Adam joined his wife in sin (instead of atoning for her). The Suffering Servant (although Yahweh's agent) humbled himself and was numbered with the transgressors. Adam exalted himself by seeking equality with God. The contrast is between "my righteous servant" and the "servant of sin"...for, "Whosoever commits sin is the servant of sin" (John 8:34). The apostle Paul illuminates the Genesis "fall" through the lens of Isaiah and presents the reader with a number of contrasts. This begs the question of the historical identity of the Suffering Servant a question that has been completely obfuscated by a liberal scholarship that asserts that the Servant Songs in Isa 42:1-53:12 are the product of an unknown post-exilic author styled "Deutero-Isaiah". However, the correct setting of the Servant Songs is the reign of Hezekiah,[3] and failure

---

[1] Martin, *An Early Christian Confession*, 23-24. [Ed. JWA]: Re "poured out". The precise form of Isa 53:12's Hebrew term הֶעֱרָה/h⁽rh translated 'poured out' connects with 'make bare' or 'expose' in Lev 20:18-19 related to 'uncovering' (cf. גלה) nakedness. 'Exposed his soul' – what Jesus did to himself – would then profoundly benefit from connecting with Col 2:15 and thus better measure the ironic counterpoint in that NT text re Christ's 'undressing' principalities and powers also in his death.

[2] Hurst, "Re-enter the Pre-existent Christ in Philippians 2.5-11?", 457 n. 39; C. A. Wanamaker, "Philippians 2.6–11: 'Son of God or Adamic Christology'?" *NTS* 33 (1987): 179-193 (182).

[3] See H. A. Whittaker, *Isaiah* (Cannock: Biblia, 1988), G. Booker and H. A. Whittaker, *Hezekiah the Great: The Songs of Degrees* (Birmingham: CMPA, 1985).

to correctly contextualize the oracles leads to aberrant understandings. The oracles seem to admit of both a collective and an individual role for the Servant. Collectively, the Servant is the faithful Judean remnant[1] but the passages that speak of individual suffering are based on Hezekiah. As the king, he was not only the divine agent, but also the representative of the people; in other words, a mediator and type of the messiah.

No one would insist that either Adam or the Suffering Servant pre-existed. The ideas of agency and God manifestation (not incarnation) are integral to both roles—especially in the account of Adam's "fall". Even though Paul types Christ as the "second Adam" (1 Cor 15:47), Trinitarians fiercely resist "Adam Christology" because the parallel with Adam places Christ in a role that is subordinate to the Father. However, it is the "natural" that is first and then the "spiritual" (1 Cor 15:46). If Christ existed before Adam the contrast breaks down. As the "second Adam" Jesus refused to follow in the footsteps of the "first Adam" instead embracing the role of the suffering servant.

The Philippians are not being exhorted to forego a pre-existent "god-like" status in exchange for a humbler "human" form.[2] Instead, the community, who already had an exalted status in Christ and the powers of the future age, should follow his example (not the example of Adam's overweening ambition), who although made in the express image of God, did not snatch at divinity. Nor did he selfishly abuse his powers, nor did he claim his rightful place as King of the Jews, nor did he lord it over his brethren. He put to one side the privileges of a son for those of a servant. Adam blamed God for his fall; "The woman whom You gave to be with me, she gave me of the tree, and I ate" (Gen 3:12) but Christ declared; "Those whom you gave me I have kept...." (John 17:12). Jesus humbled himself to death on the cross in order to save his bride...be ye likeminded.

---

[1] [Ed. AP]: Or Judah.

[2] "For all seek their own, not the things which are of Christ Jesus". (Phil 2:21 NKJV)

Seals, trumpets and vials

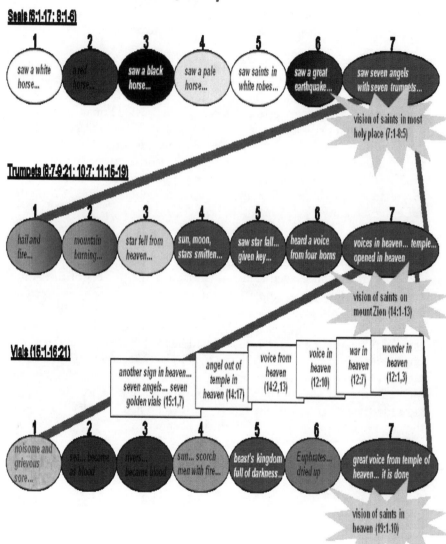

Seals (6:1-17; 8:1-5)

1	2	3	4	5	6	7
saw a white horse...	a red horse...	saw a black horse...	saw a pale horse...	saw saints in white robes...	saw a great earthquake...	saw seven angels with seven trumpets...

vision of saints in most holy place (7:1-8:5)

Trumpets (8:7-9:21; 10:7; 11:15-19)

1	2	3	4	5	6	7
hail and fire...	mountain burning...	star fell from heaven...	sun, moon, stars smitten...	saw star fall... given key...	heard a voice from four horns	voices in heaven... temple... opened in heaven

vision of saints on mount Zion (14:1-13)

Vials (15:1-16:21)

another sign in heaven... seven angels... seven golden vials (15:1,7)

angel out of temple in heaven (14:17)

voice from heaven (14:2,13)

voice in heaven (12:10)

war in heaven (12:7)

wonder in heaven (12:1,3)

1	2	3	4	5	6	7
noisome and grievous sore...	sea... became as blood	rivers... became blood	sun... scorch men with fire...	beast's kingdom full of darkness...	Euphrates... dried up	great voice from temple of heaven... it is done

vision of saints in heaven (19:1-10)

P. Heavyside

The Spirit of the Lord in the History Books
A. Perry

Introduction

Various OT accounts use "Spirit of the Lord".[1] In the collected state of these traditions, they combine to produce a composite picture of the Spirit of the Lord as an "agent" in the narrative—a kind of hypostatization of the power of God.

History Books

In the history books, the narrative pattern is that the Spirit of the Lord comes upon a deliverer or king (Othniel, Gideon, Jephthah, Samson, Saul and David) who is then empowered to act on behalf of the Lord. This pattern is reinforced with allusions to the Exodus and an implicit comparison is struck between the deliverer-judge and Moses (cf. "groanings", Jud 2:18; Exod 2:24). The people "cry" unto the Lord (Jud 3:9; 6:6; 10:10; Exod 2:23; 3:7), and the Lord "raises up" (Jud 3:9; cf. Deut 18:15) a judge to deliver them (Jud 13:5).

The Spirit of the Lord acts in regular ways: i) coming upon the judge (Jud 3:10; 11:29); ii) clothing[2] Gideon prior to battle (Jud 6:34); iii) initiating the troubling through dreams of a judge to action (Jud 13:25; cf. Gen 41:8; Ps 77:5; Dan 2:1, 2); iv) rushing suddenly upon a judge prior to acts of physical prowess (Jud 14:6, 14:19; 15:14); and v) the physical transport of a prophet ("taking up" and "casting down", 2 Kgs 2:16).

In traditions about Saul, there is a similar "deliverance" motif and allusions to Exodus traditions are employed. Thus, God "looks" upon the people when he hears their "cry" (1 Sam 9:16; Exod 2:25; 3:7); Saul is selected to perform a "Moses" role; his choice is confirmed with "signs"; and God is "with" him (1 Sam 10:7; Exod 3:12). One of the signs is that the Spirit of the Lord will come suddenly upon Saul and he will prophesy (1 Sam 10:6, 10; 11:6). The Spirit of the Lord subsequently departs from Saul and comes

---

[1] We will present this evidence in terms of the MT rather than the LXX, noting only those instances where the LXX offers significant differences of detail in the episodes.

[2] J. R. Levison cites Assyro-Babylonian texts to support his interpretation that "clothing" is indicative of possession by a spirit-being—"The Angelic Spirit in Early Judaism" *The Society of Biblical Literature 1995 Seminar Papers*, 34 (1995): 464-493, (469).

upon David (1 Sam 16:13-14), and speaks by him, and places his word in his tongue (2 Sam 23:2).

The first information the reader is presented with in Judges is that the Spirit of the Lord comes upon a judge and he is thereby empowered to lead the people (Jud 3:10; 6:34; 11:29). No specific actions are specifically attributed to the Spirit in the cases of Othniel, Gideon or Jephthah—there is no instrumental statement to the effect that the Spirit caused Othniel to go out to war, but insofar as Hebrew narrative regularly indicates causation by conjunction, it is the conjunction of a statement that the Spirit of the Lord came upon a judge followed immediately by a statement about what the judge did that secures the causal link. The metaphor here of "coming upon" is that of the "Spirit-as-agent" because the action of the Spirit is what the judge immediately does in the story.

With Samson, the narrator does not initially say that the Spirit of the Lord came upon him, but instead he ascribes an action to the Spirit of the Lord.

> And the Spirit of the Lord began[1] to stir him in Mahaneh-dan, between Zorah and Eshtaol. Jud 13:25 (NASB)

Against the backdrop of Othniel, Gideon and Jephthah, this statement is describing the Spirit *as it is already in Samson*; this kind of phraseology refers to *what* stirs Samson to action, and the metaphor is one of agency. The LXX translators read the metaphor in this way,

> And the Spirit of the Lord began to go out with him in the camp of Dan, and between Saraa and Esthaol. Judg 13:25 (LXX-A)[2]

In later stories about Samson, the Spirit of the Lord comes upon him mightily so that he performs feats of strength (Jud 14:6; 15:14). This idea

---

[1] The auxiliary Hiphil of חלל is regularly used with Qal or Hiphil infinitives to denote the beginning of an action by a character.

[2] *Targum Jonathan* has "a spirit of power from before the Lord began to strengthen him", but this seems to be motivated by Samson's subsequent behaviour rather than the sense of "troubling" which is linked to the "trouble" caused by dreams in MT usage and therefore prophetic inspiration. The LXX has συνεκπορεύομαι—"the Spirit of the Lord began to go out with him" which likewise does not render "troubling" but retains a notion of agency.

of "coming mightily upon Samson" indicates that the Spirit of the Lord is an agent coming mightily upon Samson.

The same close connection between the Spirit of the Lord and behaviour is seen in David's claim that the Spirit spoke by him (2 Sam 23:2). This description is an example of agency: the Spirit is in David but David refers to the Spirit as if it is an agent speaking through him.

However, other actions related to the Spirit of the Lord imply the Spirit is a **spirit-being** because the action is *external* to the individual (it relates to the body of a person):

- Lifting up Elijah and carrying him off (1 Kgs 18:12)
- Taking Elijah up to a mountain and casting him down (2 Kgs 2:16)

These actions indicate transport by a being and are thereby marked out as different. The transport of Elijah is described in vigorous terms as a "casting down" upon a mountain. This detail is sufficient to indicate the Spirit of the Lord here is a spirit-being from the Lord.[1]

The final case in the history books is the example of Micaiah's prophecy (1 Kgs 22:24; 2 Chron 18:23). Here a spirit goes from the throne of God in heaven to be a lying spirit in the mouth of Ahab's prophets. It is this spirit about whom Zedekiah asks: "Which way went the Spirit of the Lord from me to speak to thee"? This is another example in which the Spirit is described as a spirit-being.

These last two examples do not indicate metaphorical presentation of the Spirit as an agent; it is not the spirit *in* Elijah that carries him off and casts him down, and the cosmology of Micaiah's vision also clearly indicates spirit-beings.

Discussion

The data so far presents a varied picture and it blocks certain interpretations. Standard literary treatments of the notion of "character" or "agent" offer a basis for distinguishing these terms. Formalist and Structuralist theory works with more austere definitions of "character".[2]

---

[1] Later Jewish writings include the transport of individuals by angels.

[2] S. Chatman, *Story and Discourse* (Ithaca: Cornell University Press, 1978), 111-113.

Theorists emphasize plot and make characters into products of the plot.[1] They have a functional status, and their actions are their defining quality. Aristotle[2] gave primacy to the notions of an "agent" and "action" in a story, and regarded "character" as a superimposition. This allows theorists to reserve the term "agent" for a case where there is no development of character.

The textual data we have so far considered does not support the interpretation that the Spirit of the Lord is presented with a metaphor of a mimetic character.[3] Psychological and mimetic aspects of characterization are not mirrored in Spirit of the Lord traditions. Thus, there are no grounds for asserting a full-blown personification. Using J. Paxson's terms, the metaphor lacks "voice and face"; only David's claim to inspiration adds voice.[4]

In terms of plot and story-form, the Spirit of the Lord is a "helper" or a "donor",[5] and there is a sense of empowering individuals. Furthermore, there are uses of the expression as a term of reference for a spirit-being.

Conclusion

Our conclusion is that the narrative historical traditions of the OT are describing extraordinary human behaviour and referring to the Spirit of the Lord as the cause of this behaviour. In order to secure an informative reference to the Spirit, the narrator uses an ontological metaphor of agency—the Spirit-as-agent. The austerity of the predicates associated with the expression "Spirit of the Lord" gives no basis for anything more substantial, such as a Trinitarian conception.

---

[1] This standard distinction and this terminology derive from E. M. Forster, *Aspects of the Novel* (London: Penguin, 1962), 75.

[2] This can be seen throughout his *Poetics*, but it is particularly clear in ch. 6 and the discussion of tragedy.

[3] For one treatment of mimetic characterization see, R. Scholes and R. Kellogg, *The Nature of Narrative* (Oxford: Oxford University Press, 1966), ch. 5.

[4] J. L. Paxson, *The Poetics of Personification* (Cambridge: Cambridge University Press, 1994), 42.

[5] These terms derive from the folktale analysis of V. Propp, but we use them here as an inference from the story traditions that involve the Spirit of the Lord rather than as a model applied to these traditions; on this see, J. Culler, *Structuralist Poetics* (London: RKP, 1975), 230-238.

Quirinius
A. Perry

There are many characteristics of the gospels that indicate their accuracy; additionally, there are a small number of well-known so-called inaccuracies. Positive assessments of the nuts and bolts of the gospel records have been written by conservative scholars. Since the gospels are a social history of a charismatic teacher and his followers, any inaccuracies would be limited to the "public" side of Jesus' ministry—names, dates, places and the cultural environment. Thus, for example, we are able to verify Luke's political facts—the emperor Augustus, Herod the Great, Quirinius and Pilate, or Annas, Caiaphas and Ananias. Furthermore, we are able to verify Luke's reliability as a historian by examining his follow-up book, Acts.

Inaccuracies in historical texts are expected by the historico-critical method; there is no presumption that the gospel texts are divinely inspired in such a method and so historians will point out errors where there is other evidence that points to different facts of the matter. For example, the reference to a tax census of Quirinius sometime in 6-4 B.C.E. has been dubbed an error because he is known to have become the legate of Syria in 6 C.E. and initiated a census in that year (Josephus, *Ant.* 18.1.1; cf. Tacitus, *Annals* 3.48).[1]

There are two preliminary points to make about this "error": first, it is representative of the type of error that could be identified in the gospel records, i.e. errors to do with the more public facts of names, dates and places—the possible errors in this regard are very few indeed; secondly, where there is a conflict between two different sources (Josephus and Luke), critical scholars will favour the non-Biblical evidence and conservative scholars will favour the biblical evidence.

It is accepted by conservative scholars[2] that Quirinius was a legate of Syria in 6-7 C.E. and that there was a census then, which caused unrest in Judea (a province of Syria), and which is referred to by Luke in Acts 5:37 "After this man, Judas of Galilee rose up in the days of the census and drew away *some* people after him; he too perished, and all those who followed him were scattered" (NASB). Luke's use of the expression "the census" and his

---

[1] This view is defended in the standard academic bible dictionary—D. S. Potter, "Quirinius" *ABD*, 5:588-589.

[2] A representative treatment is that of W. Brindle, "The Census and Quirinius: Luke 2:2" *JETS* 27/1 (1984): 43-52.

reference to Judas the Galilean establishes that he is referring to the census of 6-7 C.E. against which Judas led a rebellion.

The census at the time of Jesus' birth is mentioned in this way:

> And it came to pass in those days, that there went out a decree from Caesar Augustus, that all the world should be taxed. (*And* this taxing was first made when Quirinius was governor of Syria.) And all went to be taxed, every one into his own city. Luke 2:1-3 (KJV revised)

In this narrative aside[1] Luke refers to a first census, or a "former" or "earlier" census than the one made in 6-7 C.E. This is an important qualification as it coheres with Acts 5:37 which refers to the later and more famous census. Since there is no record of any more census enrolments happening after 6-7 C.E. in relation to Quirinius, we can deduce that the census of Luke 2:2 is not that of 6-7 C.E. but an earlier one. Because Josephus does not record two such census enrolments, critical scholars work with just one and infer that Luke makes a mistake with his placement of a first census at the end of the reign of Herod the Great.

However, an incidental detail of Luke's account makes it unlikely that he is making a simple mistake (after all, his chronology in Luke 3:1 is flawless). Mary and Joseph travel to Bethlehem of Judea to enrol for tax purposes. Just before the birth of Jesus, Herod was ruler of Judea and Galilee and a census initiated in his region could have been one that required travel to Judea for those born in the south. After Herod's death, the kingdom of Judea was divided and Galilee came under the jurisdiction of Antipas. In the census of 6-7 C.E. there is no particular reason why those residents in the north would have been required to travel south for enrolment. This makes the census of Luke 2:2 more likely to have been a different and earlier one than that of 6-7 C.E.

Although no extant record other than Luke's requires the suggestion, some scholars have therefore proposed that Quirinius could have been a special military legate anytime between 6-4 B.C.E. in addition to the domestic governor of Syria at the time (who was Sentius Saturninus until 6 B.C.E.

---

[1] For a discussion of this narrative aside see S. M. Sheeley, *Narrative Asides in Luke-Acts* (JSNTSup 72; Sheffield: JSOT Press, 1992), 102-103.

and thereafter Quintilius Varus between 6-4 B.C.E.[1]). It is known that Quirinius was conducting a long campaign from the north of Syria (and maybe Galatia) against the Homonadensus at this time and had been since about 10 B.C.E. He could have assumed a temporary legateship in Syria during any interim period between the two documented governors.

Upon hearing of Jesus from the Wise Men, Herod sought to kill the children in Bethlehem up to two years of age, but Mary and Joseph had been warned to flee this danger. They fled to Egypt and only returned when Herod had died which is dated to 4 B.C.E. The inference therefore is that Jesus was born most likely in the years 6-5 B.C.E. and that the census Luke mentions took place in one of these years.[2] A temporary interim military governorship on the part of Quirinius (possibly during a handover period between Sentius Saturninius and Quintilius Varus in 6 B.C.E.) is not implausible. Herod's relationship with Augustus had broken down by the end of his reign and a direction from the military legate of Syria to conduct a census would have been heeded.

Our discussion of Luke's chronology is an example of the kind of discussion that conservative and critical scholars have about the reliability of the gospel records. It is a choice to allow Luke's evidence to stand in a reconstruction of Roman History, but it is because Luke shows himself to be reliable on other names and dates that it is best to do so in this case and conjecture a second interim legateship on the part of Quirinius. In the relatively few cases where the historical veracity of the gospels can be challenged with apparently contrary external evidence,[3] conservative scholarship has provided plausible harmonisations of the data.

---

[1] It is known from Josephus (*Ant.* 10, 9-10) that Quintilius Varus was legate until at least 4 B.C.E. and the death of Herod but not thereafter— when it is next known that Gaius Julius Caesar was the governor in 1 C.E.
[2] Tertullian, *Adv. Marc.* 4.19, dates the census to the governorship of Sentius Saturninius.
[3] A. N. Sherwin-White, *Roman Law and Roman Society in the New Testament* (Oxford: Oxford University Press, 1963), 162-171 (162) observes that the presence of Quirinius' name has caused the most controversy in Luke's Roman History.

Pre-historic Genealogies
A. Perry

The Old Testament scholar, K. A. Kitchen, offers a standard discussion of the genealogy of Genesis 5 in relation to the king lists and reign lengths of Mesopotamian monarchs. In Sumerian and Akkadian king lists, for the period prior to the flood there are 8 or 10 kings stretching back until kingship was "lowered from the heavens". In the Sumerian King List, for example, the total number of years for the reigns of the eight kings is 241,000 years whereas the total number of years for the reigns of the kings after the flood is 24,510 and 2310 years for a sequence of 23 and then 12 kings.[1] Whereas the Sumerian King List documents a long pre-history before the Flood in terms of an 8 to 10 series of kings and their reigns (depending on the tablet), the genealogy of Genesis 5 works with 10 generations and less years.[2] Both counts break at the Flood, each has large numbers and the years decline dramatically after the Flood. Their "8/10" framework[3] allows the suggestion that we have here a notional use of numbers to structure an unknown and long period of time.

A second point to make here is that the genealogy in Genesis 5 is not necessarily consecutive—the father-son relationship may in some instances be a father-grandson relationship or there may be a multiple of intervening generations. The opening entries of the genealogy are,

> And Adam lived an hundred and thirty years, and begat a
> son in his own likeness, after his image; and called his

---

[1] ANET, 265; K. A. Kitchen, *On the Reliability of the Old Testament* (Grand Rapids: Eerdmans, 2003), 439f.

[2] This comparison is true in a general way if both Genesis and the Sumerian King List are using a decimal system; however, the King List is actually using a modified sexagesimal system. J. H. Walton, *Ancient Israelite Literature in its Cultural Context* (Grand Rapids: Zondervan, 1989), 127-131, shows how the two decimal and sexagesimal systems align very closely in their totals after conversion, if the original compiler of the Sumerian King List was using the Genesis 5 genealogy and misunderstood its digits as a modified sexagesimal number. In this way, Walton makes a conclusive case for the Genesis genealogy being the older text.

[3] The use of "ten generations" as a motif to exhaust a period of time is seen in the law, "An Ammonite or Moabite shall not enter into the congregation of the Lord; even to their tenth generation shall they not enter into the congregation of the Lord for ever" (Deut 23:3, KJV).

name Seth: And the days of Adam after he had begotten Seth were eight hundred years: and he begat sons and daughters: And all the days that Adam lived were nine hundred and thirty years: and he died. And Seth lived an hundred and five years, and begat Enos: And Seth lived after he begat Enos eight hundred and seven years, and begat sons and daughters. And all the days of Seth were nine hundred and twelve years: and he died. And Enos lived ninety years, and begat Cainan: And Enos lived after he begat Cainan eight hundred and fifteen years, and begat sons and daughters: And all the days of Enos were nine hundred and five years: and he died.   Gen 8:3-1 (KJV)

We would normally read this today as a consecutive sequence without any gaps. However, the early story of Genesis 4 documents the birth of Cain and Abel before Seth. The genealogy of Genesis 5 gives no hint of a Cain or an Abel or any other sons and daughters before Seth, but a reader should take this information and use it to condition his understanding of the genealogy of Genesis 5. Seth is a first generation son of Adam (Gen 4:25), and Enos is likewise a first generation son of Seth (Gen 4:26); but Cainan may be a grandson, or a great-grandson, or a more distant "son" of Enos; the genealogy may therefore have gaps. The fixing of the birth of Cainan to Enos' age at 90 may be a fixing of a *forbear* of Cainan, the individual in whose line Cainan was born.

An extensive time period after Enos, in which men and women multiply on the earth, is implied in the conclusion to Genesis 4,

> To Seth also a son was born, and he called his name Enos. At that time <u>men</u> began to call upon the name of the Lord. Gen 4:26 (RSV)

If we read the genealogy of Genesis 5 as a literal consecutive sequence, this change in the "times" is not given enough time to develop between the generations of Enos and Cainan. The time marked by "Enos" is one where there are men (some but not all) who call upon the name of the Lord. This conclusion to Genesis 4 is deliberately placed after the genealogy of Cain[1]

---

[1] The presence of two genealogical traditions in Genesis corresponds to Mesopotamian texts where in addition to the prehistoric listing of kings, there is a tradition of the seven successive wise sages who teach the skills

in which the development of human skills is recorded rather than any "walking with God". In the light of this development in human history, the characterization of the era after Enos' birth is about a return to God on the part of some, and this implies that there had been an apostasy from God by men and women generally. This information is important as it should prevent a reader from treating the genealogy of Genesis 5 as a simple consecutive sequence of father-son relationships—there is a great deal of time after Enos and before Cainan.

This interpretation makes sense in the light of the nomination of only 10 generations; there are ten names that structure the family history of Noah. The colophon in Gen 6:9, "These are the records of the generations of Noah" (NASB), makes the genealogy part of Noah's ancestry.[1] The ten-fold stylised arrangement is mirrored in the genealogy of Cain: although it is a 6 generation framework, both end with an individual who has three sons, and both have similarly named ancestors.

A further indication that the genealogy of Genesis 5 is to be read in a non-consecutive way is the absence of the added information of "calling the name of the son": this detail is recorded for Seth in Gen 5:3, Enos in Gen 4:26, and for Noah in Gen 5:29 but not for the other "sons"; the number of generations in the middle of the genealogy is therefore unknown.

The other difficulty that modern readers have with the genealogy is the longevity of the individuals; the oldest man lived for 969 years and this is dismissed as an unbelievable "fantastic" number. Again, a modern reader is assuming that the ages given are literal, but the case against the ages being real consists simply of the estimates of death given by archaeological anthropologists of the dead that they uncover in grave sites in the Near East from any point in the past. Furthermore, there is no basis in paleo-biology for supposing that human life-spans were much different 10,000 years ago. If we assume that men and women lived to what we regard as normal ages, we should ask: *why* are long ages given here in Genesis 5 and in the Mesopotamian king lists?

---

of human wisdom; hence, Cain's genealogy has a 6-fold listing of human skills.

[1] R. K. Harrison, "From Adam to Noah: A Reconsideration of the Antediluvian Patriarchs' Ages" *JETS* 37/2 (1994): 161-168 (162); P. J. Wiseman, *New Discoveries in Babylonia about Genesis* (4th ed.; London: Marshall, Morgan & Scott, 1946), chap. 5.

One kind of response would be to reject the ages given as 'real' and regard the numbers as false; we could then reject the historicity of the genealogy as a whole, and use this conclusion to cast doubt on the historical value of the primeval history. This kind of reaction would be extreme, and we should instead ask: if those who composed the genealogy knew very well how long humans typically lived, *why* would they employ long ages? A preliminary point would be that we are assuming the long ages given were ubiquitous among humans, but the only data we have relates to ten individuals. Equally, we are assuming that archaeological anthropologists are right to assume the same rate of ageing for the past as we have today.

Some conservative scholars see literal ages in the genealogy and they observe that long ages are given for the birth of the "sons" as well as the death of the "fathers" in the genealogy; further, Enoch lives for 365 years and Lamech's 777 years are cut short by the Flood—these ages are determined by external events and are not easy to dismiss. Moreover, the reduction of human ages after the Flood to between 100-200 years and then to around 70 years was gradual over a few generations. Thus, it is suggested that God intervened after the Flood so that human beings had shorter life-spans; the precedent for this is Gen 6:3, "And the Lord said, My spirit shall not always strive with man, for that he also *is* flesh: yet his days shall be an hundred and twenty years" (KJV).

This approach is problematic for critical scholars of the Bible because it involves the idea of divine intervention. This is a "problem" that occurs in several other places in the Old Testament where the miraculous is recorded or implied. In response, other conservative scholars have tried different approaches. For example, it has been said that the Hebrew digits are not decimal (Base-10) but Base-2 or some other base; or, the numbers are aligned with an old cosmological scheme related to the planets; and, even, the years are not solar years but some other (perhaps lunar) "year". These suggestions, and others, show that scholars do not dismiss the genealogy as poor history; there is a good case[1] to be made for it being older than Mesopotamian king lists in composition. Rather, they seek to explain the *use* of large numbers in the genealogy. Of these approaches, the best harmonizing suggestion is that the numbers are **notional** and serve the purpose of structuring an unknown long period of time. Can we expand on this suggestion?

The ages that are given mostly cluster above the 900 mark—just short of a thousand years. Lamech's life is cut short because of the Flood and Enoch

---

[1] Walton, *Ancient Israelite Literature in its Cultural Context*, 127-131.

is a special case, but otherwise the 900 +/- pattern is carefully chosen, because the choice of a "thousand years" as a limiting period isn't arbitrary. In the "Prayer of Moses", it is said that, "…a thousand years in thy sight *are but* as yesterday when it is past, and *as* a watch in the night" (Ps 90:4, KJV). The comment is, no doubt, a metaphor for the passage of time and how the ages are marked by God. The New Testament writer, Peter, makes a comment with this verse when he says, "But, beloved, be not ignorant of this one thing, that one day *is* with the Lord as a thousand years, and a thousand years as one day" (2 Pet 3:8, KJV).

This language is relevant to Genesis 5 because in Genesis 2 God had declared that were Adam to sin, he would die in the day that he sinned (Gen 2:17). If the poetic understanding of time expressed in the Prayer of Moses is at work in Genesis 5, the limitation of the antediluvian ages to just under a thousand years is one way in which the compiler of these traditions (traditionally Moses) shows the fulfilment of God's edict of death: the refrain of the genealogy is "and he died" (8x). If a thousand years are as a day in God's eyes, all these men did die in the kind of "day" that God had decreed for Adam's dying.

It is beyond the scope of this essay, but there is a good case supporting the view that Moses compiled or collected together the early traditions of Genesis which are dubbed "historical records" (Gen 2:4; 5;1; 6:9; 10:1, 32; 11:10, 27; 25:12, 13, 19; 36:1, 9; 37:2),[1] and so the understanding implicit in the Prayer of Moses is relevant to our reading of Genesis 5. Furthermore, the prayer starts off (vv. 1-5) as a meditation on the early chapters of Genesis with its references to "all generations", "giving birth to the earth", "children of Adam", "destruction" and a "flood". If a long and unknown period of time was going to be structured with ten generations, ages just under a thousand years would be chosen to conform to God's attitude to the passage of time and the edict that Adam was to die in the "day" that he sinned. The opening verses of Moses' prayer reconcile the apparent contradiction between Genesis 2 and 5 in its meditation.

The Old Testament account of creation is often ridiculed because the genealogy of Genesis 5 is totalled up to give an age for the earth of around 6000 years. The historical reliability of the whole of the Old Testament is then thrown into doubt. This is a poor stance to adopt. The genealogy is "of its times" in using large numbers, if we reject the literality of the

---

[1] W. C. Kaiser, *The Old Testament Documents: Are they Reliable and Relevant?* (Downers Grove: InterVarsity Press, 2001), 57-58; Wiseman, New Discoveries in Babylonia about Genesis, chap. 8.

numbers, this does not mean the individuals are not historical individuals. However, once we observe that there is no name-calling from Cainan onwards until Noah, we have a basis for treating the genealogy as having substantial gaps and the pre-history of Genesis becomes an indeterminate period. The genealogy itself does not engage in totalling up. Whether we treat the ages mentioned in a literal way or a notional way is an open question.

Was the Ark a practical size?
J. Burke

Sceptics objecting to the size of Noah's Ark frequently point to smaller 19th century timber ships which were unseaworthy due to their large size, such as the 19th century American schooners 'Wyoming' and 'Great Republic, two of the largest all timber vessels ever built. It is claimed that the chronic leaking, warping, and hull separation from which such ships suffered (despite reinforcement with iron bracing), proves the Ark could not have survived the flood.

Though frequently compared with sailing ships, or even ships with steam engines, the Ark was actually a barge. Barges are not subject to the same stresses as a sailing ship, such as the weight of sails and rigging, and they are not subject to hull stresses caused by the wind bending the masts. The Ark did not have to carry the tremendous weight of cannon which burdened the timber ships with which it is often compared, nor did it have to deal with the weight and stresses of a steam engine or steam bilge pumps, or the rigors of sea travel (it stayed within the Mesopotamian flood plain).

One of the largest wooden ships, the Appomattox, is often compared with the Ark. Measuring 97.2 metres long (319 feet), with a beam of 12.8 metres (42 feet), it had to be reinforced with steel bracing just to stay together, and pumped continuously by steam bilge pumps due to constant leaking, as stresses on the hull caused the timbers to separate. Sceptics frequently point to this as an example of the vulnerability of wooden ships over 300 feet long, and argue that this demonstrates Noah's Ark could not possibly have been practical.

However, the Appomattox was designed completely differently to the Ark, being a steam powered ship not a barge. It was also subjected to other stresses caused by having to tow a large unpowered barge behind it. This barge, the Santiago, is a far more relevant vessel with which to compare the Ark. Like the Ark it was made entirely of timber, carrying no steel bracing, and was not powered either by steam or sail. It was even larger than the Appomattox, 102.4 metres long (336 feet), with a beam of 14 metres (46 feet). Its service history (1899-1918), was over twice as long as that of the Appomattox, despite serving on the Great Lakes, notorious for their storm conditions and unpredictable waters.

From as early as the 17th century, comparisons have been drawn between the Ark and various ancient vessels considered similar in dimensions and construction. Defending the practicality of the Ark, Walter Raleigh argued that it was smaller than a ship built in the reign of Hiero II of Syracuse (3rd century BC), and smaller than the giant fighting ship Tessarakonteres built by Ptolemy IV Philopater (3rd century BC). The Tessarakonteres remained a common point of comparison to the Ark throughout the 19th century for Christian apologists, naval historians, nautical engineers, and scientific journals.

Historians recognize a number of ancient large ships comparable to the Ark as genuine vessels.

- **1,480 BC**: An obelisk barge built in Egypt for Queen Hatshepsut, 95-140m long (311-459ft), 32m wide (104 ft);[1] a wall relief shows it carrying two obelisks end to end, indicating a length well over 100 metres.

- **c. 200 BC**: The Thalamagos, a large pleasure barge built Ptolemy IV Philopater, 114m long (377 ft), described by the Greek historian Athenaeus.

- **c. 200 BC**: The Tessarakonteres, a warship built for Ptolemy IV Philopater, 128m long (420ft), described by the 1st century Roman historian Plutarch.

- **c. 200 BC**: A timber warship described by the 1st century Greek historian Memnon of Heraclea, 100m long (300ft).

- **1st century**: The 'Nemi Ships', two timber barges built for the Roman emperor Caligua, 70m long (229ft), 18m wide (60ft).

- **1st century**: A large cargo barge built for Caligula, used to transport an obelisk from Egypt to Rome, 104m long (341ft), 20.3m wide (66ft).

---

[1] Estimates vary depending on interpretations of the historical evidence.

The successful wooden ships of this size required nothing more sophisticated than such timber technology as mortise and tenon joinery, tension cables (called 'hogging trusses'), and bulkheads or internal bracing, such as transverse lashing and lateral or longitudinal strength beams. In some cases, only three out of these five techniques were used, whereas Noah's ark demonstrably used at least four of these techniques.

Noah was a Mesopotamian, who would have used contemporary Mesopotamian construction techniques, meaning the Ark would have used mortise and tenon joinery, longitudinal strength beams, tension trusses, and hogging trusses, just like other ships built in the Bronze Age. In Mesopotamia, copper was used to make hammers and nails, adzes, chisels, axes, and drill bits from before 3,500 B.C.E, mortise and tenon joinery was used from at least the same time, whilst timber boats using sails and copper nails appear as early as 3,500 B.C.E.

Egyptian inscriptions as early as the reign of Khufu I (2,589-2,566 B.C.E.), show ships built with internal bracing techniques such as lateral and longitudinal strength beams, and transverse lashing. Longitudinal strength bulkheads are found in the Egyptian Middle Kingdom era (between 1,991 BCE and 1,648 B.C.E.), showing that this technology was used from a very early date in the Ancient Near East.

While only the obelisk barge of Hatshepsut is chronologically proximate to the Ark, these vessels prove that pre-modern societies were capable of building timber ships far larger than even their Industrial Age counterparts. It can be proved that the technology used by these cultures was capable of building such large vessels.

Importantly, these ships were built using the same construction techniques used in the Early and Middle Bronze Age, including mortise and tenon joinery and a 'hull first' construction method, rather than the 'frame first' construction method used by later Western maritime engineers.

Even more significant is Caligula's 'Giant Ship', mentioned previously. It had six decks, displaced between 7,000 and 8,000 tons, and carried a crew of 700-800. It was built using the same construction method as the two pleasure barges (the 'Nemi Ships'). The dimensions of this ship are not contested, since its physical remains have been found at Port Claudius in Italy (near Rome International Airport), where it was sunk and filled with stones to create a foundation for the port's lighthouse.

Prior to this discovery, mention of super barges in Roman historical literature (such as Pliny the Elder), had been dismissed as either legend or wild exaggeration. Not only was it considered impossible to build such a large vessel from timber, it was also considered impossible that the Romans had the technology necessary for such an achievement. But the physical evidence overturned these preconceptions.

It became clear that the simple maritime techniques known not only by the Romans but by the Ancient Near East in the Early Middle Bronze Age were more than enough to construct sea going vessels larger than any Western timber ship up to the mid-19th century. Even more startling was the fact that this super barge of Caligula's was a reliable sea-going vessel, unlike many 19th century timber ships over 90 metres long (295 feet).

It is therefore clear that the technology required to build a timber ship the size of Noah's Ark was already available long before the 19th century, and had been used to construct vessels almost as large as the Ark.

Marginal Notes

Isa 41:3 – AP

> He pursued them, *and* passed safely; *even* by the way *that* he had not gone with his feet. Isa 41:3 (KJV)

The reference to "by the way *that* he had not gone with his feet" is a puzzle to commentators. The RSV has "by paths his feet have not trod" and the NASB has "By a way he had not been traversing with his feet". The Hebrew is singular "a way/path" and the verb is very common and translated mostly as a variant of "come" (KJV, 1435x), although a variant of "go" is also used (KJV, 123x). The verb is Imperfect, but the tense is determined by the opening verb of this passage, "Who **raised** up righteousness from the east..." which is Perfect. Hence, the KJV is to be preferred which translates the Hebrew verbs that follow "raised" as past tense. The claims of Isa 41:2-3 are about something that has been done by Yahweh,

> Who <u>hath wrought and done *it*</u>... Isa 41:4 (KJV)

The verbal form changes back here to the Perfect. We can therefore translate v. 3 as,

He pursued them, *and* passed safely; *even* by a way *that* he did not go with his feet. Isa 41:3 (KJV revised)

A conqueror had gone but not with his feet; he had pursued kings but not with his feet. A common suggestion is that he made his pursuit on mounted cavalry, but since cavalry and infantry were common in the armies of the day, it hardly seems something worthy for notice in an oracle. Furthermore, given that we have a "pursuit" being mentioned, one would expect cavalry. A text from Sennacherib's Annals casts light on the oracle:

> I led the way like a fierce wild bull with my picked bodyguards and merciless battle troops. I traversed wadis, torrents, ravines, and dangerous slopes <u>in my sedan chair</u>. Where it was too hard going for my sedan chair, I took to my feet and went on in pursuit to the high peaks, like a gazelle.[1]

This text coincidently has the same ingredients as the oracle: a way; a pursuit; and not using the feet. The boast of Sennacherib is that he pursued his prey at a sedate pace in a sedan chair; it was measured and certain because it was safe to do so — his troops controlled the area. This connection is one of the many indications that the oracles of Isaiah 40-48 relate to the days of Hezekiah rather than that of the Babylonian Exile.

Book Notice – Coming in 2011

Reasons (editor: Thomas Gaston)
The objective for this book is to present reasons for seeking God and for believing in the God of the Bible, Jesus as his son and the saviour of men and women, and the Bible as the Word of God. The book will be a compilation of essays by various authors, supported by a team of reviewers, all committed Christadelphians with relevant expertise.

This work will fill a current gap in the writings of our community with an up-to-date overview of relevant issues from philosophy, science, history and biblical studies. It is hoped that this will serve as useful primer and positive reinforcement for young Christadelphians facing a world increasingly hostile to religious faith. It is also hoped that this book will function as a preaching tool to help encourage others to seek after God.

---

[1] Cited from H. W. F. Saggs, *The Might That Was Assyria* (London: Sidgwick and Jackson, 1984), 254.

Table of Contents

Foreword

Introduction: Faith in the Modern World - Thomas Gaston (UK)

Part One: Reasons for Seeking God
1. Philosophical Arguments for the Existence of God - Mark Vincent (US)
2. The Fine-Tuning of the Universe - Peter Jeavons (UK)
3. The Origins of Life - Paul Boyd (UK)
4. Our Conscious Selves - John Launchbury (US)
5. The Moral Capacity - Thomas Gaston (UK)

Part Two: Reasons for Believing God
6. The Historical Jesus - Andrew Perry (UK)
7. The Resurrection of Jesus - Simon Dean (UK)
8. The Old Testament and History - Andrew Perry (UK)
9. Bible Prophecy - David Alexander (Aus)
10. Israel: God's Chosen People - Reg Carr (UK)

Appendix
Textual Criticism, Inspiration and Canon - Jonathan Burke (Taiwan)

Letters

Dear Editor,

Thanks for the latest edition of EJournal which I enjoyed reading. The omission of 'scholarship' content certainly makes for easier reading but I realize that footnotes and reference to scholars is necessary for a complete treatment of the subject.

Your discursive essay "The New Age" (July 2010) highlights some interesting topics and your comments on the new covenant were of particular interest.

The reference to a new covenant in Jeremiah 31 is repeated in all the prophets either explicitly or implied. The writer to the Hebrews in chapter eight is clearly referring to this new covenant. The covenant referred to in Heb 9:14 involves both the Abrahamic covenant and the new covenant with Israel. There appears to be some ambiguity as to which covenant is new. There is no new Abrahamic covenant but it might be considered as a two part covenant: the first part concerns Christ as the promised 'seed' and all those who are Christ's at his coming; the second part which will be new, concerns the mortal descendants of Abraham and the literal possession of the land. The literal defining of the boundaries of the land in the promise to Abraham apply only to the mortal descendants of Abraham. When Abraham and his seed receive the promise of immortality, being spirit beings, they will not need to dwell in the land in the same way as mortal beings, which exist in a two dimensional space and time.

The two parts of the covenant are rarely mentioned, yet the symbolic representation of God's kingdom with the 'Heavens & Earth' clearly illustrates this twofold aspect. The Earth is defined in Genesis 1 as the dry land which was separated from the waters that covered the surface of the planet, designated as the seas. The symbol Earth aptly describes Israel whom God separated from the sea of nations. The Heavens are defined in Genesis 1 as the space between the water covering the planet and the waters above. This is generally understood to mean the atmosphere. The atmosphere is the complete life support system for all living things on the planet. It provides the air for all creatures living on the dry land, it acts as a filter for all dangerous cosmic radiation, which would destroy living things, and it ensures an equitable temperature and provides the vital element of water, to name but a few of the marvels of this extraordinary element. The Heavens in a symbolic application would be the complete life support system for the nation of Israel and I believe the angels under God's direction fulfilled this function. The kingdom came to an end and it is characterised as such in 2 Peter 3:12, and a new Heaven and Earth is promised in Isa 55:17. It is clear from Heb 2:5 that the restored kingdom will not be in subjection to angels, but to Christ and his princes, i.e. all who are granted immortality at the second coming of Christ and constitute the new Heavens. The new age begins when the new Heavens and Earth are installed and this can only be at the return of Christ. The key element to the fulfilment of the covenant is the life, death and resurrection of Jesus which ratified the covenant, the complete fulfilment being realised during the Millennium.

Trevor Evans

Web Resources
Codex Vaticanus
A collection of photos of all pages from the old photo facsimile of Codex Vaticanus is available online. It is a large download broken up into ZIP/RAR files. The black and white photos are taken at an

angle to the codex and at a fairly high resolution (about 4,000 by 3,000 pixels).

http://www.mediafire.com/?sharekey=a63c12e4771ee14fa0f2f20c509059
d97730a72b63f0eb48b8eada0a1ae8665a

The older photos can be compared with the more recent colour photographs at www.codexsinaiticus.org.

Peer Review

In an article "Scholars test Web Alternative to Peer Review" in the NY Times, (http://www.nytimes.com/2010/08/24/arts/24peer.html?_r=1), P. Cohen observes that the traditional peer review of articles for academic journals has in a couple of recent cases given way to experiments in web-based review. She says,

> Instead of relying on a few experts selected by leading publications, they advocate using the Internet to expose scholarly thinking to the swift collective judgment of a much broader interested audience.

and,

> Today a small vanguard of digitally adept scholars is rethinking how knowledge is understood and judged by inviting online readers to comment on books in progress, compiling journals from blog posts and sometimes successfully petitioning their universities to grant promotions and tenure on the basis of non-peer-reviewed projects.

Her comments are apposite for the Christadelphian EJournal as we rely on the audience for peer review, and have made small changes to published material as a result.

News

A new editor has joined the EJournal and will be involved from January 2011 issue onwards, Bro. D. Burke, responsible for "Theology and Apologetics". He is taking a degree in Theology at Tabor College, Adelaide, which is a Christian college with a conservative evangelical ethos.

Postscript
A. Perry

Speakers are not necessarily good writers and writers are not necessarily good speakers. The apostle Paul was evidently a good writer but not a good speaker (2 Cor 10:10); Moses was a good writer but somewhat diffident about speaking (Exod 4:10). This is not to deny inspiration, but just to observe something about the human dynamics. The problem here is that good speakers need good content, and this is why, in the world, a good speaker will often use a speech writer.

The community is a social organisation and speaking dominates its formal structures: fraternals, exhortations, bible classes, and lectures. Most meetings are a one-to-many speaking-listening arrangement. Oratory is therefore very important in the community; if you are good at oratory, then you will get asked to speak far and wide. As an orator you get to know other orators and a kind of elite is created in which orators recommend each other and the silent many have to continually listen to a small group of good speakers.

The structure is inherited from the cultural origins of the community as this system is common in the churches. The question is this: is the dominance of a one-to-many speaking structure a good thing? There is obviously nothing wrong with one-to-many speaking, we can cite biblical precedent; the question is whether the **dominance** of this structure is damaging to the community.

It is not too difficult to think of disadvantages to the current situation but there is no need to do this now. More importantly, at congregation (the memorial meeting), there is biblical precedent for many-to-many:

> If therefore the whole church be come together into one place, and all speak with tongues… But if all prophesy, and there come in one that believeth not, or *one* unlearned, he is convinced of all, he is judged of all… How is it then, brethren? when ye come together, every one of you hath a psalm, hath a doctrine, hath a tongue, hath a revelation, hath an interpretation. Let all things be done unto edifying… If any man speak in an *unknown* tongue, *let it be* by two, or at the most *by* three, and *that* by course; and let one interpret… Let the prophets speak two or three, and let the other judge… For ye may all

> prophesy one by one, that all may learn, and all may be
> comforted... 1 Cor 14:23-31 (KJV)

Although this passage presumes the exercise of the spirit gifts, there is a pattern here for the main ecclesial meeting that involves the many brethren rather than the one brother.

The 'one-speaker' system is derived from the churches and their preference for priests, vicars and pastors. The biblical model for congregation is for a many-to-many style (or perhaps a 'few-to-many'). This facilitates the **sharing** of the knowledge of Jesus Christ among equals and helps to avoid the rather human tendency to elevate the orators amongst us.

The orator system militates against the spirit of coming together and spiritual sharing that is essential for growth in Christ, and it does so precisely because it requires a very passive audience week after week. The main meeting of the ecclesia should therefore be one in which the orator system is not commonplace. This may be difficult for the speakers in the community to accept but it is an important change that needs to be considered in the ecclesias. This system would act as a counter-balance to the one-to-many occasions such as large fraternals or Bible schools. Good speakers are a tremendous blessing, although they may not be good writers; their place is the bigger occasion. The weekly day-to-day work of spiritual sharing needs the many-to-many model.

END

Supplement

In this supplement we present two cases for an early and a late date for the Book of Revelation.

A Late-Date for Revelation: A Church-Centric Interpretation
T. Gaston

Introduction

A common hermeneutic in Biblical Studies is to consider a text alongside its historical context (i.e. "What might the text have meant to its initial readers?"). Many would advocate this hermeneutic for the Book of Revelation and indeed much of modern scholarship has focused on the search for a first-century application. It is partly for this reason that scholarly consensus has moved away from the traditional Preterist-Historicist-Futurist battlegrounds and turned the attention towards the Roman persecution of Christians in the first century as the major catalyst for the composition of the book. The Beast is identified with Nero for a mid-60s dating or Nero-Redivivus (i.e. Domitian) for a mid-90s dating. The author comforts his readers with pipe-dreams of the advent of Christ and renewal of the world. A clear application for the first century reader; as for future generations, well, predictive prophecy isn't fashionable these days anyway.

I have argued elsewhere that a Nero-centric interpretation will not work, not least because 666 will only equal "Nero" if you choose to spell the name incorrectly.[1] Regrettably, the scholarly consensus is that Nero is the Beast, rendering most modern scholarship useless as to the question of dating the composition of the book. This is not to deny the importance of historical context as a hermeneutic, yet taken to the absolute such a principle binds the message of the book within the constraints of human scholarship. I want to propose that Revelation is bigger than that. The date of composition is just a starting-point; the warning is for all generations.

Almost all OT prophecy, and Jesus' Olivet Prophecy, is Israel-centric. If we date Revelation to the mid-60s – the Jews are still in the Land, Jerusalem is still standing, the Temple remains intact – then the wealth of

---

[1] T. E. Gaston, *Come and See: An Exposition of Revelation* (Hyderabad: Printland Publishers, 2007), 402-416.

OT allusions throughout the book might lead us to an Israel-centric interpretation for the book. However, if the book is dated post-70, i.e. to the mid-90s – the Jews are scattered, Jerusalem is in ruins, the Temple rituals have ceased – then perhaps Spiritual Israel should be our focus.

In this essay, I will put forward the case for a late-date for Revelation, a case based largely upon external evidence.[1] Having done so, I will propose the basis of a Church-centric interpretation.

Persecution

For many commentators it is the issue of persecution that is central to the dating of Revelation, and specifically which period of persecution best fits the composition of Revelation. Two Roman emperors are accredited with persecuting Christians in the first-century, Nero and Domitian.

The persecution by Nero is well-attested by Roman historians Tacitus (*Annals* XV.44.2-8) and Suetonius (*Life of Nero* XVI.2). According to Tacitus, the reason for the persecution was to fasten the guilt for the burning of Rome on Christians and so deflect accusations that Nero himself had started the blaze. Whatever the excuse, the Christians were clearly hated by the Roman populace and the initial reaction to the state-sanctioned persecution was probably favourable. However, Tacitus records that Nero's tortures were so cruel that many began to feel compassion for these otherwise despised Christians.

It is probable that it was during this persecution that both the apostles Peter and Paul were put to death.[2] Prior to his death, Peter writes to the Christians in Pontus, Galatia, Cappadocia, Asia and Bithynia of the sufferings being experienced by "your brotherhood in the world" (1 Pet 5:8-9; cf. 1:6, 4:12-13). This confirms that the Neronic persecution was not confined to the city of Rome and implies that some edict for the persecution of Christians was enacted throughout the provinces.

The evidence of persecution during the reign of Domitian is less substantial. Tertullian makes passing reference to Domitian, "who almost equalled Nero in cruelty", initiating a short persecution of Christians but he gives no particulars (*Apology* 5.1-4). Eusebius records the persecution in greater detail, quoting a story (probably apocryphal) from Hegesippus relating to the grandsons of Jude appearing before Domitian. Eusebius

---

[1] Also see *Come and See,* 381-397.
[2] Clement of Rome, *1 Corinthians* 6.1-2.

does give some particulars, stating that Flavia Domitilla, niece of a Roman consul, was exiled because she was a Christian (*History of the Church* 3.18.3). However, the Roman historian Dio Cassius records the charge against Domitilla as "atheism" and "Jewish ways" (*Epitome* LXVII.14). There is scarce little evidence of a state-initiated persecution in Asia Minor during this period.

However the emphasis placed upon these two emperors is probably unwarranted. Tertullian seems to indicate that the laws against Christians were never repealed (*Apology* 5.5-8) so that there may have been a legal basis for the persecution of Christians from the reign of Nero onwards. The correspondence between Pliny, governor of Bithynia (c.112), and the emperor Trajan demonstrates that a governor could initiate proceedings against Christians without any edict from Rome, indeed Trajan states that "nothing can be laid down as a general ruling" but that Christians are nevertheless to be punished (*Epistle* X.97). As for individual cases, such as that of the apostle John, a Roman governor was the supreme judicial authority in his province – no governor would need the emperor's sanction to banish someone deemed to be a trouble maker.

The seven letters to the churches does not reflect a situation of universal persecution. Whilst at Pergamum Antipas has been killed (Rev 2:13) and the church at Smyrna will shortly suffer troubles (Rev 2:10), the other churches seem unaffected – Laodicea is described as being materially rich (Rev 3:17)! Even John's exile, assuming he was exiled (this is not stated in Revelation), appears to be past ("I **was** on the island of Patmos ...", Rev 1:9). Persecution, then, was not unique to any particular period(s) during the first century and the sporadic troubles suffered by the seven churches may be consistent with any date (though perhaps less suitable for a Neronic dating).

External Testimony

Early Christian writings provide important testimony for the dating of Revelation. Though these testimonies are divided between the Neronic and Domitian dating, it is the later date that has the strongest support amongst these writers.

The earliest testimony we have is from Irenaeus of Lyons who writes, regarding the number of Beast (c.174):

> However, we will not risk a pronouncement on this or
> assert positively that he will have this name, for we know
> that if his name had to be proclaimed openly   at present,

it would have been spoken by the one who saw the Apocalypse. It was seen not long ago but nearly in our generation, toward the end of the reign of Domitian (*Against Heresies* 5.30.1)

Victorinus of Pettau (c.305) records in his commentary that:

When John said these things he was in the island of Patmos, condemned to the labour of the mines by Caesar Domitian (*Comm. Apoc.* 10.1)

Jerome, also, states that:

In the fourteenth year then after Nero, Domitian having raised a second persecution, he was banished to the island of Patmos, and wrote the Apocalypse, on which Justin Martyr and Irenaeus afterwards wrote commentaries (*Lives* IX)

Other writers concur with this testimony, including Eusebius, Crosius, Sulpicius Severus and Primasius. The weight of this testimony may be called into question by the fact that Irenaeus is the only source for Eusebius' testimony on this matter. Jerome also appears to be dependent upon the commentaries of Justin and Irenaeus, and it is not clear whether he or Victorinus have independent verification of this detail. Despite this, the testimony of Irenaeus is still significant as he is the earliest witness to the date of Revelation and he, apparently, knew Polycarp who knew John.

The witness to an early date is weak in comparison, and seems confined to the Syriac Church. The Syriac version of the Apocalypse states that John was banished during the reign of Nero, but the earliest known copy to bear this information dates from c.600. An apocryphal work, also written in Syriac, entitled *The History of John the Son of Zebedee*, also records that John was banished during the reign of Nero, presumably based upon the same tradition. Other writers that include this information include Arethas, Theophylact and Photius – all from the Eastern Church and all considerably later than Irenaeus.

Internal Evidence

Indications from within the book as to its date of composition are less conclusive. It may be argued that the circumstances of the churches described in the seven letters better fits a later date, however, in every case our lack of knowledge is a determining factor.

- The city of Laodicea was devastated by an earthquake in 60 AD. Is six years too short an interval for the church at Laodicea to become materially rich (Rev 3.17)?
- Paul, writing c.61, commends the Ephesians[1] for their faith (Eph 1:15f). Is it conceivable that the church could have left its first love so quickly (Rev 2:4)?
- Some of the churches named in the seven letters are not mentioned in Acts or the other NT writings; it may be that they did not exist at this point. Is the early date too early for the establishment of these churches?

These, and similar arguments, are inconveniences for the argument for the early-date of Revelation but are not real hurdles in themselves. They only lend credibility to the date established by external testimony.

Perhaps more fruitful internal data comes from literary allusions of which Revelation abounds, though mostly alluding to the OT. The tricky part comes from identifying which way the river flows. Take the repeated phrase "he who has an ear, let him hear" (Rev 2:7, 11, 17, 29; 3:6, 13, 22). It has clear resonances with the gospel sayings of Jesus (cf. Matt 11:15; 13:9, 13:43), but there are a variety of explanations for this resonance. While this may be an allusion to the gospels, it may equally be an allusion to an oral tradition of the sayings of Jesus. Though it is almost certain that Jesus is not alluding to Revelation when he uses these words, it is possible that both are alluding to OT texts (cf. Deut 29:4; Ezek 12:2). More importantly, we cannot rule out the explanation that unity of language is based upon unity of inspiration. Nevertheless, from the perspective of a reader, certain allusions are only meaningful if it is assumed that they imply knowledge of the gospels. For instance, the Seals sequence parallels the Olivet prophecy (cf. Rev 6; Matt 24), the harvest of the earth parallels the judgment parables of Jesus (cf. Rev 14:14-20; e.g. Matt 13:24-30) and the marriage of the Lamb parallels the wedding parable (cf. Rev 19:6-10; Matt 22:1-14). The reference to the Gentiles treading the holy city under foot (Rev 11:2) is almost certainly an allusion to Luke 21:24.

If then Revelation presupposes that its initial readers were familiar with the contents of one or all of the synoptic gospels then this has implications for what date we can reasonable suppose Revelation to have been written. The

---

[1] [Ed. AP]: Of course, the date of the Letter to the Ephesians is contested and could be earlier in the Caesarean Captivity.

earliest estimates for the synoptic gospels place their composition in 50s,[1] which might accommodate a mid-60s date for Revelation. However if we date the gospels any later, mid-60s, or even mid-70s, then a late-date for Revelation is more probable. In fact, the UBS/GNT[4] appendix finds allusions and parallels with almost every NT book, including all four gospels and later epistles like Hebrews (4:10; cf. Rev 14:13) and 1 John (4:1; cf. Rev 2:2). It seems preferable to suppose that Revelation was one of, if not the, last books of the NT to be written, a fitting corollary for its position as the closing chapter of our Bibles.

The Continuous-Historic Interpretation

The traditional Christadelphian approach to Revelation has followed the scheme developed by expositors like Joseph Mede and adopted in most of its particulars by John Thomas. The scheme follows a "telescopic" model. The Seals, the Trumpets and the Vials correspond to periods of European history, starting immediately from the book's composition and ending with return of Christ. The Seventh Seal encompasses the period of the Trumpets; the Seventh Trumpet encompasses the period of the Vials. The seventh instance of each series ends with the establishment of the Kingdom; the "telescopic" scheme means that as we approach the *eschaton* we have more and more detail.

The Continuous-Historic (C-H) interpretation, as detailed in John Thomas' *Eureka*, presupposes the late-date for the composition of Revelation. The First Seal is identified as the period between the death of Domitian and the accession of Commodus (96-183), apparently a period of peace and righteousness corresponding to the white horse (Rev 6:2). I have outlined elsewhere why I feel this interpretation to be inadequate.[2] In principle, a continuous historical interpretation could begin with another start date and so the date of composition need not determine our general approach to the book.

The C-H interpretation has often been criticised for focusing heavily on secular Western European history. This is a natural consequence of the Western European origins of the C-H interpretation, but it can feel constrictive to those from elsewhere in the world. This criticism is valid, as far as it goes, since there is no reason for the prediction of European

---

[1] [Ed. AP]: A recent doctoral thesis by J. G. Crossley (The Date of Mark's Gospel, London: T&T Clark, 2004) has argued for a date for Mark in the early 40s.

[2] T. E. Gaston, *The Continuous-Historic Interpretation Examined* (2006), 30-1.

history *per se*. However, inasmuch as the history of Christianity is for large part centred on Europe, particularly Rome, it is not incongruous to interpret the symbols in light of European histories if a Church-centric approach is adopted. The late date for the composition of the book forces us to move away from the Israel-centric hermeneutic of OT prophecies and look instead towards a Church-centric interpretation, i.e. focusing on the fortunes of the Church and warning against future corruptions of Lamb's bride.

A Church-Centric Approach to Revelation

In the fourth appendix of Graham Pearce's *The Revelation – Which Interpretation?* an interesting hermeneutic is briefly discussed. The writer ("A.C.") notes how seven separate lampstands signify the seven churches, evoking the seven-branched lampstand of the Temple. Thus, it is argued, the book directs own attention to the "new constitution" (i.e. Christianity), and away from the Jewish nation, by applying OT symbols to the "Ecclesia of Christ".[1] I have previously written that this is a "hasty" conclusion but also criticised traditional C-H expositors for not applying this principle, ignoring OT precedents for Revelation's symbology.[2] Nevertheless, I believe that this is one indication, which, when coupled with several other observations, points to the fact that Revelation concerns the Christian Church and not the Jewish nation.

Twice in the seven letters to the churches we find the phrase "those who say they are Jews and are not" (Rev 2:9; 3:9). This phrase distinguishes two types of Jews: there are those who say they are Jews and those who actually are Jews. This reinforces a distinction made elsewhere in the NT between natural Jews and spiritual Jews; "know that only those who are of faith are sons of Abraham" (cf. Matt 3:9; John 8:39-44; Rom 2:28-9). It is apparent that by the time Revelation was being written there had already been a parting of ways between Jews and Christians. There is now a definite division between the ecclesia of Christ and the "synagogue of Satan". This corresponds better with a late-date for Revelation, but also indicates that Revelation is not concerned with natural Israel.

We find this principle again when we meet the 144,000. In Revelation 7, these "servants of God" are said to be from "all the tribes of the children

---

[1] A.C., "A Principle of Interpretation" in *The Revelation – Which Interpretation?* (ed., G. Pearce; Torrens Park: Christadelphian Scripture Study Service, 1982), 136.
[2] Gaston, *The Continuous-Historic Interpretation Examined*, 26-27.

of Israel" (Rev 7:4) and so might be supposed to be natural Jews. Yet when we meet the 144,000 again in Revelation 14 they are described as "firstfruits to God and to the Lamb", who are "redeemed from the earth" and "redeemed from mankind" (Rev 14:3-4). The 144,000 of Israel are not natural Israel but spiritual Israel – "who follow the Lamb wherever he goes".

Again, this principle is evident in descent from heaven of "the holy Jerusalem", which is clearly identified by the angel as "the bride, the Lamb's wife" (Rev 21:9-10). The city has twelve gates with the names of the twelve tribes of Israel (Rev 21:12) and the foundations are of twelve stones like those of the breastplate of the High Priest (Rev 21:19-21; cf. Exod 28:17-20). The city also bears the names of the twelve apostles, its wall measures 144 cubits, and the city has no temple (Rev 21:14, 17, 22). This city, called both "new Jerusalem" (Rev 21:2) and just "Jerusalem" (Rev 21:10), has nothing to do with natural Israel but is a symbol of spiritual Israel, that is, the ecclesia of Christ.

Now we may choose to take a dispensionalist view of these facts. We might say that the dispensation of Israel is past, and Revelation is concerned with the dispensation of the Church. However, I think something more subtle is going on. We saw that the seven letters refer to "those who say that are Jews but are not", indicating that true Jews were not defined naturally but spiritually. Followed to its natural conclusion this would mean that true Israel is that continuous line of believers from Abraham to the followers of Christ, including Gentiles. Revelation does not make a distinction between Israel and the Church, but rather makes a distinction between true Israel (i.e. those who follow the Lamb) and false Israel (i.e. "the synagogue of Satan").

Applying the Principles

What then do I mean by a Church-centric approach to Revelation? I mean that the book of Revelation is Christ's warning to his worldwide ecclesia. Revelation as a whole is structured as a letter (cf. Rev 1:1-8; 22:21). More specifically, it follows the structure of the seven letters, beginning with a vision of Christ and ending with a vision of the Kingdom. It should not be surprising then that the book of Revelation contains warnings, just as the seven letters do; warnings of both persecutions without and apostasy within. A good interpretation of Revelation will draw out these warnings for believers. To illustrate this principle, I wish to focus on the two women of Revelation – who I believe are, in fact, one woman.

In Revelation 12 is recounted the vision of the Woman and the Dragon. The Dragon is identified as "the Devil and Satan" (Rev 12:9) and so may reasonably be identified with Sin. However, inasmuch as the Dragon appears to be interacting with the Woman (as well as other characters in the book), I think it necessary to interpret the Dragon as Sin-manifest. The seven heads (Rev 12:3) require some association with Rome (cf. Rev 17:9); the ten horns parallel Daniel's fourth beast (Dan 7:7) reinforcing this association with Rome.

The twelve stars of the Woman (Rev 12:1) should incline us towards either the twelve tribes of Israel or the twelve apostles. As I have argued above, Revelation is not concerned with natural Israel but spiritual Israel so this Woman may be identified with spiritual Israel accordingly. The allusion to the Song of Solomon (cf. 6:10) may reinforce the point. The offspring of the Woman are those who "have the testimony of Jesus Christ" (Rev 12:17) so she cannot be identified otherwise.

As the chapter unfolds, the Woman gives birth to a male child "who was to rule all nations with a rod of iron" (i.e. Jesus Christ; cf. Rev 19:15). The child is caught up to God and his throne (Rev 12:5), a reference to exaltation of Jesus to the right-hand of God. As soon as the child is caught up, war breaks out in heaven and the Dragon (i.e. sin) is cast down; he is overcome by "the blood of the Lamb" (Rev 12:11). The Dragon is not yet defeated, and now persecutes the Woman, who bore the child. So the Woman is given two eagle's wings to fly into the wilderness and there she remains for a set time (cf. Rev 12:6, 14). The final verse of the chapter is telling; the Woman thus protected, the Dragon makes war on those who "keep" the commandments of God – this might imply that the Woman herself no longer keeps the commandments.

In Revelation 17, John is carried out to wilderness and there we meet the Woman again, but now it is not the radiant mother but the scarlet whore. Once persecuted by the seven-headed dragon, the Woman now sits upon a seven-headed beast (Rev 17:3, 7). Once protected from persecution, the Woman is now drunk with the blood of the saints (Rev 17:6). This Woman has taken the simple nourishment she was given and become rich. This is a Church that has betrayed everything for which it once stood.

Summary

The date for the composition of Revelation cannot be reliably established by attempting to determine the contemporary situation. The seven letters do not give a consistent picture of persecution, and so persecution cannot be used as a landmark for dating the book. The prophetic portions of the book could only be used to establish the historical situation if a certain interpretation of the book is presupposed AND if the identification of Nero with the Beast could be made to stick. It is my view that the book refers not to contemporary events but mainly future events and so the use of these details to establish the date of the book is impossible. The external testimony for the late date is strong and this is supported by internal evidence, including literary allusions.

The implication of a late date is that Revelation does not refer to the fortunes of natural Israel, despite the plethora of OT allusions, but necessarily refers to something else. It is the Christian community – Spiritual Israel – to whom our attentions are directed. The book as a whole follows very much the paradigm of the seven letters, providing exhortation and warning to the Christian community as a whole.

Redating Revelation: the case for an Early Date
P. Wyns

Introduction
The dating of Revelation is not merely an academic pursuit, for unlike any other NT writing, the date assigned to the Apocalypse has major interpretive implications; establishing the correct date is therefore crucial for developing an understanding of the message that Jesus Christ gave to his servants.

What do we mean by an *early* or *late* date? An early date is considered to be a date *prior* to AD 70 and a late date is any date *after* AD 70. This is not an arbitrary date as AD 70 marks a cataclysmic event - the destruction of the Second Temple and the commencement of the Jewish *Diaspora*.

The Destruction of the Temple
The impact of AD 70 on the psyche of the Jewish nation cannot be under-estimated; J. D. G. Dunn considers it "the most serious single crisis for Jewish identity".[1] Josephus[2] contended (through a proxy) almost ten years

---

[1] "If the emergence of post-exilic Judaism, and the Maccabean crisis provided two of the main crises for Jewish identity, the third most serious single crisis of the second temple period was the destruction of the temple in AD 70 and its aftermath"—J. D. G. Dunn, *Jews and Christians: the parting of the ways, A.D. 70 to 135* (Grand Rapids: Eerdmans, 1999), 185.

[2] Josephus expresses his own views through the words of his character (Eleazar son of Yair), who contends that there could not be a Judaism without the temple, so that the people in Masada were the final Jews on

after the event that "...there could not be a Judaism without the temple" – it was an event of the utmost significance in the history of Judaism.[1]   J. A. Draper says that, ". . . to most, the loss of the temple must have seemed to be a permanent loss of the presence of God with his people",[2] and according to M. Goodman there is "...every reason to suppose that the razing of the Temple horrified Diaspora Jews as much as their Judaean compatriots".[3]

The sacrificial cult may well have continued in an inferior manner after AD 70 and it is known that sacrifice on the temple mount was briefly revived during the revolt of 132–35 BC but the temple itself was no longer present. A. Guttmann maintains that the official cult after AD 70 ended and this is supported in the updated Schürer.[4] The temple building itself was not only the symbol of Yahweh's presence but also a powerful political and nationalistic Jewish symbol.

The removal of the temple held equal significance for first century Christians, especially Jewish-Christians, as it resolved the perplexing problem of temple-worship. It also proved to be a powerful polemical tool against Judaism- removal of the temple confirmed the 'New Covenant'. Henceforth, God could only be worshipped in 'Spirit and Truth' through Jesus Christ who, along with his church, constituted the eschatological temple. Christians did not support the Jewish revolt against Rome and the destruction of the temple hastened the "parting of the ways" between

---

the earth. (*C. Ap.* 2.193-198) In his summary of the Law in *Contra Apionem* he included the Temple cult as the first item in his list of the essentials of Jewish worship (*C. Ap.* 2.193-198).
[1] W. D. Davies, "Reflections on Aspects of the Jewish Background of the Gospel of John," in *Exploring the Gospel of John: In Honor of D. Moody Smith* (eds. R. Alan Culpepper and C. Clifton Black; Louisville: Westminster John Knox, 1996), 43-64.
[2] J. A. Draper, "Temple, Tabernacle and Mystical Experience in John," *Neot* 31/2 (1997): 285
[3] M. Goodman, "Diaspora Reactions to the Destruction of the Temple" in *Jews and Christians* (ed. J. D. G. Dunn; Grand Rapids: Eerdmans, 1999), 27-38 (38).
[4] A. Guttmann, "The End of the Jewish Sacrificial Cult" *HUCA* 38 (1967): 137-148. E. Schürer, The History of the Jewish People in the Age of Jesus Christ (175 B.C.- A.D. 135), (revised and edited by G. Vermes and F. Millar (and M. Black (vols. I-II), M . Goodman (vols.III.1-2)); 4 vols; Edinburgh: T & T Clark, 1973-87), I:521-523.

Christianity and Judaism—in time, essentially, Christianity became a "Gentile religion" after AD 70.[1]

The status of the temple plays a crucial role in the trial of Jesus and Stephen, who are both accused of seeking its destruction. The temples' status is also a central motif in the epistle to the Hebrews.....even though the temple is not named in the epistle! [2] For rhetorical reasons the author of Hebrews prefers to employ allusions to the 'tabernacle' - if he had been more direct his polemic would have constituted "a massive ideological assault on the Jerusalem Temple and cultus"[3] bearing in mind that even veiled criticism of the temple cult by Stephen (Acts 6:13-14) resulted in a violent reaction. Hebrews preference for 'tabernacle' allusions over direct mention of the temple stresses the superiority of the nature of the structure that was chosen as Yahweh's temporary abode (a tent) rather than David's choice of a permanent 'house' (2 Sam 7:5-7 cf. Acts 7:44,49). The temporary nature of a structure that was moved, together with the Ark, in advance of the people in order to seek out a resting place (and that required disassembly and erection) has obvious analogies with Christ. Hebrews stresses the superiority of the 'heavenly' sanctuary over the 'earthly' sanctuary, an argument that would have been unnecessary if the Second Temple was no longer standing. The removal of the Second Temple ended the debate and the need for Christian apology, for Yahweh demonstrated conclusively that the earthly temple was no longer necessary (cf. Heb 12:25-27). In conclusion, we can be certain that Hebrews was written before the fall of the Second Temple in AD 70, and we can also be

---

[1] Revelation is addressed to seven churches in Asia Minor as the Lord **anticipates** the demise of the Jewish state and the Jerusalem church. In Rev 2:9 and 3:9—'Jew' is employed as an honorific term for the religious ideal. Jesus is warning against false Jewish converts (a fifth column)—they were not true 'Jews' but still belonged to the 'synagogue of Satan'. It is unlikely that the term 'Jew' would be employed in this sense after the destruction of the temple (post 70). The seven churches reflect first century circumstances, for example, Laodicea was so rich that they took pride in being able to rebuild the city after the earthquake of 60 without help from imperial funds (Tacitus, *Ann.* 14.27; cf. *Sib. Or.* 4.107f).

[2] S. Motyer commences his article on the Temple in Hebrews with the words; "The presence or absence of the Temple in Hebrews is one of the most intriguing and significant exegetical and historical puzzles posed by the letter"—"The Temple in Hebrews: Is it There?" in *Heaven and Earth: The Temple in Biblical Theology* (eds. T. D. Alexander & S. Gathercole; Carlisle: Paternoster, 2004), 177-189 (177).

[3] Motyer, "The Temple in Hebrews: Is it There?", 180

sure that the status of the Second Temple was a bone of contention between Jews and Christians as early as the trials of Jesus and Stephen and continued to be a stumbling-block until it was removed.

Most importantly the destruction of the sanctuary was anticipated in Daniel's 490 year prophecy (Dan 9:24-27) and the same prophecy was employed by Jesus to warn of the coming destruction of the temple by Rome (Matt 24:15). The prophecy was expected to usher in "everlasting righteousness" (Dan 9:24b) the rule of God on earth, shortly after the destruction of the temple. Moreover, it was expected to result in an eschatological Jubilee Day of Atonement—"To finish the transgression, to make an end of sins, to make reconciliation for iniquity" (Dan 9:24b).

Rabbinical Judaism adapted the prophecy by compressing the period between the destruction of the first temple (586 BC) and the second temple (AD 70) in the *Seder Olam* chronicle (a Jewish calendar ca. 160 AD) to a mere 490 years, thus effectively revising history by omitting 166 years from the Persian era. With the removal of the temple cult in AD 70 attention was refocused on the codification of the oral traditions know as the Mishna and the conclusion of the 'Torah era'. This is hardly a satisfactory realization of a prophecy that signified the in-breaking of God's rule on earth and promised, *"To bring in everlasting righteousness, To seal up vision and prophecy, And to anoint the Most Holy"* (Dan 9:24b). For early Jewish interpreters like Josephus the prophecy found a fulfilment in the destruction of the temple by the Romans; Jewish commentators, such as Rashi and Metzudos, held that the 490 years ended with the destruction of the temple.

In summary, first century Jews expected the destruction of the temple to coincide with the in breaking of God's rule on earth, Rabbinical Judaism re-interpreted Daniel's prophecy when this did not occur and refocused their energies away from the temple cult, towards the law and the synagogue. The destruction of the temple was a seminal event for Judaism *and* Christianity, and it marked not only the end of an independent Jewish nation, but the end of an era. The fact that the destruction of the temple is not referred to as a 'past event' *in any* of the NT writings is the most forceful argument for dating the *whole* of the NT before AD 70. J. A. T. Robinson sums up the lack of reference to the fall of the temple as follows:

> One of the oddest facts about the New Testament is that what on any showing would appear to be the single most datable and climactic event of the period - the fall of

Jerusalem in AD 70, and with it the collapse of institutional Judaism based on the temple - is never once mentioned as a past fact. It is, of course, predicted; and these predictions are, in some cases at least, assumed to be written (or written up) after the event. But the silence is nevertheless as significant as the silence for Sherlock Holmes of the dog that did not bark.[1]

Jewish Temple Imagery indicates an Early Date

Despite prolific Temple imagery/liturgy occurring in the Apocalypse, the impact has been marginal on interpretive approaches and the *topos* is barely noted in commentaries. Recently this neglect has been addressed (1997/1999) by studies from R. Brigg[2] and A. and A. Spatafora,[3] who investigate the use of Temple imagery in apocryphal and OT sources and the subsequent development of the Temple theme in the Apocalypse. The common feature shared by these recent works is recognition of **the importance of temple imagery/liturgy** in the Apocalypse, particularly the Day of Atonement, a feature also noted by H. A. Whittaker.[4]

Why is Jewish 'temple imagery' (cf. Rev 8:3; 9:13; 14:18; 16:7) so fundamental to the Apocalypse? The vision of the 'heavenly sanctuary' was given *before* the destruction of the 'earthly temple' and *before* the Neronic persecution in order to reassure Christians. Hebrews *follows the lead given in the Apocalypse* by reminding readers that the 'earthly tabernacle' (temple) is but a **copy and shadow** (Heb 8:5) of the heavenly things (i.e., the temple that John 'entered' in his vision)—believers now have an 'open door' to the heavenly sanctuary (Rev 4:1; cf. Heb 4:16) and become 'fellow worshipers' with the angels (Rev 19:10; 22:9); the Jewish temple cult is no longer relevant and therefore Christians (particularly Jewish Christians) need not be distressed when it is removed.

---

[1] J. A. T. Robinson, *Redating the New Testament* (London: Xpress Reprints, 1976), 13.

[2] R. A. Brigg, *Jewish Temple Imagery in the Book of Revelation* (Studies in Biblical Literature; Vol. 10; New York: Peter Lang Publishing, 1999).

[3] A. and A. Spatafora observe that, "All other studies and commentaries appear to analyse the individual recurrences, but they fail to see a relationship between them"—A. Spatafora and A. Spatafora, *From the 'Temple of God' to God as the Temple: A Biblical Theological Study of the Temple in the Book of Revelation* (Rome: Loyola Press, 1997), 7-9.

[4] H. A. Whittaker, *Revelation: A Biblical Approach* (Lichfield: Biblia, 1973), 104-105.

The Apocalypse is structured around a three-and-a-half year cycle of Jewish Feasts, and is replete with implicit and explicit allusions and echoes to the Jewish Feasts. For example, Passover (Rev 5:1f); Tabernacles (Rev 7:15); Hanukkah (Rev 11:4); Purim (Rev 11:10); Atonement (Rev 8:1f); and Tabernacles (Rev 21:3; 21:6; 22:1; cf. the water pouring ceremony of John 7:37). The Fourth Gospel shares the same interest in Feast Days with the narrative punctuated by references to the Jewish calendar (John 2:13; 5:1; 6:4; 7:2; 10:22; 11;55ff).

First Century Expectations indicate an early date

Whereas many pious first century Jews expected the 'end of the age' in the first century, Christians held the expectation that Christ would return during their lifetime (cf. Matt. 10:23; Matt. 24:34; 1 Thess. 4:15;[1] 2 Thess. 2:1-2; 2 Thess. 2:1-2). G. K. Beale has noted[2] that the formula translated in Rev 1:1 (and also 4:1 and 22:6) as **"what must….take place"** is found in only one other place in the Bible, namely in Greek versions of Daniel 2, where it occurs in verses 28, 29 and 45:

> […..]….he showed . . . what things must take place in
> the latter days
> (Dan 2:28, LXX)

> […..]…to show . . . …what things must take place
> quickly (Rev 1:1)

According to Beale, the verbs translated "show" are "semantic equivalents", both used to describe the "role of the prophets in revealing what God has 'shown' them". The important matter to note is the change from the expression "in the latter days" to "quickly," which "appears to indicate that fulfilment has begun (that it is being fulfilled) or will begin in the near future. Simply put, John understands Daniel's reference to a distant time as referring to his own era and he updates the text accordingly. What Daniel expected to occur in the distant 'latter days' -- the defeat of cosmic evil and the ushering in of the divine kingdom -- John expects to

---

[1] In 1 Thessalonians (an early epistle) Paul expected that at least some of his audience (including himself?) would still be alive when the Lord returned. The immediacy of the problems facing the Thessalonians, including their communal living arrangements, indicated that first century Christians expected an early return.

[2] G. K. Beale, *The Book of Revelation: A Commentary of the Greek Text* (NIGTC; Grand Rapids: Eerdmans, 1998), 153-4, 1130.

begin 'quickly,' in his own generation, if it has not already begun to happen."

Therefore, Rev 1:1a anticipates (via Daniel) an imminent fulfilment in the first century. This is reinforced by Rev 1:7, "Behold, He is coming with clouds" (NKJV), an allusion to Dan 7:13, followed by a description of the "Son of man" in Danielic terms in Rev 1:13-17 (cf. Dan 7:9; 10:6). Significantly, Jesus warned the judges at his trial that they, "...**will see** the Son of Man...coming on the clouds of heaven" (Matt 26:64), indicating that they would personally experience *his coming in judgement.* All of the allusions to Daniel in the first chapter of the Apocalypse point to an imminent first century fulfilment of Daniel's prophecies. The use of Daniel by Jesus in Rev 1:1 corresponds with Jesus' use of Daniel in the Olivet Prophecy regarding the destruction of Jerusalem and the temple. The conclusion is inescapable that the prophecy of Daniel/Olivet/Revelation had at least **a partial fulfilment in the first century.**

The Breach Principle

The "coming of the Son of Man" in AD 70 was an act of judgment **that only partially** realized the terms of Daniel/Olivet/Revelation.[1] First Century Christians expected the in-breaking of the kingdom to quickly follow. We might ask why the kingdom was not inaugurated immediately and if there is a scriptural precedent for this. Scripture does indeed have a precedent for delaying the promised inheritance....it is known as the breach principle:

> After the number of the days in which ye searched the land, *even* forty days, each day for a year, shall ye bear your iniquities, *even* forty years, and ye shall know my breach of promise. Num.14:34 (KJV)[2]

The **same warning** based on the **same incident** was given to first century Jewish-Christians in the epistle to the Hebrews (Heb 4:3-8). The warning

---

[1] For connections between the Olivet prophecy and the Seals see, T. Gaston, *Come and See* (Hyderabad: Printland Publishers, 2007), 104-5, and Whittaker, *Revelation: A Biblical Approach*, 67-68. Unlike the synoptics, the Fourth Gospel did not feel it necessary to include the Olivet prophecy because John had already incorporated it into the Seals!

[2] [Ed. AP]: Another example of delay is Isa 48:9, "For my name's sake will I defer mine anger, and for my praise will I refrain for thee, that I cut thee not off".

was not heeded—the Jewish nation was swept away—the Jewish-Christian church was swept away—the kingdom on earth did not materialise and Christianity became a 'Gentile religion'. This frustrated first century eschatological expectations of Christians *and* Jews—the prophetic clock *stopped ticking*. All the prophecies *could* (should) have been realized in the first century *but they were not*.

Both 2 Peter and Hebrews (and possibly others) **were aware** of the "Revelation of Jesus Christ", and were consciously alluding to or echoing the warnings given by Christ regarding the coming judgement on Judaism in AD 70.[1] Jewish-Christians were warned not to apostatize by reverting to Judaism as it would soon be swept away. In this context the words of Heb 1:2 take on new significance and resonate with meaning:

> Has <u>in these last days spoken</u> to us by *His* Son, whom He has appointed heir of all things, through whom also He made the worlds... Heb 1:2 (KJV)

The first verses of Hebrews should be placed in the context of Heb 12:25,

> See that you do not refuse Him who speaks. For if they did not escape who refused Him who spoke on earth, much more *shall we not escape* if we turn away from Him <u>who *speaks*</u> from heaven... Heb 12:25 (KJV)

The one who 'spoke on earth' was either the Angel of the Presence who spoke on God's behalf and bore the divine *Yahweh* name (Exod 23:20-23), or it was Moses who was God's divine agent (cf. Acts 7:35). The one who speaks to the Hebrews <u>from heaven</u> is now the resurrected Christ who speaks with God's authority through his servant John:

> Knowing this first, that no prophecy of Scripture is of any private interpretation, for prophecy never came by the

---

[1] A strong case has been made for both the epistle to the Hebrews and the Gospel of John being directed at the Jewish-Christian community at Ephesus. The epistle to the Hebrews has extensive allusions to the warning given to the Ephesians in Rev 2:1-7. See, P. Wyns, "The Fourth Gospel and Hebrews" and "The Fourth Gospel and Revelation" in *The Christadelphian EJournal of Biblical Interpretation Annual 2009,* (ed. A. Perry *et al*; Sunderland: Willow Publications, 2009), 154-163, 163-170 (168-169). For intertextual links between 2 Peter and Revelation 2, see Robinson, *Redating*, 227.

will of man, <u>but holy men of God spoke</u> *as they were* <u>moved by the Holy Spirit</u>. 2 Pet 1:20-21 (KJV)

<u>I was in the Spirit</u> on the Lord's Day, and I heard behind me a loud voice, as of a trumpet. Rev 1:10 (KJV)

However, when He, the <u>Spirit of truth</u>, has come, He will guide you into all truth; for He will not speak on His own *authority,* but <u>whatever He hears He will speak</u>; and He will <u>tell you things to come</u>. John 16:13 (KJV)

In Heb 12:25-27 and 2 Pet 1:17-21 we have different examples to emphasize the same point (the example employed by Hebrews probably appealed more to Jewish-Christians). Hebrews draws on the wilderness experience and the revelation on Mount Sinai, Peter draws on the revelation on the transfiguration Mount:

Exodus 19	Hebrews 12	2 Peter 1 (Transfiguration)
18. Mt. Sinai	**18.** Mt Sinai	**18.** The holy mount
19. God answers Moses by a voice	**25.** Him (God) that warneth from heaven	**18.** This voice (God's) which came from heaven we heard
18. Whole mount quaked greatly	**26.** Voice shook the earth	
19. The people feared (Exod 20:19).	**21.** Moses feared	The disciples feared (Luke 9:35)
9, 16. A thick cloud	**21.** Tempest	A cloud (Luke 9:34)
If thou shalt indeed <u>obey his voice</u>... (Exod 23:22) (the voice of the angel of the presence who spoke to Moses on earth)	**25.** ...refused Him <u>who spoke on earth</u>	**17.** This is my beloved son in whom I am well pleased, <u>hear ye him</u>. (Jesus) (Luke 9:34)

Both Hebrews and 2 Peter emphasize that the resurrected Jesus now speaks with the full authority of God and has recently given a revelation *from heaven* to his servant John—they would do well to heed Jesus' warning from heaven regarding the coming judgement on Judaism.

Internal versus External Evidence

The late dating of Revelation is usually established by reference to external evidence. The external evidence is by no means unanimous, with the strongest testimony being that of Irenaeus (*ca.* 180), which establishes a date of AD 96 under the persecution of Domitian. This evidence has been challenged: the testimony of Irenaeus is ambiguous and subject to alternative readings,[1] and the persecution under Domitian[2] was localized and not as severe as that under Nero.[3]

Essentially, the question of dating comes down to the relative weight that is placed on the external evidence as opposed to the internal (Biblical) evidence. With external evidence both the motive[4] behind the testimony

---

[1] See the alternative reading put forward by Robinson, *Redating*, 221-222.

[2] A number of late date advocates either contradict themselves or do not even attempt to use the Domitian persecution to establish the date. See J. P. M. Sweet, *Revelation* (London: SCM Press, 1979), 24-25; G. E. Ladd, *A Commentary on the Revelation of John* (Grand Rapids: Eerdmans, 1972), 8; R. H. Fuller , *A Critical Introduction to the New Testament* (London: Duckworth, 1966), 187; L. Morris, *Revelation* (Leicester: Inter-Varsity Press), 36; and D. H. van Daalen, *A Guide to Revelation* (London: SPCK, 1986), 3. L. L. Thompson has demonstrated clearly that there was no empire-wide persecution of Christians inaugurated by Domitian—*The Book of Revelation: Apocalypse and Empire* (Oxford: Oxford University Press, 1990), 95-115. D. Warden concludes, "...a Domitianic persecution based on literary evidence from the milieu of the imperial capital is essentially irrelevant"—"Imperial persecution and the Dating of 1 Peter and Revelation" *JETS* 34/2 (1991): 203-212, (212). See also J. C. Wilson, "The Problem of the Domitianic Date of Revelation" *NTS* 39 (1993): 587-605.

[3] K. L. Gentry concludes his assessment of the evidence with the words: "The evidence of a general persecution against Christianity under Nero is strong and almost universally recognised. Its cruelty, extent, and length are most compatible with the requirements of the Revelational record. Not only so, but the Domitianic evidence is meagre and, if accepted, Domitian's persecution pales by comparison"—K. L. Gentry, *Before Jerusalem Fell: Dating the Book of Revelation. An Exegetical and Historical Argument for a Pre-A.D. 70 Composition* (Tyler: Institute for Christian Economics, 1989), 298-9; see also 17-18, 24-38.

[4] T. B. Slater asserts; "Moreover, Thompson has shown conclusively that the writings of the Roman historians who were Irenaeus' primary sources had themselves intentionally given a poor depiction of Domitian in order

and the accuracy[1] of the testimony can be challenged. This is not the case with internal evidence—the authority of the testimony is not in question and the motive behind the testimony is pure. Nevertheless, we should remember that internal evidence is subject to other issues, such as direction of quotation (who is quoting whom?) and interpretation.

When was Revelation written?

Perhaps the clearest internal indicator for dating is Rev 17:10-11 which places the Apocalypse during the reign of the sixth Roman emperor—Nero (54-68), as the "<u>one that is</u>" (e.g. in power at the time of writing), commencing the count with the first emperor, Julius Caesar. The problem for commentators is identifying the "seventh" emperor, who "has not yet come", with various candidates being suggested none of whom is particularly relevant.[2] This "other" who, "has not yet come" and will exist for only a "short time" is associated with the re-emergence of the beast. The future protagonist is equated with the "eighth" (head) and is "of the seven" (heads). The problem is caused by the failure to recognise the *prophetic interruption* caused by the *breach of promise*. The "one who is to come" and the reincarnated beast are eschatological figures that appear *right at the end*, just before the appearance of Jesus—the "short time" is analogous with the three-and–one-half year witnessing that sees the "resurrected" beast murder the witnesses (Rev 11:7). The witnessing is *based on* the "Faithful Witness" (Rev 1:5) who was murdered in Jerusalem (cf. Rev 11:8) by an imperial power in collusion with an institutionalized religion (beast). First century events act as a kind of transparency through which to view the end and Nero is the archetype for the blaspheming, persecuting "man" (666) who "has not yet come".

Nero's persecution of Christians was not accidental. A minority sect like the Christians would not have come to his attention, were it not for the trouble that Judaizers stirred up (cf. Acts 18:2). The suggestion to use

---

to ingratiate themselves to Trajan and his new imperial family. Thus, for these reasons, Irenaeus is not the most reliable source for dating the Apocalypse to John and can only be used as a supporting witness, if then"—"Dating the Apocalypse to John" *Bib* 84 (2003): 252-258 (254).

[1] Robinson, *Redating*, 221, remarks, "the external testimony is only as strong as the internal and must be assessed critically". R. B. Moberley states, "We would not normally regard so distant, belated and second-hand opinion as, by itself, evidence"—"When was Revelation Conceived?" *Bib* 73 (1992): 376-393 (367, 381).

[2] See Gentry, *Before Jerusalem Fell*, 146-164.

Christians as a scapegoat and blame them for the great fire probably came from his mistress, Poppea, who was a recent convert to Judaism.[1]

It is often asserted that Nero's name does not calculate the gematria value of 666 (Rev 13:18), but the Aramaic spelling of Nero Caesar - *Nrwn Qsr* (attested at Qumran) does, moreover, when the Latin spelling of 'Nero Caesar' is transliterated into Hebrew it calculates the alternative numerical value 616 a textual variant found in some manuscripts![2] So both the Aramaic *and* the Latin form indicate the number of **a** man - Nero Caesar. However, the numerical riddle 666 is supra-historical in its significance, going beyond identifying the particular (**a** man) to identifying the universal hubris and self-divinization of **man**.[3]

Such was the tyranny of Nero that myths accreted about his reappearance (that he was possibly not dead) and as early as 69 AD an imposter emerged to be quickly followed by other pseudo-Neroes. Commentators often aver that passages such as Rev 13:3, 14 and 17:8, 11 (describing the beast that survived a mortal wound) form the basis of the *Nero Redivivus* (Nero Returns) myth. The myth is employed by late date advocates (as a prophecy after the event) *and* by early date advocates! K. L. Gentry suggests that the myth was already well established early in the reign of the superstitious Nero, who sought predictions from astrologers.[4]

The explanation offered here is that the Book of Revelation (given early in the reign of Nero) *contributed* to the myth of his "return". By coincidence (sic) the number of **man** calculated the value of Nero Caesar (who was an archetype) and together with the prophecies concerning the reincarnation (recovery/resurrection) of the beast this encouraged the spread of the *Nero Redivivus* myth amongst pagan pretenders, who acquired (and misunderstood) it from Christian sources. This testifies to the terror that Nero invoked even after his death. The beast with its seven heads equates to the totality of the beast-heads in the vision of Daniel 7 representing the

---

[1] Josephus (*Ant.* 20.8 .11) recounts how Poppea pleaded with Nero on behalf of Ismael the high priest and Helcias the temple treasurer, who were held hostage at Nero's court, in order to force the Jews to demolish a wall that blocked Herod Agrippa's view of the Temple precinct.

[2] For detailed analysis of 666 and 616 see Gentry, *Before Jerusalem Fell*, 193-203.

[3] Empire building (cf. the beasts of Daniel's vision) is an act of human assertion and glorification (cf. Dan 4:30; 1 Kings. 10:14) and something that Jesus refused (Matt 4:8-10).

[4] Gentry, *Before Jerusalem Fell*, 300-317 (305).

sum total of the "kingdoms of men". In the first century, the "beast" was Roman and the Harlot (unfaithful woman) supported by imperial power (riding the beast) was Jerusalem— the perfect combination of ruthless Gentile power and institutionalized Jewish religion. This duality (Jerusalem/Rome) found common purpose when they crucified the Lord and threw the Christians to the lions but their agreement did not last and Rome eventually destroyed Jerusalem (cf. Rev 17:16). The events of the first century are a preview of future events.

Conclusion

Serious problems exist in accepting a late date for Revelation. The vantage point of the seals is retrospective (just before the Nero persecution), looking backwards to the foot of the cross.[1] This gave first century Christians the reassurance that the 'resurrected Lamb' was immediately empowered to lead and encourage his church through the coming tribulations (not 66 years later!). Jesus was aware of all the hardships and martyrdoms endured by the primitive church—persecutions that would "fill up the measure of his sufferings" until the coming retribution of 70.

Of particular interest is the importance of the Day of Atonement which thematically informs the Trumpet section. The Day of Atonement is considered by Jews to be the holiest and most solemn day of the year and is a national holiday. Why does the liturgy of a *Jewish Feast* related to *national atonement* form a central theme in the Book of Revelation? The Day of Atonement has no relevance to any other nation, nor is it relevant to the church or the "church age". Instead of forgiveness, the Day of Atonement in the Apocalypse results in a process of national punishment and retribution.

---

[1] The first seal commenced at Passover, at the resurrection, and the last seal was completed **42 years (?) later** on the day after Passover (Josephus, *Wars* 10.9.1.), with the fall of the last fortress and suicide of the Jewish defenders at Masada. The seals are all related to the church history recorded in Acts and the secular history recorded in Josephus. The conquering Gospel (Rev 6:2; Acts 9:15), Herodian Persecution (Rev 6:4; Acts 12:1-2), Claudian famine (Rev 6:5-6; Acts 11:28), disintegration of the Jewish state (Rev 6:8 cf. *Josephus*, [Thackeray Loeb edition] who reports assassins, robbers, a false prophet [253-70] and the suppression of rebellions in this period [253, 260, 263, 269f]), Nero persecution (Rev 6:9-11; 1 Pet 5:8) and the Jewish war concluding with the fall of Jerusalem and last fortress at Masada (Rev 6:12-17)—six Seals, each lasting approximately seven years.

In 1973 the nation of Israel suffered a surprise attack **on the Day of Atonement** – it was a war they almost lost. The Day of Atonement war was the divine response to *prayers asking for national forgiveness* and it is this event that *re-started the prophetic clock*. We are now living in the period immediately prior the witnessing to the Jewish nation.

Many interpretations of Revelation are politically motivated - the Continuous-Historic approach originated as Protestant polemic against the Catholic Church[1] and the Catholic response was full Preterism[2] (the notion that it was *completely* realized in 70). Exegetes should move away from politically motivated interpretations and adopt an approach grounded in a biblical hermeneutic. Revelation was obviously not *completely* realized in the first century but it is just as obvious that it was written early and that it had an application to our first century brethren and sisters and to the Jewish nation (and still does).

---

[1] Martin Luther and John Calvin adopted a Historicist approach during the Reformation.

[2] A Preterist response was issued during the Counter Reformation by the Jesuit Luis De Alcasar.